THE KINGS AND KINGDOMS OF ISRAEL AND JUDAH

KNOW YOUR BIBLE SERIES

• • • • • • • • • • • • • • • • • • •

A STUDY COURSE OF
THE KINGS AND KINGDOMS
OF ISRAEL AND JUDAH

• • • • • • • • • • • • • • • • • • •

White Wing Publishing House and Press
Cleveland, Tennessee U.S.A. and Other Nations
ACD
31698

> James Stump
> 11545 Us Highway 220
> Stoneville, NC 27048

The Kings and Kingdoms of Israel and Judah
Copyright ©2002
Published by White Wing Publishing House
P.O. Box 3000 • Cleveland, Tennessee, U.S.A. 37320-3000
(423) 559-5425 • 1-800-221-5027
http://www.wingnet.net
All rights reserved
Cover art: Sixto Ramírez
Reprint 2002

ISBN # 1-889505-40-4

CONTENTS

Important Instructions 5

Lesson One
The Kings and Kingdoms of Israel and Judah 7
Lesson Two
The Kingdom Demanded 12
Lesson Three
The United Kingdom
Saul: The First King 18
Lesson Four
David: The Second King 26
Lesson Five
Solomon: The Third King 41
Lesson Six
The Divided Kingdom 51
Lesson Seven
Nadab: Second King of Israel 60
Lesson Eight
Elah: Fourth King of Israel 66
Lesson Nine
Ahab: Seventh King of Israel 72
Lesson Ten
Ahaziah: Eighth King of Israel 83
Lesson Eleven
Jehu: Tenth King of Israel 95
Lesson Twelve
Jehoahaz: Eleventh King of Israel 103
Lesson Thirteen
Shallum: Fifteenth King of Israel 113
Lesson Fourteen
Pekah: Eighteenth King of Israel 119
Lesson Fifteen
The Kings of Judah
Rehoboam: First King of Judah 126
Lesson Sixteen
Asa: Third King of Judah 136
Lesson Seventeen
Jehoshaphat: Fourth King of Judah 142
Lesson Eighteen
Athaliah: Seventh "Ruler" of Judah 152

Lesson Nineteen
    Amaziah: Ninth King of Judah 160
Lesson Twenty
    Jotham: Eleventh King of Judah 168
Lesson Twenty-one
    Hezekiah: Thirteenth King of Judah 175
Lesson Twenty-two
    Manasseh: Fourteenth King of Judah 188
Lesson Twenty-three
    Josiah: Sixteenth King of Judah 196
Lesson Twenty-four
    Jehoiakim: Eighteenth King of Judah 204
    Examinations 215

FOR BIBLE TRAINING INSTITUTE

THE KINGS AND KINGDOMS OF ISRAEL AND JUDAH

—Lesson One—

THE KINGS AND KINGDOMS OF ISRAEL AND JUDAH

Required Scripture Readings: Deuteronomy 17:14-20; Hosea 13:9-11.

Pronunciation Helps: Nineveh—NIN-e-va; Ramah—RA-ma; Assyria—a-SEER-i-a; Babylonia—BAB-a-LON-i-a; Ishbosheth—ish-BOSH-eth; Rehoboam—REE-o-BO-am.

A BROAD-SCOPE PREVIEW

The journey is long from Ramah in the land of Benjamin to Nineveh in Assyria and Babylon in Babylonia—some 600 miles "as the crow flies," and more than half a millenium of sunrises and sunsets.

The demand for a king and a kingdom was made at Ramah in about 1095 B.C., and this period of history came to its conclusion at Babylon in about 587 B.C. The journey was fraught with disasters and failures due to sin; yet there were generous sprinklings—and occasional outpourings—of divine glories and blessings as the rewards of repentance and obedience.

In this panoramic study we will make the journey in retrospect. However, lest we become wayworn and weary from literally volumes of available commentary on the Bible record of this period, plus the additional historical offerings, we will endeavor to be wisely selective. Interest in particular areas will vary from student to student. Some may feel inspired to pursue certain areas more extensively.

Perhaps the ensuing lessons will fulfill some or all of the following purposes:

(1) To enrich your perception of the workings of God among His chosen people

(2) To broaden your knowledge and understanding of the Old Testament Scriptures

(3) To make character studies of the different kings

(4) To observe the effects of their leadership on the kingdoms

(5) To encourage the practice of keeping factual information in the context of the times and circumstances

(6) To note the constant forward movement of events toward the larger fulfillment of the plan of God

(7) To make pertinent application of Israel's history to current situations, with an eye to becoming better servants of God

SOURCE MATERIALS FOR THE STUDY

The Bible is first and always the determinative Source Book. All commentary, opinion, logic, assumption, or historical information not from the biblical historical books, must be kept subordinate to the Inspired Text written by "holy men of God" who "spake as they were moved by the Holy Ghost" (2 Peter 1:21).

The Bible record begins with 1 Samuel 8, and ends with 2 Kings 17 for "Israel," and with 2 Kings 25 and 2 Chronicles 36 for "Judah." Much reading from the Bible will be imperative, since the inclusion of the full Bible text would require much space in the body of the course.

Supplementary materials may vary according to what is available to the class or individual student of the course. Suggested helps include:

(1) Reputable *commentaries* by men generally known as conservative or fundamental in their interpretation of the Scriptures—*Matthew Henry's Commentary; Clarke's Commentary; The Pulpit Commentary,* and others.

(2) *Lessons in Bible Training, Volume One*—Bible Training Institute textbook.

(3) *The Works of Falvius Josephus*—Jewish historian of the First Century A.D. He had available to him volumes of Israelite history held as being authentic, though, of course, not written by divine inspiration in the same sense as the Holy Scriptures.

(4) *Bible Dictionaries*, most of which are reliable. They are good for information in condensed form; however, brevity sometimes leads to assumptions and personal interpretations, so keep your Bible handy for verification.

(5) *Bible Atlases*, which deal largely with geography and historical briefs on events related to the specific historical locales. The *maps* used seldom include everything referred to in the Bible records. It is often necessary to refer to more than one map. Also, changes in the names of places make additional research necessary.

The territory possessed and occupied will vary with the different maps referred to. The general areas will agree, however. Frequent use of the maps will prove helpful.

CHRONOLOGY

This deals with calendar dates and time periods, and their consecutive order. There are numerous systems of biblical chronology. The fact that they differ indicates that the true dates are not known. This is particularly the case in the period under study (as well as prior to it), and especially up to the time of the Exile.

In this course, we will not always give the date of accession for each king. When dates are used, they will conform to those used in the *Thompson Chain-Reference Bible* only, for the sake of uniformity.

It will be noted that the *United Kingdom* period begins with Saul's accession as the first king on Israel's throne, about 1095 B.C. (1 Samuel 9). David's accession is given as 1056 B.C. (2 Samuel 2), which would be thirty-nine years for Saul's reign; however, in Acts 13:21, Paul says forty years. David reigned forty years (2 Samuel 5:4), and Solomon reigned forty years (1 Kings 11:42); but it appears that Solomon actually began his reign before David's death (1 Chronicles 23:1; 28:1-21; 29:1). It may be that they co-reigned two or more years, but the *Divided Kingdom* era is dated to have begun about 975 B.C., which allots one hundred twenty years to the kings of the *United Kingdom*. This is an example of the uncertainties of chronology.

In the Bible text, the number of years of each king's reign is given; however, the totals of their reigns do not agree with the number of years given by chronologists between the beginning of the *Period of the Kings* and the date of each kingdom's exile. This must be due either to overlapping reigns or a miscalculation in the date for the beginning of the period. Also, portions of years may be counted as full years. Since there were forty-three kings in all, "here a little and there a little" could make a considerable difference in the chronology.

DIVISIONS OF THE STUDY

There are three distinct divisions of this period:

(1) *The Kingdom Demanded*: This was a brief span, evidently a matter of weeks, or a few months at the most. It is covered completely in 1 Samuel, chapters eight and nine.

(2) *The United Kingdom*: This included the reigns of the first four kings: Saul, Ishbosheth, David, and Solomon. It covered a period of not more than one hundred twenty years—1095 to 975 B.C. approximately. The reign of Ishbosheth is omitted in most listings, but it should be counted since it is a matter of record, as we shall see.

(3) *The Divided Kingdom*: The division sprang from Solomon's sin of taking many wives—"strange women" from heathen nations (1 Kings 11:1, 2), who "turned away his heart" (verse 3). The Lord, in His anger, rent the dynasty away from Solomon's house following the reign of his son Rehoboam. (See 1 Kings 11:9-13, 26-40, and 12:1-24.)

The division resulted in what is referred to as "Israel" (the Northern Kingdom), and "Judah" (the Southern Kingdom). "Israel" was ruled by a succession of nineteen kings, from about 975 to 721 B.C., when it went into exile in Assyria. "Judah" had a succession of twenty kings, from 975 to 586 B.C., when it was exiled in Babylonia.

THE STUDY PROPER

Because of the large number of personalities to be studied, it will be necessary to be somewhat brief, except in the cases of those particularly used of God in carrying out His will in His overall plan.

First, the kings of the *United Kingdom* will be studied; second, the kings of "Israel," because the Northern Kingdom was the first to fall; and third, the kings of "Judah," since the Southern Kingdom outlived "Israel" by about one hundred thirty-five years. In the Bible, the reigns of the kings of both kingdoms are treated concurrently, but for clarity and convenience, they will be grouped separately for these lessons. Attention will be called to concurrent reigns from time to time.

Where possible and relevant, the prophets who bore God's messages of warning and promise will be mentioned as contemporaries of the various kings.

Now—once again—do not try to study this course without reading all the *Required Scripture Readings* listed at the beginning of each lesson, plus all the references given as you proceed.

Happy traveling! And may God go with you!

—Lesson Two—

THE KINGDOM DEMANDED

Required Scripture Readings: 1 Samuel, chapters 8 and 9 and 10:1.

Pronunciation Helps: Jebus—JEE-bus; Gibeah—GIB-e-ah.

RELEVANT FACTS
Chief characters: Samuel and Saul.
Location: Ramah, in the land of Benjamin, about eight miles north of Jebus (Jerusalem).
Time span: Possibly as many as 17 years—1112 to 1095 B.C. (*Thompson's Chain-Reference* chronology).

THE HISTORICAL SITUATION
The *Period of the Judges of Israel* was expiring. Samuel was not only the judge, but also a priest and a prophet. He had already served Israel many years, and he had been an excellent leader. But now he was about seventy-five years old, and, to relieve himself of an overload of responsibilities and some of the traveling from place to place, he made his two sons judges.

The sons, Joel and Abiah, were not walking in the upright way of their father. They had become covetous, and were perverting judgment for bribes. This was grievous to the people. Perhaps they were reluctant to complain to their aged judge about his sons, thinking he may not have been aware of their dishonest conduct, and that the work might have been too much for him to bear. But after this had continued for several years, the elders of Israel fell upon a plan.

Considering the periodic waywardness of the people of Israel, it is probably that their plan had deeper roots than the mere unhappiness with Samuel's sons as their judges. At any rate, we find Israel in a state of dissatisfaction, which they expressed in the following words:

"Behold, thou art old, and thy sons walk not in thy ways: now make us a king to judge us like all the nations" (1 Samuel 8:5).

Samuel was displeased, for he knew the people's request was not of God. He was also hurt, or wounded in spirit, feeling that their unrest was a personal rejection. He knew that God had made him what he was; and he knew he had served in the fear of the Lord.

He took the matter to the Lord in prayer. Of course, God, who knows all things at all times, had not been taken by surprise, as had Samuel. So, if Samuel had been astonished at the people's desire, he probably was moreso at the Lord's answer:

"Hearken unto the voice of the people in all that they say unto thee: for they have not rejected *thee*, but they have rejected *me*, that I should not reign over them.

"According to all the works which they have done since the day that I brought them up out of Egypt even unto this day, wherewith they have forsaken me, and served other gods, so do they also unto thee.

"Now therefore hearken unto their voice: howbeit yet protest solemnly unto them, and shew them the manner of the king that shall reign over them" (8:7-9).

THE MANNER OF KINGS

A momentous change was at hand! A change of government, from theocracy to monarchy! Surely Israel was not blind as to the implications of this drastic transition. Their history was rife with proof that they had been in oppression and servitude to heathen kings time after time. Besides, even in times of peace, they had mingled all too freely with the peoples of kingdoms, and they had every reason to know *the manner of kings*.

Evidently the choice was premeditated and deliberate; but God would leave them without excuse. So Samuel did as the Lord had said:

"And he said, This will be the manner of the king that shall reign over you: He will take your sons, and appoint them for himself, for his chariots, and to be his horsemen; and some shall run before his chariots.

"And he will appoint him captains over thousands, and captains over fifties; and will set them to ear his ground, and to reap his harvest, and to make his instruments of war, and instruments of his chariots.

"And he will take your daughters to be confectionaries, and to be cooks, and to be bakers.

"And he will take your fields, and your vineyards, and your oliveyards, even the best of them, and give them to his servants.

"And he will take the tenth of your seed, and of your vineyards, and give to his officers, and to his servants.

"And he will take your men-servants, and your maid-servants, and your goodliest young men, and your asses, and put them to his work.

"And he will take the tenth of your sheep: and ye shall be his servants.

"And ye shall cry out in that day because of your king which ye shall have chosen you; and the Lord will not hear you in that day " (8:11-18).

The people really knew all of this; and it must have sounded good to them. At least they would be "like all the nations." They would no longer have to "suffer" the humiliating embarrassment of being "a peculiar treasure," or a "holy [set apart] nation" unto the invisible God!

Their response to Samuel, God's spokesman, was very emphatic: *"Nay; but we will have a king over us*; That we also may be like all the nations; and that our king may judge us, and go out before us, and fight our battles" (8:19, 20).

Again God said to Samuel, "Hearken unto their voice, and make them a king" (8:22). And Samuel sent them away. They knew him well enough to understand that when he had further word from the Lord about the king, he would let them know. We are not told how long Samuel waited for that word. There may have been a time-lapse of as many as seventeen years between chapters eight and nine. It is clearly apparent, however, that Samuel did not go up and down through the land searching for the requested king. God knew who the king would be, and where he was; and that was good enough for this prophet, priest, and judge.

THE EMERGING KING

As God would have it, the "king" would seek the prophet. So, on a certain day, "the Lord told Samuel in his ear" that the next day, at about the same time, He would send him a Benjamite. Samuel was to anoint this man to be "captain" over Israel.

Some two or three days earlier, *as God would have it*, some asses belonging to a Benjamite named Kish who lived near Gibeah, about halfway between Jebus and Ramah, grazed their way out of bounds and became lost to their owner. Kish had a son named Saul; and, *as God would have it*, Kish bade Saul take a servant with him and go in search of the lost asses.

Does it seem strange that this seeker after dumb brutes should be described so specifically, and that he was: (1) a choice young man, (2) a goodly young man—no goodlier person than he among the children of Israel, and (3) a tall young man—from his shoulders and upward taller than any of the people? Even a moment's meditation convinces us that all these impressive attributes were not necessary in one seeking lost asses. Perhaps the significance will appear in a later lesson.

For three days they sought, with those "beasts of burden" successfully eluding them! On the third day, the goodly young man reasoned that his father would be more concerned about his absence than about the lost brutes. But, *as the Lord would have it*, the servant remembered that the prophet Samuel dwelt in the city nearby, and that he might give them the needed direction.

After some inquiry, Saul and the servant entered Ramah— *just as Samuel was coming out*, en route to the place of sacrifice, for there was to be a feast there that day! "And when Samuel saw Saul, the Lord said unto him, Behold the man whom I spake to thee of! this same shall reign over my people" (9:17).

When the self-introductions were over, Samuel began a series of somewhat bewildering statements: "Go up before me unto the high place; for ye shall eat with me to-day, and to-morrow I will let thee go, and will tell thee all that is in thine heart."

Saul may have wondered—"Is this aged man a little senile? Why should he invite me, a stranger, and very obviously a farmer, to eat with him and spend the night in his home? He says, 'I will *let* thee go tomorrow.' Is he presuming to tell me I *must* stay? What does he mean—'I will tell thee all that is in thine heart'? Well—*who can know the heart?*"

Then, as if by after-thought, Samuel tells him to be no longer concerned about the asses—which, by the way, had been lost three days ago—for they had been found.

"How does this man know about the lost asses?" Saul may have pondered, observing that he knew the number of days they had been searching for them. "And can he be sure they have been found?"

But before any of this could make sense, the seer astounded him with a truly baffling question: "And on whom is all the desire of Israel? Is it not on *thee*, and on all thy father's house?"

Was the old prophet sarcastically belittling him and his family? But Saul must show respect for God's prophet, so he tells him that he is a Benjamite, of Israel's smallest tribe; and that his family is the least of all families in that least of all the tribes. Then he ventures a question: "Wherefore then speakest thou so to me?"

Samuel didn't bother to answer. Instead, he continued his strange procedure. If Saul and the servant were dressed in "farm clothes," Samuel seemed not to see or care. Into the "parlour" he ushered them! In the "chiefest place" he seated them! And right in the midst of thirty bidden guests!

"What is all of this?" Saul may have cried out within his heart. But the guests seemed not to show any amazement. Perhaps they all knew that the elderly seer had outlived his sanity!

Next, Samuel directed the cook to bring forth some "portion" which had been pre-arranged. And when it was brought forth—lo, it was set before Saul, and Samuel said, "Unto this time it hath been kept for *thee*...."

"This has to be a mistake," Saul may have reasoned, "but it is hardly a thing to be settled in the presence of the host's guests."

"So Saul did eat with Samuel that day."

At Samuel's home in Ramah, they went onto the housetop where "Samuel communed with Saul"—about what we are not told. But in the morning they were up early, and Samuel, true to his word, sent Saul away. But, as a courteous host of his day and time, he accompanied him some distance. Near "the end of the city," Samuel requested that the servant be bidden to go on ahead—"that I may shew thee the word of God" (9:27).

When they were alone, "Samuel took a vial of oil, and poured it upon his head, and kissed him, and said, Is it not because the Lord hath anointed thee to be captain over his inheritance?" (10:1).

At that moment—though none but the two may have known it—Israel became a KINGDOM, and Saul, son of Kish, became THE FIRST KING!

FOR OUR ADMONITION AND LEARNING

As the apostle Paul has said, "Now all these things happened unto them [Israel] for ensamples [types]: and they are written for our *admonition* [to advise, warn, or reprove] upon whom the ends of the world are come" (1 Corinthians 10:11).

He also said, "For whatsoever things were written aforetime were written for our *learning*, that we through patience and comfort of the scriptures might have hope" (Romans 15:4).

By Israel's blatant demand to be *like all the nations* we are warned of the late Twentieth Century boldness of "secular humanism." Its insidious design is to *dethrone God* and *enthrone man!* Satan planted the seed in Eden. Israel's periodic idolatry was a subtle assertion of man's "right" to defy the true God.

The seed burst forth in a horrendous display when Israel "came out of the closet," *boldly demanding a king!* God told Samuel what they really *meant*. And God knew! They meant that *they did not want Him to order their lives!* God gave them their desire. And we may be *admonished* and *taught* if we will follow the history of that bold demand to its awful conclusion in 721 B.C. and 586 B.C.!

Now we, "upon whom the ends of the world are come," will do well to refuse the least ground in our lives to the current surge of "humanism," which, in some quarters, confesses to be a "religion"! Our Bible (if we will study it) will clearly expose this deception as *the spirit of Antichrist*. The time seems near when it will temporarily *dethrone God* and *enthrone that "man of sin"!*

—Lesson Three—

THE UNITED KINGDOM

SAUL: THE FIRST KING

Required Scripture Readings: 1 Samuel, chapters 10 through 31; 2 Samuel 1; 2 Samuel 21:12-14; 1 Chronicles 10. Since the reading for this lesson is so extensive, it is advised that it be read chapter by chapter as the lesson progresses.

Pronunciation Helps: Ahinoam—a-HIN-o-am; Malchi-shua—MAL-ki-SHOO-a; Abinadab—a-BIN-a-dab; Merab—MEE-rab; Michal—MI-kal; Jabesh-gilead—JA-besh—GIL-e-ad; Nahash—NA-hash; Amalekites—AM-a-lek-ites; Goliath—go-LI-ath; En-gedi—EN-ged-i; Ziph—ZIF; Endor—EN-dor; Gilboa—gil-BO-a; Geba—GE-ba; Michmash—MICK—mash; Keilah—Kee-I-lah.

RELEVANT FACTS
Chief characters: Saul, Samuel, and David.
Time span: 40 years—1095 to 1055 B.C., approximately.
Seat of government: Gibeah, about 5 miles north of Jebus (Jerusalem).
Contemporary personalities: Samuel, the prophet and priest.
Lineage and family: (See 1 Samuel 9:1, 2; 1 Chronicles 8:30-34 and 9:36-40.) Tribe of Benjamin. Father: Kish. Wife: Ahinoam (1 Sam. 14:50). Sons: Jonathan, Malchi-shua, Abinadab, and Ishbosheth (Esh-baal). Daughters: Merab and Michal (1 Sam. 14:49).
Age at time of accession: Not know; but his son Jonathan was an adult soldier.
Death: Fell in battle at Gilboa (1 Samuel 31; 2 Samuel 1).

THE HISTORICAL SITUATION (See also under Lesson Two.)
Almost 400 years before this time (about 1491 B.C.), the children of Israel had experienced the exodus from Egypt under Moses. Soon afterwards, God brought them under covenant as a nation and gave them the Law. From that time

they had been a theocracy—governed by God through a divinely appointed leader.

With Israel's fleshly demand for a king, theocracy was rejected and a monarchy, or kingdom, was established. Scripture indicates that a kingdom was in the plan of God in due time, but not by a premature demand of man. God initiates every development in His eternal plan. But God was merciful to Israel. As it was written later, "The Lord is merciful and gracious, slow to anger, and plenteous in mercy" (Psalms 103:8). But eventually they would reap their fleshly sowing!

SAUL THE KING

Saul's selection by God and his secret anointing by Samuel must have left him mystified. This appointment required some unmistakable confirmation. This God provided by three signs after he left Samuel (1 Samuel 10:2-9). The third sign wrought a great change. The Spirit of the Lord came upon Saul, and he was "turned into another man," as Samuel had said (10:6, 9-12).

Others heard him prophesy, along with a company of prophets. They understood this to mean that God had made him a prophet. Saul was understanding more clearly now, but he told no one what had transpired between him and Samuel.

Soon after this, Samuel called for a gathering of the people at Mizpeh, about six miles northwest of Gibeah, Saul's home city. No mention was made of the previous anointing. Samuel proceeded with the ceremony by lot, that the people should see the hand of the Lord in the selection of their king. But when the lot fell on Saul, he could not be found. In this we are given the opportunity to see the humility of this *choice, goodly* (possibly handsome), *very tall* young king, who had "hid himself among the stuff" (10:22).

At last he stood before the people—now his subjects—and Samuel proclaimed: "See ye him whom the Lord hath chosen, that there is none like him among all the people?"

And the people were happy. They had asserted their "rights," and they now had a king and a kingdom "like all the nations"! In acceptance, they shouted, "GOD SAVE THE KING!" Then the people went their way, and Saul returned to his wife and children in Gibeah.

On the east side of the Jordan, the Ammonites encamped against Jabeshgilead, a city of the half-tribe of Manasseh. The inhabitants would have submitted to Ammonite rule, but the Ammonites' king, Nahash, proposed to thrust out their right eyes, as a matter of reproach on Israel.

The elders of Jabesh asked for seven days in which to decide whether to fight or submit to the reproach. This granted, they appealed to their new king, Saul, for help. Saul was still filling the humble role of a herdsman, but when he heard of the Ammonites' threat, the Spirit of the Lord came upon him, along with a holy anger (11:6)! Successfully and quickly he rallied an army of 330,000 men, and within the allotted week they attacked their enemy and won a great victory.

This victory inspired a second proclamation and confirmation of the kingship, so Samuel called for a gathering at Gilgal. It was a joyful occasion; but Samuel took the opportunity to remind the people of their sin in demanding a king, also assuring them that God would not forsake them if they would fear Him and serve Him; otherwise, His hand would be against them (12:12-25).

Two years passed in peace and quiet, although Israel always considered the Philistines a threat to their security. Saul had raised up a "standing army," even as all the nations did. However, his Ammonite victory, along with his having been so greatly lauded by his people, may have made him restless for engagements on other fronts.

The Philistines had garrisons here and there, but nothing is said about them posing a charge. However, Jonathan, Sauls' son, supposedly at his father's command, smote the garrison at Geba. This so inflamed the Philistines that they mustered a mighty army and pitched at Michmash where Saul's troops had been, but he had withdrawn to Gilgal.

Israel saw that they were hopelessly outnumbered. The spirit of fear and alarm spread, and the people began to hide "in caves, and in thickets, and in rocks, and in high places, and in pits," and some fled to the east of Jordan (13:6, 7).

Saul remembered that Samuel, two years before, had spoken of some occasion for meeting him at Gilgal, and that he was to tarry seven days for the prophet-priest to come and offer a sacrifice (1 Samuel 10:8). He reasoned that this must be the time, so he tarried.

Now the seventh day was fast getting away, but Samuel had not come. The people were scattered from him. Israel truly needed the Lord's help. But there was no priest to make intercession! Expedience seemed to demand action!

"And Saul said, Bring hither a burnt offering to me, and peace offerings. And he offered the burnt offering" (13:9).

Samuel arrived just as the ceremony was ending. Saul went out to salute him, but he was met with a rebuke—"WHAT HAST THOU DONE?"

Saul was free with his arguments of self-justification, but Samuel only answered his own first question—"Thou has done foolishly: thou hast not kept the commandments of the Lord thy God...." Now Saul's kingly dynasty would not continue beyond the end of his own reign!

Samuel departed abruptly. And Saul was left with six hundred men against the Philistine hordes! The Philistines saw Israel's disadvantage and considered the country conquered; so instead of waging battle, they plundered the land and took the spoil.

But the confrontation was not over. (Read chapter 14.) Some days later, Jonathan and his armorbearer, unbeknown to Saul, approached a Philistine garrison that was pitched in a strategic site. (Josephus says it was "just after the break of day," and that the Philistines were sleeping.) When they made their presence known and had slain about twenty men, the relaxed Philistines immediately fell into confusion, thinking all Israel had come out of hiding and was making a surprise attack. That "the earth quaked" (verse 15) would seem to indicate an intervention of God. The host fled, killing one another in their frustration.

Hearing of this, "all the men of Israel" (verse 22) came out of hiding and pursued the enemy. "So the Lord saved Israel that day." But despite the victory, Israel was distressed over a foolish order of Saul that no one should eat anything until evening. Jonathan had not known this, so he had eaten some honey. Saul would have killed his son had not the people rescued him (14:42-45).

Henceforth, Saul "vexed" all his enemies (14:47, 48), apparently becoming increasingly vain in his own might. He sought God only when in trouble. He made up his army with a fleshly eye—"any *strong* man, or any *valiant* man, he took unto him" (14:52).

The next major confrontation was with the Amalekites. (Read chapter 15.) God sent Saul a very detailed order by Samuel: "Now go and smite Amalek, and *utterly destroy all that they have*, and spare them not; but slay both man and woman, infant and suckling, ox and sheep, camel and ass" (15:3).

With 210,000 men, God gave Saul another victory; but Saul's self-will and self-righteousness worked his doom! "But Saul and the people spared Agag, and the best of the sheep, and of the oxen, and of the fatlings, and the lambs, and all that was good, and *would not utterly destroy them* . . . ." (15:9).

God was watching! he sent Samuel to deliver His final verdict to Saul!

When Samuel arrived, Saul met him with his plausible excuses clothed in pious garb. But Samuel would not "negotiate." God's message was clear:

" . . . Hath the Lord as great delight in burnt offerings and sacrifices, as in obeying the voice of the Lord? Behold, to *obey* is better than sacrifice, and to *hearken* than the fat of rams.

"For *rebellion* is as the sin of witchcraft, and *stubbornness* is as iniquity and idolatry. Because thou hast rejected the word of the Lord, *he hath also rejected thee from being king*" (1 Samuel 15:22, 23).

Saul was no longer "little in his own sight" (15:17); but neither was he any longer "king" in God's sight. He would finish his reign, but he would henceforth know that he was only a "figure head."

God had the shepherd boy, David, anointed as the future king (1 Samuel 16:1-13). The Spirit of the Lord came upon him; but an evil spirit from God troubled Saul. And God used that evil spirit to bring David before Saul to refresh him with music (16:16-23). But this "refreshing" in Saul turned to jealousy and hatred after David had slain the towering Philistine, Goliath, and the singing women had credited him with slaying his "ten thousands" to Saul's "thousands"! (1 Samuel 18:7).

Even in making David his son-in-law, Saul's design was to snare him (18:20-30)! When his design failed, David's favor in Israel increased, as did Saul's jealousy! At last David was compelled to live as a fugitive from Saul's murderous wrath for some seven years (chapters 19-30)! Time and time again, the fickle-hearted king would confess that David was kinder to him than he deserved, for time and time again David refused to touch God's anointed. But Saul would never invite David home. The evil spirit was there to stay!

He ordered Jonathan and his servants to kill David (19:1); he threw the javelin at him (19:10); he followed him to Samuel's city of Ramah to slay him (19:18-24); he had the priests slain who dared to protect David (22:11-19); he sought David's life after David had won a battle for Israel at Keilah (chapter 23); he followed David to En-gedi, where David spared him (chapter 24); again he sought him in the wilderness of Ziph, and again David spared his life when Saul's own captain, Abner, was remiss in this duties (chapter 26).

We come now to Saul's last year. The Philistines were still plaguing Israel, and once more they came out for warfare (28:1). Samuel was dead, so Saul could no longer hear from God (28:6). The two armies had pitched; the fighting could begin anytime. As the God-forsaken king of Israel waited in fear and trembling, a last-resort thought presented itself. He said to his servants, "Seek me a woman that hath a familiar spirit, that I may go to her, and inquire of her" (28:7).

Now Saul had "put away" all such persons (28:3), but the servants knew of one woman at Endor who had escaped. So Saul disguised himself and asked the woman to bring up Samuel from the dead. She was afraid, but Saul *swore unto her by the Lord* that she would not be punished.

Did Samuel come forth? Lengthy expositions on 1 Samuel, chapter twenty-eight, have been written pro and con. *Matthew Henry* and *The Pulpit Commentary* are almost vehement in their arguments that it was *not* Samuel who ascended out of the earth. They lay it all to deception on the part of the woman and the devil. *Henry* says, "We have here the conference between Saul and Satan." *The Pulpit Commentary* says, "Whence this voice came it is difficult to say. St. Augustine thought that the woman really conjured up a demon, who took the form of Samuel.... We cannot believe that the Bible would set before us an instance of witchcraft employed with the Divine sanction for holy purposes."

On the other hand, *Josephus* accepted it as unworthy of discussion—that it *was* Samuel who came up. One *William*

Lee has said, "The history [Bible] appears to leave us in no doubt, namely, that . . . *Samuel himself,* under whatever inexplicable conditions, delivered the dread message which is put into his lips."

It is safe to stay with the Bible, even when we do not understand it. Most misunderstandings of Scripture result from men's unwillingness to accept it *unaltered.*

At any rate, the rather one-sided battle was engaged in Mount Gilboa. "And the battle went sore against Saul, and the archers hit him; and he was sore wounded by the archers" (31:3). Reading 1 Samuel 31:4 with 2 Samuel 1:1-10, *C. I. Scofield* offers the following:

"(1) Saul is 'hit'—wounded mortally, potentially 'slain,' by the Philistines; (2) either to escape agony, or insult the enemy, he falls upon his sword, and his armour-bearer, supposing him to be dead, slew himself; (3) but Saul was not dead; raising himself upon his spear, he besought the Amalekite to put him to death."

Saul's three sons—Jonathan, Malchi-shua, and Abinadab—died that same day, and Israel fell unto the Philistines, all as "Samuel" had said.

1 Chronicles 10:13, 14 briefly states the sad but accurate conclusion:

"So Saul died for his transgression which he committed against the Lord, even against the word of the Lord, which he kept not, and also for asking counsel of one that had a familiar spirit, to enquire of it;

"And inquired not of the Lord: therefore he slew him, and turned the kingdom unto David the son of Jesse."

FOR OUR ADMONITION AND LEARNING

Most races are won somewhere between the "Get set, GO! line" and the "Finish line." If Saul had been more mindful of his conduct between those two points, we would be reading a better story of his life.

It is never necessary to do anything which violates the clearly stated Word of God. Nothing worthwhile is ever gained, but all may be lost, by following that course. *God's attitude* toward such a spirit is set forth in the consequences of Saul's self-will, and his usurpation of authority not his own at Gilgal. And God's attitude has not changed. Grace gives room for repentance and restitution, but in the end, sin will be punished if it remains!

The "bleating" and "lowing" of stark, evidential truth cries out above the din of hypocritical lies and sanctimonious sacrifices! How much better it would have been if Saul's first words to Samuel had been a straightforward, penitent confession—"I HAVE SINNED"!

Saul's early humility had costumed itself in the guise of "holy expediency" when Samuel delayed his appearance to offer the sacrifice. Even good men must be careful *in patience to possess their souls*! Sacrifices are good, and they are required; but only Christ could offer (or *be*) the other man's sacrifice.

Satan takes his advantage as a "ruler of the darkness of this world" when Christians allow themselves momentarily to get out of touch with God. He stands ready with the temptation to seek "help" through the medium of *spiritism*, or of the *occult*!

—Lesson Four—

DAVID: THE SECOND KING

Required Scripture Readings: 1 Samuel 16-30; 2 Samuel 1-24; 1 Kings 1:1 to 2:12; 1 Chronicles 3:1-9; 1 Chronicles 11-29. Since many of these chapters were read in the study of Saul, it is advised that they be scanned again as we proceed with this lesson. Portions will require careful reading.

Pronunciation Helps: Ahinoam—a-HIN-o-am; Maacah—MAY-a-ka; Haggith—HAG-ith; Abital—a-BIT-al; Absalom—AB-sa-lom; Adonijah—ad-o-NI-ja; Tamar—TA-mar; Adullam—a-DULL-am; Abiathar—a BI-a-thar; Achish—A-kish; Ishbosheth—ish-BOSH-eth; Mahanaim—May-a-NAY-im; Asahel—A-sa-hel; Joab—JO-ab; Abishai—a-BISH-a-i; Kirjath-jearim—KIR-jath-JEE-a-rim; Ebenezer—eb-e-NEE-zer; Adriel—A-dri-el; Merab—MEE-rab; Ziba—ZI-ba; Mephibosheth—mef-IB-o-sheth; Machir—MAY-ker; Lo-debar—LO-de-bar; Uriah—u-RI-ah; Amnon—AM-non; Ahithophel—a-HITH-o-fel; Hushai—HU-sha-i; Amasa—a-MAY-sa; Naphtali—NAFF-ta-li; Araunah—a-RAW-na; Ornan—OR-nan; En-rogel—EN-RO-gel; Shimei—SHIM-e-i.

RELEVANT FACTS

Chief characters: David, Samuel, Saul, Jonathan, and Solomon.

Time span: 40 years as king, plus an uncertain number of years between 1 Samuel 11 and 2 Samuel 2. He reigned seven and one half years over Judah at Hebron, and 33 years over all Israel at Jerusalem.

Seats of government: Hebron and Jerusalem (2 Sam. 5:5).

Contemporary personalities: The prophets Samuel, Nathan, and Gad.

Lineage and family: (1 Sam. 16:1, 13; 2 Sam. 3:2-6 and 5:13-16; 1 Chr. 2:12-15 and 3:1-16; Matt. 1:1, 6; Luke 3:31, 32) Born about 1085 B.C. Tribe of Judah. Father: Jesse. Wives: Michal, Abigail, Ahinoam, Maacah, Haggith, Abital, Eglah, and Bath-sheba. (See 2 Sam. 5:13.) Sons born in Hebron: Amnon, Chileab (Daniel, 1 Chr. 3:1), Absalom, Adonijah, Shephatiah, Shammuah, Shobab, Nathan, Solomon, Ibhar,

Elishua, Nepheg, Japhia, Elishama, Eliada, and Eliphalet.
Daughters: Tamar (1 Sam. 13:1), and possibly others.
Age at time of accession: 30 years (2 Sam. 5:4, 5).
Death: About 1015 B.C., age about 70 years (1 Chr. 29:26-28).

THE HISTORICAL SITUATION

Pre-King Years: David's history begins with his being sought out by Samuel, at God's direction, and being anointed the future king of Israel (1 Samuel 16:1-13). When Saul learned of this, he became insanely jealous. The *Thompson Chain-Reference* chronology makes David about twenty-two or twenty-three years old at that time (1063 B.C.), but this is unlikely, considering the context. *Josephus* says he was "no more than a child in age" when he was first brought to Saul with his harp to "refresh" the king when the evil spirit troubled him (16:14-23). Also, he seems too young for military service at the time of his slaying of Goliath (1 Samuel 17).

Scripture indicates that David did "a lot of living" between the time of his early anointing and his accession to the throne (1 Samuel 16-30). One of the outstanding incidents was his victory over Goliath. Three of his older brothers were in Saul's army, fighting against the Philistines. Jesse sent David with food for his brothers. He sought them out, and while they were talking, the Philistine giant, Goliath, came out, challenging the army of Israel to select just one man to fight with him. Whichever prevailed, his nation would rule over the other nation. As David watched and listened, the men of Israel fled in fear. He inquired, "Who is this uncircumcised Philistine, that he should defy the armies of the living God?" (17:26).

Receiving the answer, he continued: "Let no man's heart fail because of him; thy servant will go and fight with the Philistine." He was taken before Saul, who tried to dissuade him; but he related to the king how he had slain a lion and a bear single-handedly when they had come out to attack his father's sheep. Then, as though emboldened by the Spirit of God, he declared: "The Lord that delivered me out of the paw of the lion, and out of the paw of the bear, he will deliver me out of the hand of this Philistine."

Then, with Saul's blessing, but refusing his clumsy armor, he went forth, selecting five smooth stones for his sling from the brook as he went. When Goliath saw a mere youth approaching him, he cursed him by his gods in boastful disdain. David confidently replied:

"Thou comest to me with a sword, and with a spear, and with a shield: but I come to thee in the name of the Lord of hosts, the God of the armies of Israel, whom thou hast defied. This day will the Lord deliver thee into mine hand; and I will smite thee, and take thine head from thee; and I will give the carcases of the host of the Philistines this day unto the fowls of the air, and to the wild beasts of the earth; that all the earth may know that there is a God in Israel. And all this assembly shall know that the Lord saveth not with sword and spear: for the battle is the Lord's, and he will give you into our hands" (17:45-47).

The words were God's words; only the tongue and voice were David's! for with the first of the five stones he felled the giant; then with Goliath's own sword he cut off his head! The men of Israel took up the fight and drove out the Philistines, pursuing them some twenty miles northwest to Ekron and twenty miles southwest to Gath.

Strangely enough, Saul seemed not to know David; and when he was brought before the king, apparently there was no commendation or honor bestowed. But Saul's son Jonathan observed David closely, and his soul was knit with David's soul from that time forward (18:1-4).

Though Saul was remiss about honoring the young "giant-killer," the women were not. But their song of praise triggered a period of some seven years of danger and hardship for the future king. They played instruments of music, with singing and dancing, saying, "Saul hath slain his *thousands*, and David his *ten thousands*."

Saul's jealousy raged! The evil spirit which had come upon him after Samuel's rebuke rose up again, and Saul seemed determined to do away with his young competitor. He began with a hypocritical show of affection, offering him his daughter Michal as his wife—if he would risk his own life by obtaining a dowry. (See 1 Samuel 18:20-29.) When this snare failed, Saul's hatred was aggravated by a fear of his new son-in-law. To him, David's death seemed the only solution.

Reading the account, one wonders when Saul found time to rule the kingdom, his time being constantly consumed by his efforts to pursue David to his death! (NOTE: Review the brief outline of this pursuit in Lesson Three, concerning Saul.)

The ensuing years were extremely difficult for David, but the Spirit of the Lord that was upon him preserved him in two outstanding ways: (1) His life was spared from the hand of Saul and those whom he engaged to help him carry out his evil design; and (2) the spirit of revenge never possessed him. Once he had fled the city of Gibeah and Saul's immediate presence, with the help of his wife Michal, he did not return until after Saul's death. We quote here a paragraph from *Zondervan's Pictorial Bible Dictionary* which summarizes those years briefly:

"David fled to Philistine Gath, but his motives became suspect. Only by a stratagem and by God's grace (1 Sam. 21:12, Psa. 56:3, 34:6-8) did he reach the cave of Adullam in Judah (Psa. 142:6). Here David was joined by the priest Abiathar, who had escaped Saul's retaliatory attack upon Nob (cf. Psa. 52:1), and by a variety of malcontents (1 Sam. 22:2). On three separate occasions, Saul attempted to seize David: [1] when fellow-Judeans from Ziph betrayed his presence, after his deliverance of Keilah (1 Sam. 23, Psa. 54:3); [2] at the cave of En-gedi by the Dead Sea, where Saul was caught in his own trap (1 Sam. 24, Psa. 7:4, 57:6); and [3] upon David's return to Ziphite territory, when he again spared his pursuer's life (1 Sam. 26). Near the end [of the pursuit], however, David in despair sought asylum in Gath ... (1 Sam. 27 and 28)."

It seems that David reached the ultimate test of his faith at this point. It was as though he had decided to forsake Israel and dwell among the Philistines, who, after all, were more kind to him than his own king and people. David's greatest enemy—Satan—was pleased with his spirit of despair, even making Saul give up the pursuit when he learned where David had gone. But God would not forsake His chosen successor to the throne. This was merely "the darkest hour just before the dawn"!

King Achish, of Gath, befriended David and his six hundred men, and gave him the city of Ziklag. They went out and made gains for Achish, in appreciation for his kindness

(27:7-12). We see the depths of David's despair in his willingness to accompany Achish to war against Israel (28:1, 2; 29:1-11). It seems clear that God caused the Philistines to refuse David's assistance in this war.

When David and his men returned to Ziklag, the Amalekites had smitten the city, and had taken their wives and children captive (chapter 30). The Lord told David to pursue the captors. All were recovered; also the abundant spoils that the Amalekites had taken in their pillaging of other cities, including some in Judah.

David evidently was more encouraged now, for he shared the spoils by sending some of them to "the elders of Judah, even to his friends" (30:26). In the meantime, the Philistines, under King Achish, went to Jezreel, near Mount Gilboa (some 100 miles north of Ziklag) and pitched against Saul's army. Saul's time had run out, and he fell in that battle, along with three of his sons. It was a great Philistine victory, and God had so directed that David was not involved.

On the third day after David's return to Ziklag, he learned of Saul's defeat and death. The greatness of the man is seen in his grief for the one who had sought his life for seven years; also his lamentation for Jonathan was great and deep. (See 2 Samuel 1:19-27.) Soon after this, David was directed of the Lord to go to Hebron, about twenty miles north of Ziklag, in Judah.

Momentarily, Israel was without a king. It was widely known in Israel that Samuel had anointed David to be their future king, but some of his escapades while fleeing from Saul had been misunderstood. There had been times when they were not sure whether he as "friend" or "foe."

Ishbosheth, the "King" Who Should Not Have Been

Abner, who had been captain of Saul's host for many years, made an effort to be loyal to the memory of Saul. One son of Saul, Ishbosheth, had not fallen in battle, if indeed he had even been a soldier. *Matthew Henry* portrays him as a weak character, and one whom Saul thought not fit for battle; also that he would not have sought his father's throne on his own. Be that as it may, Abner took advantage of Israel's disarray, and his own posture in their eyes under the confusing circumstances. He took Ishbosheth to Mahanaim in Gilead, on the east side of the Jordan, and made him king over Gilead (2 Samuel 2:8-10). Mahanaim was situated in the borders of the tribe of Gad and the half-tribe of Manasseh. The Philistines had not crossed the Jordan, so Abner possibly deemed this safe territory for Saul's dynasty to begin to rebuild.

But when Saul had been rejected by the Lord, Samuel had declared that his kingdom (or dynasty) would not continue (1 Samuel 13:14; 15:26). This meant that none of Saul's posterity should inherit the throne; therefore, Ishbosheth was the "king" who should not have been king. But his reign was short-lived, as we will see from a later development.

DAVID THE KING

When David, his family, and his men went to Hebron, as the Lord had directed, "the men of Judah came, and there they anointed David king over the house of Judah" (2 Samuel 2:4). It is not clear if Ishbosheth had been made king over Gilead as yet, but David's first official action was to commend the men of Jabesh-gilead for their kindness to Saul, and for giving him a proper burial. At the same time, he announced his kingship over Judah.

Apparently, Abner was more in command in Gilead than was Ishbosheth. His first move was to set conflict in motion between Judah and Gilead (which was representative of all Israel except Judah). The Bible record is a trifle vague in the introduction of this conflict, but most historians and commentators agree that Abner initiated the meeting of "the two sides" at Gibeon for the purpose of trying to gain Judah for Ishbosheth (2:12-14). If so, he cleverly began the day's "activities" with something of a "sports event"—akin to the gladiatorial games of long ago. Neither David nor Ishbosheth were present. Joab represented David as his captain of the host.

The twenty-four competitors soon were all dead by one another's swords! If war had not been intended, it had nonetheless quickly developed into "a very sore battle." Abner and his men of Israel were beaten. He evidently took flight, and one of Joab's brothers, Asahel, pursued him and was slain by Abner. This resulted in enmity between Joab and Abner. (NOTE: Both Joab and Asahel were sons of David's half-sister, Zeruiah, making them David's nephews.)

Joab and his other brother, Abishai, then pursued Abner until sundown. The children of Benjamin came out and joined Abner on a hilltop, and Abner called out accusations to Joab, accusing him of instigating the trouble—the opposite of which was true. Joab refrained from any further pursuit. It was a sad beginning for David, who was a man of peace at heart; for the Bible says that "there was long war between the house of Saul and the house of David: but David waxed stronger and stronger, and the house of Saul waxed weaker and weaker" (2 Samuel 3:1). The reference is probably to the seven years that David was king only over Judah.

Ishbosheth soon provoked Abner to anger with an apparently false accusation. (See 1 Samuel 3:7-11.) From that time, Abner began to negotiate for the consolidation of all the tribes; not that he particularly desired it that way, but in his heart he knew that God has anointed David to be king over all Israel. He met with David in Hebron and promised that he would persuade all the other tribes to come under David's reign. David sent him away in peace. But when Joab heard the news, he had Abner brought back without David knowing it, and taking him aside, he slew him. While outwardly it may have seemed that this was Joab's vengeance for Asahel's blood, it is possible also that Joab feared that David would make Abner captain once all Israel was together.

Ishbosheth felt like "a ship without a rudder" when Abner was dead, and all his people were troubled. Abner had not lived to bring them all together. Two of Ishbosheth's captains conspired against him and secretly slew him. They expected David to appreciate their doing away with his opposition, but instead, David had them put to death. In his sweet, peaceable spirit, David had had no quarrel with Saul, either in his life or in his death. He had depended on God as his defensive. Others tried to come to his aid, but their fleshly devices were of no avail.

Ishbosheth had been king only two years. This leaves five years of leadership unaccounted for with regard to all the tribes except Judah. Opinions vary, but it seems clear that David made no effort to persuade the other tribes to accept him. Israel, as a whole, was under Philistine domination. It may have been very much as it had been in the time of the judges.

In God's good time "came all the tribes of Israel to David unto Hebron, and spake, saying, Behold, we are thy bone and thy flesh. Also in time past, when Saul was king over us, thou wast he that leddest out and broughtest in Israel: and the Lord said to thee, Thou shalt feed my people Israel, and thou shalt be captain over Israel" (2 Samuel 5:1, 2; 1 Chronicles 12:23-40). So David was at last anointed king over all Israel in about 1048 B.C. The seat of government was moved to Jebus, henceforth called Jerusalem (5:6-12; 1 Chronicles 11:4-9), and Joab was made David's chief and captain by virtue of his being the first to smite the Jebusites.

Then the Philistines made two attacks, but by divine direction David repelled them (5:18-25). However, the intervals of peace with them were "spasmodic," to say the least. The last outright war with the Philistines during David's reign was in about 1021 B.C., or shortly thereafter (2 Samuel 21:15-22).

It seems probable that the first five or six years of David's reign in Jerusalem saw the building of the conquered city, including a fortification called Millo, and Zion, a hill south of what later became the temple area. David called this hill of Zion "The City of David," and he dwelt there until his house, or palace, was erected sometime later.

It may be that David thought of one accomplishment, above all others, as the one which gave him the most satisfaction: *The bringing of the sacred "ark of the covenant" to Jerusalem and Mount Zion.* The chronology indicates that it was about the year 1042 B.C. when he accomplished this feat (2 Samuel 6). The "ark" had been in Kirjath-jearim, about ten miles west of Jerusalem, since shortly after the Philistines had taken it in a battle at Ebenezer in about 1140 B.C. (See 1 Samuel 7:1, 2.) Commentators explain that the "twenty years" spoken of there had reference to the number of years before Israel was again in a spiritual condition to give thought to the ark. It had been put in safe keeping in the house of one Abinadab, with a priest assigned to look after it. We assume that this arrangement had continued these near-100 years until the time of David's reign. (Psalms 132:3-8 should be of interest here.)

Through ignorance or presumption (perhaps both), there was some difficulty in getting the ark moved to Jerusalem.

(See 2 Samuel 6:1-11.) But it was a joyous occasion when it was finally brought in and set in its place "in the midst of the tabernacle that David had pitched for it"(6:17). There was shouting, trumpet-blowing, and dancing. David himself leaped and danced before the Lord—to Michal's embarrassment. (NOTE: The Lord made Michal barren because of her attitude on this occasion. The "five sons of Michal . . . whom she brought up for Ariel" [2 Samuel 21:8 and 1 Samuel 18:19] were her sister's sons by Adriel. Michal reared them for her brother-in-law after her sister Merab's death.)

Immediately after getting the ark situated, David seems to have been smitten with conviction over the fact that he, as king, was living in a house of cedar while the ark of God was "within curtains" (7:2). He greatly desired to build a house, or temple, for the Lord. He mentioned this to Nathan the prophet, who at first spoke unadvisedly in telling David to proceed. But that night God made His will known to Nathan. Second Samuel, chapter seven, is rich indeed in a very intimate dealing of the Lord with this man who was after His own heart. *First,* the Lord told David that He did not desire a house of this kind at that time. *Then,* He introduced the principle of a "spiritual house" which He would establish sometime in the future. He involved David in that house, saying that "the Lord telleth thee that *he* will make *thee* an house" (7:11).

From there, the Lord began to speak of the coming Christ, who would be "of the house and lineage of David" (Luke 2:4). Evidently the "house" and the "kingdom" that would be "established for ever" (verse 16) was a prophecy of the Church and the coming kingdom. Undoubtedly Stephen referred to this in his great sermon just before his martyrdom (Acts 7:45-50); also Paul in his sermon at Antioch in Pisidia (Acts 13:22-37).

In an incident too often treated as coincidental, we are privileged to get a veritable glimpse into the very heart of this great man of God. It took place some fifteen years after he had become king over Judah. Evidently some reminiscence about his fond relationship with Saul's son Jonathan inspired the thought. He asked, "Is there yet any man that is left of the house of Saul, that I may shew him kindness *for Jonathan's sake?*" (9:1). Ziba, who had been a servant in the house of

Saul, informed him that Jonathan's son, Mephibosheth, was living in the house of a man named Machir, in Lo-debar. Mephibosheth was lame in both feet. (See 2 Samuel 4:4.) At this time he was probably in his early twenties, and had a son named Micha (Micah, 1 Chronicles 8:34).

David had Mephibosheth (and evidently his family) brought from Lo-debar, thought to have been located east of the Jordan near Mahanaim. The meeting of the two was touching and tender (9:6-8). David restored to Mephibosheth all the land that Saul had owned, and directed Ziba to look after the increase of the property. Although this made Mephibosheth a wealthy man, David's great heart could be satisfied only by having him live in Jerusalem, eating at the king's table as one of his own sons.

Even Great Men Can Fail

At a time when there was a change of kings in Ammon, David sought to make friends, but was rejected, and his servants were treated shamefully (10:3-5). The Ammonites got the Syrians to go with them against Israel. In the battle, the Syrians fled, then the Ammonites followed suit. The Syrians gathered recruits and came against Israel again, and were beaten. But David purposed to overthrow the Ammonites. (*Josephus* attributes this to the manner in which they had treated his servants.) David did not go with his army to this second battle with the Ammonites, but directed Joab, who gathered a host from "all Israel" (11:1).

As David was walking upon the roof of his house in the evening, he allowed himself to be tempted of Satan when he beheld a beautiful woman at some distance who was washing herself. She was the wife of Uriah, one of his soldiers who was in the war against Ammon. Her name was Bath-sheba. David had her brought to him, and he fell into the sin of adultery. Later, when he found that she was with child by him, he attempted a scheme whereby he hoped to make it appear that the child was by her own husband.

He sent for Uriah, feigning to learn of him how his captain Joab was doing, and how the war was prospering (11:6, 7). Then he bade him go home, on leave briefly, as it were. But Uriah was so concerned for Israel's welfare in the face of war, and for those who were on the field facing the foe, that he would not go home, but slept at the door of the king's house with the servants. David gave him two more days, making him to become drunken so that he would forget his soul-burden; but still Uriah did not go home.

Then David ordered Joab to put Uriah "in the forefront of the hottest battle . . . that he may be smitten, and die" (11:15). This second scheme worked; Uriah was killed in battle. When Bath-sheba's mourning for her husband was past, David had her brought to him, and she became his wife and bore him a son.

Of course, David had committed a heinous sin and crime, and although he was beloved of the Lord, his sin could not go unpunished. God sent Nathan the prophet to confront him about the matter. Nathan approached him with something of a parable, which David apparently thought had reference to an awful crime done by someone in his kingdom. (Read 2 Samuel 12:1-4.) He was greatly angered at the selfish cruelty of the rich man in Nathan's parable, and ordered that he be put to death, after full restitution had been made.

Then Nathan said to David, *"Thou art the man."* Then he showed David his own selfishness and lust, after God had blessed him with everything his heart could desire. He had sinned against God as well as against Bath-sheba and Uriah. Then came the sentence: (1) The sword would never depart from David's house, *because he had despised God!* This first led to the second; (2) God would raise up evil against him out of his own house, or family; and (3) the child born of his adultery would die.

David repented. "I have sinned against the Lord," he said to Nathan. The depth and sincerity of the repentance cannot be seen in these six simple words, but only in God's response, for only God knew the man's heart. Had the repentance been sorrow only because his sin had been found out, the death sentence of the Law would have been his due. But the prophet said, "The Lord also hath put away thy sin; thou shalt not die."

The last pronouncement of the sentence was the first to fall upon the king. The child was struck with sickness, and although David fasted and prayed for him seven days, he died (12:15-23). But God gave him another son by Bath-sheba, " . . . and he called his name Solomon: and the Lord loved him" (12:24).

The other pronouncements haunted David the rest of his life. Three of his sons were slain, apparently by the sword; and one of those same sons fulfilled the prediction concerning his "wives," and also tried to steal the throne from his father.

First, Amnon, David's son by Ahihoam, was slain through the vengeance of his half-brother Absalom (2 Samuel 13:23-39). *Next,* Absalom, David's son by Maacah, who was much praised for his "beauty" and blemishless physique (14:25, 26), stole the hearts of ten of the tribes away from his father, and made himself king for a short season in Hebron. But when he came to Jerusalem to take David's throne, complications developed through Absalom's counsellor, Ahithophel, and David's friend, Hushai (16:15-23; 17:1-23). Included in Ahithophel's wicked counsel was the matter Nathan had prophesied about David's wives (concubines, 16:20-22). But the treachery ended in a battle at Mount Ephraim between the followers of Absalom and the followers of David, in the course of which Absalom met his death (18:1-17). *Lastly,* Adonijah, David's son by Haggith, was slain (shortly after David's death) by Solomon (1 Kings 2:13-25).

Despite Absalom's treachery, David loved him greatly and mourned over his death so excessively that Joab rebuked him soundly (2 Samuel 18:33; 19:1-8). Then David returned to the throne in Jerusalem, but "the sword" continued to plague his "house," though more remotely.

Possibly because of a continued underlying grief over Absalom, David unwisely made Absalom's captain of the host, Amasa, his captain in Joab's stead (2 Samuel 19:13; 20:4). Both Joab and Amasa were David's nephews, but Joab had been totally faithful to him, even in carrying out his evil design against Uriah. But Joab had had a part in Absalom's slaying, and despite the fact that Amasa had been on the side of enmity, now he was being elevated.

Upon David's return to Jerusalem, the old spirit of division flared up again. Sheba, a son of Belial, swayed the ten tribes away from David (20:1, 2). David commanded Amasa to assemble an army from among the men of Judah within three days. Amasa took a little longer, so David put Joab's younger brother, Abishai, temporarily in charge, lest Sheba's host get an advantage. Joab was thus further incensed, but he went with Abishai's host to the field. But when Amasa and the men he had gathered out of Judah met them in Gibeon, Joab pretended to greet him, but slew him with his sword! Joab joined Abishai in pursuing Sheba, but the people looked to Joab. At the city of Abel, in Naphtali, they overtook Sheba. A woman in the city cooperated with Joab in beheading him (20:13-23), and Joab again became captain of the host.

Here we repeat: *Even great men can fail.* And David failed again. The Philistines stirred up trouble again (21:15-22), but David was victorious. However, about a year later (possibly less than two years before his death), it seems that "the man of war" spirit in David had not been stilled. Israel seemed always to be war-hungry, and David had come to share their yearning. God had given him great deliverances, but now David seemed to attribute too much of his success to himself. He determined to "number Israel and Judah." This in itself was not wrong; but in this case God knew it to be entirely a matter of *military prowess* and *personal pride.*

Joab objected, but the king's word prevailed. But no sooner had the total been arrived at than "David's heart smote him" with conviction of his great sin (24:10). Again he repented, saying, "I have sinned greatly in that I have done: and now, I beseech thee, O Lord, take away the iniquity of thy servant; for I have done very foolishly."

Through the prophet Gad, the Lord gave David three choices of punishment: (1) seven years of famine in the land, (2) three months of flight before his enemies, or (3) three days of pestilence in the land. David chose the three days of pestilence, counting on the mercy of the Lord. At the end of "the time appointed," 70,000 men had died, and God stayed the hand of the destroying angel.

David was by the threshing floor of a man named Araunah. The angel of the Lord appeared to him there, and David further repented and begged that the people be spared and the sin laid to his charge (2 Samuel 24:17). Then the angle commanded the prophet Gad to direct David to set up an altar on the threshing floor (1 Chronicles 21:18). David went to Araunah (Ornan, in Chronicles) to buy the floor. Araunah wanted to give it to him without charge, but David replied:

"Nay; but I will surely buy it of thee at a price: neither will I offer burnt offerings unto the Lord my God of that which doth cost me nothing" (2 Samuel 24:24).

He built the altar and offered burnt offerings and peace offerings. "So the Lord was entreated for the land, and the plague was stayed from Israel."

David's Last Year

"Now king David was old and stricken in years . . . " (1 Kings 1:1), and "Then Adonijah . . . exalted himself, saying, I will be king . . . " (1:5).

Adonijah proceeded with preparations for his coronation, with Joab and Abiathar the priest assisting him. But David and those closest to him did not know what was taking place until Nathan the prophet informed Bath-sheba. Nathan knew that it was David's desire that Solomon succeed him on the throne, because God had so ordered it (1 Chronicles 22:9).

Both Bath-sheba and Nathan went before David, relating to him all that Adonijah was doing. David gave them detailed instructions as to what should be done. (Read 1 Kings 1:32-35.) All were carried out while Adonijah and those with him were feasting at En-rogel, not knowing what was being done.

Just "as they had made an end of eating" (1:41), Jonathan, the priest's son, brought them the message: "Verily our lord king David hath made Solomon king . . . . And also Solomon sitteth on the throne of the kingdom" (1:43, 46). Fear fell upon the whole assemblage, and "they went every man his way," leaving Adonijah to fear for his life at the new king's hands! But Solomon was patient with him, and Adonijah bowed himself before Solomon.

David spent his last days counselling the people publicly, and Solomon privately. Certain men were to be slain for their past misdeeds, particularly Joab and Shimei; others were to be rewarded for their kindnesses. Apparently, he died with the building of the temple on his mind and heart. He had not been permitted to build it, having been a man engaged in much war; but he had gathered much of the material that would be required, and had given generously of his own means. God had shown him much of the pattern, and he charged Solomon to build accordingly (1 Chronicles 28:11-21).

"And he died in a good old age, full of days, riches, and honour: and Solomon his son reigned in his stead" (1 Chronicles 29:28).

FOR OUR ADMONITION AND LEARNING

Much can be learned from a close scrutiny of the life of David from his youth to his death. There is much to follow by way of example; then there are the warnings and admonitions. Wealth, power, and success have been the undoing of once-humble people of all generations, but they need not be any man's ultimate ruin.

Undoubtedly the thing which troubles the minds of most people concerning David is his exalted place in the overall plan of God, even to the end, though at times his guilt was so great as to seem almost unpardonable. From this very thing, in the light of the gospel of God in His Son Jesus Christ, we can receive the greatest of all truths pertaining to man's relationship with God.

Man is not capable of seeing as God sees. Outward appearance colors some things irretrievably if we do not see the truth of the gospel. We were all *utterly depraved sinners* before God; but while we were yet sinners, Christ died for us. Even yet, if the Father did not see us in His Son, He could not look upon us. But the most abominable element of *our fleshly nature in Adam* has received complete and perfect satisfaction by means of our sins having been imputed to Christ on Calvary and His righteousness having been imputed unto all who believe—who will trust and obey.

Only God knows the *sincerity* of a man's conviction, godly sorrow, confession, and repentance. It is more difficult for *men and women* to forgive the backslider to the point where full confidence is restored. We tend to hold in reserve the possibility that their repentance falls short of God's acceptance. This is something each of us must wrestle with for himself. But we must entertain no doubt about the Bible record, such as that of David, and some others. If *God* has accepted them and restored them, who are *we* to object?

"*Calvary covers it all*"—for others—and for you and me! Praise God!

—Lesson Five—

SOLOMON: THE THIRD KING

Required Scripture Readings: 2 Samuel 12:24, 25; 1 Kings, chapters 1 to 11; 1 Chronicles, chapters 28 to 30; 2 Chronicles, chapters 1 to 9; Matthew 1:6, 7.

Pronunciation Helps: Phoenician—FEE-nish-i-an; Abishag—AB-ish-ag; Shunammite—SHOO-na-mite; Zadok—ZA-dok; Abiathar—a-BI-a-thar; Benaiah—ben-A-ah; Ahijah—a-HI-jah; Hadad—HAY-dad; Rezon—REE-zon; Jeroboam—jera-BO-am.

RELEVANT FACTS
Chief characters: Solomon; all others decidedly secondary in the context.
Time span: 40 years (1015 to 975 B.C.)
Seat of government: Jerusalem.
Contemporary personalities: Nathan the prophet; Ahijah the prophet; and Iddo the seer (2 Chr. 9:29).
Lineage and family: Son of David and Bath-sheba. Tribe of Judah. Born about 1034 B. C. Wives: 700 (1 Kings 11:1-3), including a daughter of Pharoah, king of Egypt (1 Kings 3:1); Naamah, the Ammonitess (1 Kings 14:21). Son: Rehoboam (1 Kings 14:21); perhaps others.
Age at time of accession: About 19, according to the *Thompson Chain-Reference* chronology, in about 1015 B.C. However, *Josephus* says he was "but a youth in age."
Death: About 975 B.C. (1 Kings 11:41-43; 2 Chr. 9:29).

THE HISTORICAL SITUATION
At the time of David's death, Israel was in more of a victorious condition than they had been for many years, if ever before. The kingdom was greatly enlarged, extending from the Euphrates River on the northeast to the River of Egypt on the southwest.

The Philistines had been the most formidable foe, but David had crushed their power. In fact, militarily, all their neighboring nations had been subdued, and there was a standing army in constant training (1 Chronicles 21:5; 27:1-24). There was an important alliance in effect with Phoenician Tyre (2 Chronicles 2:3-14).

The "ark of the covenant" was in place at Jerusalem, and God had already given the plan for the temple, along with the directive that Solomon would supervise its construction. David had turned the hearts of his people to the one true and living God. The financial economy was sound. What better time for a new, young and wise king to inherit the throne?

SOLOMON THE KING
His Early, Good Years

We have seen how Solomon came to power within the year before David's death, this move having been made necessary by Adonijah's attempt to enthrone himself. But the people at large loved David, and his word and desires had been respected. Besides, the man of *God's choice* was now anointed and crowned.

"Then Solomon sat on the throne of the Lord as king instead of David his father, and prospered; and all Israel obeyed him.

"And all the princes, and the mighty men, and all the sons likewise of king David, submitted themselves unto Solomon the king.

"And the Lord magnified Solomon exceedingly in the sight of all Israel, and bestowed upon him such royal majesty as had not been on any king before him in Israel" (1 Chronicles 29:23-25).

"And Solomon the son of David was strengthened in his kingdom, and the Lord his God was with him, and magnified him exceedingly" (2 Chronicles 1:1).

Among Solomon's first official duties was the carrying out of his father's deathbed requests, the first being the execution of Joab (1 Kings 2:5, 6). Joab had made this easier for Solomon by his part in Adonijah's conspiracy (1 Kings 1:7).

But then Adonijah made a move which commentators and historians agree was a second effort to make the first conspiracy yet serve its purpose. It is difficult for the Bible reader to see this as a "scheme" unless it is understood that there were some very rigid rules concerning a ruler's concubines.

It is reasonably sure that the incident of 1 Kings 1:1-4 was recorded only as necessary to the understanding of the matter of Adonijah and Abishag (1 Kings 2:17ff). This in turn requires some knowledge of concubines, as spoken of in the Old Testament. This practice did not carry the stigma attached to it today. We think in New Testament terms, as we should, of course. (NOTE: We would advise the student to consult the subject in a good Bible dictionary.)

Keep in mind that the writers of the Old Testament knew that their readers had a knowledge of the early practice of concubinage. For instance, the thorough search for the young virgin for David was understood to mean a new concubine. Abishag, a Shunammite from Issachar, became a concubine in David's harem. A ruler's concubines were inherited by his successor to the throne. Usually the regulations were so rigid that having a ruler's concubine was a definite step toward claiming the throne. (Consider the incident about Absalom in 2 Samuel 16:20-23, again remembering that the intent was generally understood at that time.)

We can now better understand the incident recorded in 1 Kings 2:13-25, along with Solomon's unbending judgment. He was surprised that his mother had overlooked Adonijah's real intent. And, since Abiathar had "helped" Adonijah in his first conspiracy (1:7), Solomon counted him unfit for the priesthood, so he removed him and put Zadok in his place (2:27, 35).

While the wheels of judgment were turning, as it were, Solomon went on to fulfill his promises to David. Joab had slain Abner and Amasa. Besides this, he had involved himself in Adonijah's conspiracy, though he knew Solomon was to be king. So Solomon had Benaiah, his captain of the host, to slay Joab.

Then Shimei, of the house of Saul, was called in. He had cursed David, and cast stones at him during the time of Absalom's rebellion (2 Samuel 16:5-13); but after Absalom was dead, he confessed his sin, and David had spared his life (2 Samuel 19:18-23). Now Solomon restricted Shimei to the city of Jerusalem. If he ever crossed the brook Kidron, he would be put to death. (Three years later, he crossed the brook, and Solomon ordered him slain by Benaiah.)

The people could see that their new king did not use idle talk, nor did he compromise with sinful disobedience. It is therefore written, "And the kingdom was established in the hand of Solomon" (1 Kings 2:46).

About a year after he became king, Solomon married the daughter of the king of Egypt. Intermarriage was at least permissable under the law, except with the nations of Canaan. However, idolatry was to be renounced. Since Solomon, at this point in time, "loved the Lord, walking in the statutes of David his father" (1 Kings 3:3), it seems clear that this marriage had nothing to do with those which came later and "turned away his heart" (1 Kings 11:1-3).

Now Solomon commenced his greatest work for God; and God was leading. He began with a great sacrifice at Gibeon. The tabernacle of the congregation and the brazen altar were still there from the days of Saul, though David had provided a tent in Jerusalem for the ark of the covenant (2 Chronicles 1:1-6).

Solomon offered a thousand burnt offerings. If this seems to be a matter of "vain show," we are reminded that Solomon's kingdom began as a prosperous reign. There was an abundance of means; therefore the offerings to God were rightfully abundant. And that God *loved* this "cheerful giver" and approved the sacrifice is confirmed by His visitation of the young monarch that night.

God Personally Visits Solomon: We often say, "You can't out-give God." As though in response to Solomon's thousand burnt offerings, God "gave him a blank check," as it were: *"Ask what I shall give thee"!* Our first thought might be that that was a dangerous proposition to make to a youth who had known practically nothing of material hardship and the need for frugality. But God knew His man.

Humility, common sense, and respectful appreciation are all in evidence in Solomon's ready reply. He first remembered his father David, and how he had walked in truth and righteousness before God; then he recognized the faithfulness of God in placing him, David's son, on Israel's throne. Confessing his own insufficiency as leader of so great a people, he made a request that would put to shame many older minds:

"Give me now wisdom and knowledge, that I may go out and come in before this people: for who can judge this thy people, that is so great?" (2 Chronicles 1:10).

At this God-pleasing request, it was as though "the windows of heaven" were opened as the Omnipotent said:

"... Because this was in thine heart, and thou hast not asked riches, wealth, or honour, nor the life of thine enemies, neither yet hast asked long life; but hast asked wisdom and knowledge for thyself, that thou mayest judge my people, over whom I have made thee king:

"Wisdom and knowledge is granted unto thee; and I will give thee riches, and wealth, and honour, such as none of the kings have had that have been before thee, neither shall there any after thee have the like" (2 Chronicles 1:11, 12).

"And if thou wilt walk in my ways, to keep my statutes and my commandments, as thy father David did walk, then I will lengthen thy days" (1 Kings 3:14).

Soon after this, God put Solomon's wisdom on display before his people through his ministration of judgment in a simplistic yet awesome way. Two harlots brought an infant before Solomon, each claiming it as hers, since the child of the other had died. The king called for a sword, and ordered that the living child be cut in half and divided between the two women. Horrified, the real mother was willing to give the infant to the other woman rather than see it slain. The other was willing for Solomon's judgment to be carried out. Then, probably looking at the true mother, the wise, young ruler said:

"Give her the living child, and in no wise slay it: she is the mother thereof" (1 Kings 3:27).

God had used the incident to even more securely establish the king in his kingdom: "And all Israel heard of the judgment which the king had judged; and they feared the king: for they saw that the wisdom of God was in him to do judgment" (1 Kings 3:28).

The promised wealth rapidly became manifest through Solomon's sound management and administration of business. (See 1 Kings 4:1-28 and 2 Chronicles 1:14-17.) Greater still, his excelling wisdom became known abroad, "and his fame was in all nations round about" (1 Kings 4:29-34). And apparently, he kept a level head—for the time being.

Solomon's Greatest Work: It appears that Solomon began almost immediately after his enthronement to make preparations for the building of the temple (1 Kings 5 and 2 Chronicles 2). In the fourth year of his reign the construction began, and continued seven years (1 Kings 6 and 2 Chronicles

3, 4). The temple was elaborate and beautiful; however, little can be gathered from the Scriptures about its typology. The New Testament consistently refers to the *tabernacle* and its furnishings, rather than the *temple*, as types and shadows.

With solemn ceremony the ark of the covenant was moved from Mount Zion (The City of David) to the holy of holies in the new temple (1 Kings 8:1-11; 2 Chronicles 5:5-14). At that time it contained only the tables of stone on which were written the Ten Commandments. When the priests had come out of the holy place behind the veil, there was much praising the Lord, and a cloud filled the house. Josephus' description is interesting:

"Now as soon as the priests had put all things in order about the ark, and were gone out, there came down a thick cloud, and stood there, and spread itself, after a gentle manner, into the temple; such a cloud it was as was diffused and temperate, not such a rough one as we see full of rain in the winter season. This cloud so darkened the place, that one priest could not discern another, but it afforded to the minds of all a visible image and glorious appearance of God's having descended into this temple, and of His having gladly pitched his tabernacle therein . . . . "

Then Solomon delivered his dedicatory sermon, and prayed an all-encompassing prayer. (Read 1 Kings 8:12-53 and 2 Chronicles 6.) Considering the king's youth (almost certainly not more than twenty-two years old, and probably less), we are made acutely aware of God's anointing upon him as we ponder the substance of his message and supplication.

God's acceptance, both of the prayer and the temple, was awesome indeed! (Read 1 Kings 8:54-61 and 2 Chronicles 7:1-3; both passages are necessary if we are to appreciate the glory of the occasion.)

This great feast of sacrificing and rejoicing lasted a week; then "On the eighth day he sent the people away: and they blessed the king, and went unto their tents joyful and glad of heart for all the goodness that the Lord had done for David his servant, and for Israel his people" (1 Kings 8:66).

God Pays Solomon a Second Personal Visit: Chronology indicates that God appeared to Solomon a second time in the middle of his reign—about 992 B.C. (Read 1 Kings 9:1-9 and 2 Chronicles 7:12-22.) Following the building of the temple, "the king's house" (including his throne) was under construction thirteen years (1 Kings 7:1; 9:1, 2; 2 Chronicles 8:1).

God's words on the occasion of this second visitation strike us as fearsome forebodings! His *promises* were great and far-reaching; but the *conditions* were emphatic and unbending! The ensuing chapters confirm the foreknowledge of God in His solemn warnings! However, until now Solomon had apparently kept the fear and love of God. One last example is seen in these words:

"And Solomon brought up the daughter of Pharaoh out the city of David unto the house that he had built for her: for he said, My wife shall not dwell in the house of David king of Israel, because the places are holy, whereunto the ark of the Lord hath come" (2 Chronicles 8:11).

The Much-Heralded Fame of Solomon: It seems that God's promised gifts of *wisdom* and *knowledge* (2 Chronicles 1:10-12), or *understanding* and *discernment* (1 Kings 3:9-12), had brought Solomon great fame in the eyes and ears of other rulers and peoples far and wide. The biblical example (highly touted to this day) is the story of the visit of the Queen of Sheba (1 Kings 10:1-13; 2 Chronicles 9:1-12). *Josephus* describes her as a woman who was "inquisitive into philosophy." Suffice it to say that, prior to her visit, she had "heard of the fame of Solomon *concerning the name of the Lord,*" and in the end she gave *God* the credit for bestowing His gifts upon him.

We tend to make much of Solomon's fame and glory because of Jesus' mention of it on the occasion of this queen's visit (Matthew 12:42 and Luke 11:31). Let us not misconstrue the intent of His statement in its context. The doubting scribes and Pharisees had challenged Jesus to prove His divinity by a "sign." He reproved them, labeling them as "an evil and adulterous generation" which could not accept the Scriptural evidences. Jonah's miraculous deliverance was a great "sign." Solomon's "wisdom" was likewise great. But the people of their day had given them a better reception than the Son of God had received.

In other words, Solomon's fame depended on outward evidence, except to the few who could discern that God was with him. Jesus, the suffering Servant who made Himself of no reputation, actually made Solomon's fame appear as nothing to those few who could see beyond visible "signs" and "wonders," and discern Him from prophecy as the very Christ of God!

Space here requires that the student turn to 1 Kings 10:14-29 and 2 Chronicles 9:13-28 for a description of what C. I. Scofield labels *"Solomon's revenue and splendour."* (NOTE: *Josephus' "Antiquities of the Jews,"* pages 253, 254, will be of interest on this subject, for those who have his writings available.)

His Last, Regrettable Years

"But ... (1 Kings 11:1). Immediately following the glowing account of his fame, influence, wisdom, possessions, and splendor, the sacred record (which is committed to "all truth") relates a different chapter (1 Kings 11):

"But king Solomon loved many strange women...."

"Of the nations concerning which the Lord said unto the children of Israel, Ye shall not go in to them, neither shall they come in unto you: for surely they will turn away your heart after their gods: Solomon clave unto these in love.

"And he had seven hundred wives, princesses, and three hundred concubines: and his wives turned away his heart.

"For it came to pass, when Solomon was old, that his wives turned away his heart after other gods: and his heart was not perfect with the Lord his God, as was the heart of David his father."

The Lord was angry. Solomon had turned disobedient. He had violated God's covenant and His statutes. He had compromised with other "religions." Despite all previous favor, punishment had to be pronounced:

(1) His kingdom would be rent from him, though not at once—"for David thy father's sake" (11:12).

(2) God stirred up an adversary, an Edomite named Hadad, and through him another, Rezon. The record here is vague, but *Josephus* seems to indicate that these two began to take over territory in Damascus of Syria, which was under Solomon's rule.

(3) Another adversary, Jeroboam—one "within the ranks" —"lifted up his hand against the king" (11:26). Commentators, as well as the historian Josephus, hold that Jeroboam tried to take the throne from Solomon. Solomon had advanced him to a prominent position in "the house of Joseph," he being of the

tribe of Ephraim, and a brave, industrious man. Upon Solomon's failure in the favor of God, the prophet Ahijah delivered God's word to Jeroboam that He would make him ruler over ten tribes, but only after Solomon's death (11:34). Apparently, Jeroboam "could not be quiet," as Josephus puts it; and the *lifting up of his hand against the king* meant a premature attempt to take the kingship over *all Israel.* Solomon would have had him slain, but Jeroboam fled into Egypt.

Chronology has it that chapter 11 covers some seventeen years of Solomon's life. They are regrettable years. He died after reigning forty years, at the age of possibly less than sixty years. There is no word to indicate that he repented when he sinned, as David had done, unless the conclusion of the book of *Ecclesiastes* is so interpreted. Comments in the "Introduction" to that book in *The Pulpit Commentary* (p. IV) are against this conclusion. *Matthew Henry* is more optimistic; he leans toward Solomon's repentance. The truth is that *we do not know.* We can only hope that he repented and obtained pardon.

And we can be admonished!

FOR OUR ADMONITION AND LEARNING

Youth or *maturity*—these matter not if God, by His Holy Spirit, uses the lips and the hands! Let the aged be admonished by the fact that Solomon fully pleased God in his youth, then greatly angered Him in his later years!

In the context of "lively stones" (1 Peter 2:5), consider the following: "And the house, when it was in building, was built of stone *made ready before it was brought thither:* so that there was neither hammer nor axe nor any tool of iron heard *in the house,* while it was in building" (1 Kings 6:7). Put that with *"The Lord knoweth* them that are *His"* (2 Timothy 2:19), and "But now hath *God* set the members every one of them in the body, *as it hath pleased Him"*(1 Corinthians 12:18). Think of all the *chiseling,* and *chipping,* and *hammering* that might be avoided in building the Church —if—.

Different "religions" often become "attention getters." Then comes the *dabbling* and *experimentation*—the "philosophical reasoning," or logic. Many things are "fascinating," "moving," "ecstatic," or even "comfortably lukewarm" (promising "need of nothing," Revelation 3:16, 17). All so-called "Christian" systems mouth the name of *God,* or cry *"Lord, Lord!"* But who is their "deity"? Some should spell them with a small "g" or a small "l"! Solomon seemed to let his heart be turned away from his father's *God* to his wives' *gods!*

Usually we expect "the last chapter" to read that "they lived happily ever after." In real life it is not always so. Solomon's is a "real life" story. We are left in suspense! We are thereby admonished to contend for the blessed assurance—*"I KNOW whom I have believed . . . "!*

—Lesson Six—

THE DIVIDED KINGDOM

Following approximately one hundred twenty years as a united kingdom, there came a great division in Israel. We have seen the *immediate cause,* stated by one commentator thus: "The origin of this separation is declared to have been a *Divine judgment* on the house of David, in consequence of the idolatrous worship introduced by the foreign wives of Solomon, and criminally permitted or partaken of by that prince . . . ."

However, the immediate circumstance was facilitated by a "slow burning jealousy," dating back for many generations, between the tribe of Ephraim (representing Joseph) and the tribe of Judah. The blessings of both Jacob (Genesis 49:8-12, 22-26) and Moses (Deuteronomy 33:7, 13-17) on each of these tribes had foretold their future eminence. Each had experienced some prominence from time to time, but Ephraim usually found it difficult to cooperate when Judah was in the lead.

When the "scepter" finally was put in Judah's hands and the prophetic Davidic kingdom was in place, Ephraim frequently was unable to swallow her pride. When Saul died, Ephraim hearkened to Abner and went with Ishbosheth instead of with David (2 Samuel 2:9). Even then, there was a temporary seven-year division—a sort of foreboding of the future Northern and Southern Kingdoms. Then, following Absalom's rebellion and death, the spirit of jealousy flared up between "Israel" and "Judah," strangely enough because "Israel" had not had a greater part in restoring David (of the tribe of Judah) to the throne. Bear in mind that this "Israel"-"Judah" terminology was almost fifty years before the "division proper"—which we will look at more particularly under the study of the first kings of the two kingdoms respectively.

Briefly at this point, observe that "Israel" became the Northern Kingdom, and included the following ten tribes: Reuben, Simeon, Gad, Issachar, Zebulun, Ephraim, Manasseh, Dan, Asher, and Naphtali. "Judah" became the Southern Kingdom, with two tribes—Judah and Benjamin. (NOTE:

Though the Lord promised only one tribe, Judah, to the Davidic succession, the tribe of Benjamin stayed with Judah also, probably because the city of Jerusalem was on the border between the two tribes, and they prided themselves in having a part in Jerusalem, where the temple and the sacred "ark" were situated. The Levites, being the priestly tribe, soon gravitated to Judah.)

It should be noted here that "the twelve tribes" did not include the tribe of Levi after God set the Levites apart, Himself being their inheritance. (See Numbers 1:45-54; 26:57-62; and Deuteronomy 18:1, 2.) Possibly because of the ill-treatment of Joseph by his brethren, his two sons, Ephraim and Manasseh, were each counted as a tribe representing Joseph. In a sense, Jacob "adopted" these two grandsons (Genesis 48). Thus there were still twelve tribes, not counting the Levites in the same sense as the others.

THE KINGS OF ISRAEL

JEROBOAM I: FIRST KING OF ISRAEL

Required Bible Readings: 1 Kings 11:26-40; 12:2, 3, 16-33; 13:1-34; 14:1-20; 2 Chronicles 10:12-19; 11:14-17; 13:8, 15-20.

Pronunciation Helps: Zeruah—ze-ROO-ah; Nebat—NEE-bat; Shishak—SHI-SHACK; Rehoboam—REE-ho-BO-am; Ahijah—a-HI-jah; Abijah—a-BI-jah; Nadab—NA-dab; Tirzah—TER-zah.

RELEVANT FACTS
Chief characters: Jeroboam, Rehoboam, and the prophets.
Time span: 22 years (975-953 B.C.) 1 Kings 14:20.
Seat of government: Shechem (1 Kings 12:25); later, perhaps Tirzah (1 Kings 14:17).
Contemporary personalities: Kings of Judah: Rehoboam, Abijam, and Asa. Prophets: Iddo (2 Chr. 9:29), Ahijah (1 Kings 11:26-29; 12:15; 14:2-18; 2 Chr. 10:15), Shemaiah (1 Kings 12:22), and one unnamed.
Lineage and family: Father: Nebat, an Ephrathite, a servant of Solomon (1 Kings 11:26: 2 Chr. 10:2). Mother; Zeruah,

a widow (1 Kings 11:26). Sons: Nadab (1 Kings 14:20), and Ahijah (1 Kings 14:1).

Death: Cause uncertain—God struck him. (1 Kings 14:19, 20; 2 Chr. 13:15, 20.)

THE HISTORICAL SITUATION

In Lesson Five, brief mention was made of Jeroboam's advancement by King Solomon (1 Kings 11:26-40). Since his mother, Zeruah, is mentioned as a widow woman, it seems evident that his father, Nebat, who was one of Solomon's servants, had died sometime before Jeroboam came to Solomon's attention as "a mighty man of valor," and "industrious" (11:28).

Solomon saw in him the potential of a capable leader, or "ruler," so he put him "over all the charge of the house of Joseph," he being of the tribe of Ephraim. God's hand was in this appointment, for He sent the prophet Ahijah to Jeroboam with an illustrated message. The prophet rent a new garment in twelve pieces and gave ten of them to Jeroboam saying:

". . . Thus saith the Lord, the God of Israel, Behold, I will rend the kingdom from the hand of Solomon, and will give ten tribes to thee . . . .

"Howbeit I will not take the whole kingdom out of his hand: but I will make him prince all the days of his life for David my servant's sake . . . .

"But I will take the kingdom *out of his son's hand,* and will give it unto thee, even ten tribes.

"And unto his son will I give one tribe . . . .

"And I will take thee, and thou shalt reign according to all that thy soul desireth, and shalt be king over *Israel"* (1 Kings 11:31, 34-37).

It is not likely that Jeroboam misunderstood the message, which was clear enough that Solomon's son would become king over all Israel, momentarily, and that God would take the kingdom of Israel "out of his son's hand," not out of Solomon's hand. Jeroboam apparently became anxious and ambitious, and therefore "lifted up his hand against the king"—Solomon (11:26).

"Solomon sought therefore to kill Jeroboam. And Jeroboam arose, and fled into Egypt, unto Shishak king of Egypt, and was in Egypt until the death of Solomon" (11:40).

When Solomon died, his son Rehoboam met with "all Israel" at Shechem where, presumably, he would be made king (1 Kings 12:1). However, commentators tend to believe that the choice of Shechem instead of Jerusalem was significant; that the people were generally aware of the rift between Jeroboam and Solomon, and that, secretly, the ten tribes entertained some hope of making their man from Ephraim king. Planned or not, the time of division was at hand.

JEROBOAM THE KING

The Bible record concerning Israel's controversy over Rehoboam's accession in the Davidic line has perplexed commentators and historians. The question is: *Just when did Jeroboam return from Egypt; and was he present during the whole period of indecision?* In chapter twelve of 1 Kings, verses two and three appear to indicate that he was there almost from the beginning, while verse twenty could be understood to mean that he actually arrived only after the ten tribes had revolted.

We cannot hope to settle, in this course, what many wise heads have failed to reconcile over the many generations. However, if Jeroboam was present early in the conference, it seems definite that he made no effort to make himself king. In fact, it appears that in the beginning it was almost assumed that the right of kingship was Rehoboam's.

On the surface at least, the basis of the controversy was a complaint that Solomon had laid too great a tax burden on the people. They implored Rehoboam to make it lighter. He asked for three days to consider that matter. After the three-day interim, "Jeroboam and all the people" (12:12) seemed hopeful that Rehoboam's decision would be favorable. It was only after he had announced his "hard-line" decision that any specific mention was made of Jeroboam being made Israel's leader. Probably Jeroboam had enough trust in the prophet's declaration so that he felt no need to put himself forward. The outcome proved this to be true. The king—Rehoboam—"hearkened not unto the people; *for the cause was from the Lord,* that he might perform his saying . . . " (12:15; 11:30-37). (NOTE: Pertinent details omitted here will be included in a future lesson on King Rehoboam, since they pertain more to him.)

"Israel" revolted against Rehoboam and the house of David, and made Jeroboam their king (12:19, 20); and God forbade that Rehoboam try to force their return militarily (12:21-24).

Jeroboam established himself in Shechem, which was about twelve miles north of the Judean border, and about thirty miles north of Jerusalem. He was no sooner settled in his domain than he began to become troubled in his mind lest his people eventually defect to Judah because of its having been the long-time place of worship. He feared lest an annual gathering at the temple should eventually result in the people being won back to the house of David (12:26, 27). He had either forgotten or was ignoring the prophet Ahijah's admonition when God had promised him a kingdom:

"And it shall be, if thou wilt hearken unto all that I command thee, and wilt walk in my ways, and do that which is right in my sight, to keep my statutes and my commandments, as David my servant did; that I will be with thee, and build thee a sure house, as I built for David, and will give Israel unto thee" (1 Kings 11:38).

In a fleshly effort to forestall a defection, he "made two calves of gold" (12:28) and set them up upon "high places" (2 Chronicles 11:15; 1 Kings 12:29-31), one at Bethel in the extreme southern part of the kingdom, and one at Dan in the extreme north. He hoped that the convenience of these locales would appeal to the people, making it unnecessary to make the long and time-consuming trek to Jerusalem.

Apparently, though he could trust God to *give* him the kingdom, he would not trust Him to *maintain* it. So he presented his line of logic to the people (1 Kings 12:28), and proceeded to ordain a sacrificial feast at each place. The biblical time for the annual Feast of Tabernacles, or the harvest, was the fifteenth day of the seventh month. It has been suggested that the eighth month may have been thought attractive to the northern tribes because of the later harvest in that area. Maybe retaining the fifteenth day would pacify any dissenters.

Notice that the *ritual* of the sacrifice was "like unto the feast that is in Judah," and that he kept the familiar use of the *altar* before the people (1 Kings 12:32, 33). But the sacrificing was "unto the calves that he had made, " and "in the month which he had devised of his own heart."

Furthermore, "he made priests of the lowest of the people, which were not of the sons of Levi" (12:31). Josephus says that at Bethel Jeroboam "undertook to be high priest himself. So he went up to the altar, with his own priests about him: but when he was going to offer the sacrifices, and the burnt-offerings, in the sight of all the people, a prophet, whose name was Jadon, was sent by God, and came to him from Jerusalem . . . ."

The Bible does not give the prophet's name, but calls him "a man of God out of Judah," who "cried against the altar in the word of the Lord . . . "(1 Kings 13:1, 2), saying:

" . . . O altar, altar, thus saith the Lord; Behold, a child shall be born unto the house of David, Josiah by name; and upon thee shall he offer the priests of the high places that burn incense upon thee, and men's bones shall be burnt upon thee.

" . . . This is the sign which the Lord hath spoken; Behold, the altar shall be rent, and the ashes that are upon it shall be poured out" (1 Kings 13:2, 3).

Jeroboam was so enraged that he would have slain the man of God; but when he put forth his hand, it withered, and he could not use it! Then the altar was rent and the ashes poured out, according to the sign spoken of by the prophet! (NOTE: For the further fulfillment some 350 years later, after the Northern Kingdom and gone into exile, see 2 Kings 23:15-20.)

At Jeroboam's request, the man of God prayed for him and his hand was restored. The king invited him to go home with him and accept a reward, but the man refused because the Lord had forbidden him, saying, "Eat no bread, nor drink water, nor turn again by the way that thou camest" (13:9). But he fell victim to a subtil "religious snare," disobeying the Lord's restriction, and losing his life (13:11-32)!

The Levitical priests began to leave their assigned cities, and their possessions, returning to Judah and Jerusalem, "for Jeroboam and his sons had cast them off from executing the priest's office unto the Lord" (2 Chronicles 11:14). Jeroboam's innovations only worked against him.

Summarily, 1 Kings 12:30 is highly significant as pertaining to Jeroboam's "new idolatry," as it were: "And *this thing became a sin:* for the people went to worship before the one, even unto Dan." The magnitude of this abominable system, as God saw it, is reflected again and again in the inspired record of after-years. (See, for example, 1 Kings 14:16; 16:26; 21:22; 22:52; 2 Kings 3:3; 10:29; 13:2, 11; 14:24; 15:9, 18, 24, 28, where this notorious practice is associated with the name of *Jeroboam the son of Nebat, who made Israel to sin.*)

Jeroboam did not stand corrected by the prophet's warning and the accompanying sign (1 Kings 13:33, 34). Josephus claims that the "old prophet of Bethel" who lied to the prophet from Judah was a wicked man and a false prophet, and that he went to Jeroboam and explained away everything that had happened, so that no place was left for the hand of God in it all. Therefore, Jeroboam's sin was punished by his house being utterly cut off. The conditions under which this was foretold were quite unusual:

Abijah, one of the sons of Jeroboam and his wife, fell sick, and Jeroboam was anxious as to what the outcome would be. A man such as he had become would hardly show his face voluntarily to one of the prophets of the true and living God, especially if he had previously known that prophet. So Jeroboam sent his wife to the prophet Ahijah, instructing her to carefully conceal her identity.

The Pulpit Commentary suggests that Jeroboam surmised that God was punishing him for his sins through his son's illness. There is no word of repentance, nor any plea for the child's healing. He could not deny that Ahijah was a true prophet, for his very kingship confirmed that fact. Now he knew the same prophet would tell the truth; but he was afraid to hear it firsthand.

Ahijah was old now, and he could not see; but the Lord had already told him who was at the door, so he said, "Come in, thou wife of Jeroboam; why feignest thou thyself to be another? for I am sent to thee with heavy tidings" (1 Kings 14:6). Perhaps these words were personal to her as a mother, for it would be "heavy tidings" to learn that her child would be dead when she next saw him. But the burden of the prophet's message lay elsewhere:

"Go tell Jeroboam, Thus saith the Lord God of Israel . . . " (1 Kings 14:7).

First, read the prophet's message from the Bible in 1 Kings 14:7-16; then we give here that message for Jeroboam in the words of *Josephus:*

"Since I made thee a great man when thou wast little, or rather wast nothing, and rent the kingdom from the house of David, and gave it to thee, and thou hast been unmindful of these benefits, hast left off my worship, hast made thee molten gods and honoured them, I will in like manner cast thee down again, and will destroy all thy house, and make them food for the dogs and the fowls; for a certain king is rising up, by appointment, over all this people, who shall leave none of the family of Jeroboam remaining. The multitude also shall themselves partake of the same punishment, and shall be cast out of this good land, and shall be scattered into the places beyond Euphrates, because they have followed the wicked practices of their king, and have worshipped the gods that he made, and forsaken my sacrifices...."

Then, to the woman, he continued (still quoting *Josephus*)—

"But do thou, O woman, make haste back to thy husband, and tell him this message; but thou shalt then find thy son dead, for as thou enterest the city he shall depart this life; yet shall he be buried with the lamentation of all the multitude, and honoured with a general mourning, for *he was the only person of goodness of Jeroboam's family.*"

We assume that his wife repeated Ahijah's message, but possibly not until the mourning for their son was alleviated somewhat. At any rate, the words of prophecy made no impression on Jeroboam, for after this we read of his military engagement against Judah, who had a new king, Abijam (1 Kings 15:1), or Abijah (2 Chronicles 13:1).

The Bible is not clear on who waged the offensive, but Josephus lays it to Jeroboam, who, he says, despised the young Abijah "because of his age." Judah's army consisted of 400,000 valiant men of war—chosen men. Jeroboam "set the battle in array against him" with 800,000—also chosen, mighty men of valour (2 Chronicles 13:3)!

With the two armies facing each other, Abijah stood upon a mountain and demanded to be heard. He spoke almost like an anointed prophet as he "read Jeroboam's pedigree," so to speak (2 Chronicles 13:4-12). But evidently while he was speaking, the hard-hearted king of Israel proceeded to situate ambushments both before and behind the army of Judah. To the natural eye, Israel "had to win"—but not so! The half-size army, by comparison, *prayed, sounded their trumpets,* and *shouted,* "... and GOD smote Jeroboam and all Israel," and they fled—all but the 500,000 who "fell down slain" (13:17)! Besides, they lost the city of Bethel, among others, to Judah.

The conclusion is brief: "Neither did Jeroboam recover strength... and the Lord struck him, and he died" (2 Chronicles 13:20). Just how God "struck him" is as yet an unsolved conjecture. It matters not, else the Bible would tell us.

After reigning twenty-two years, he died; and his son Nadab became the second king of "Israel."

FOR OUR ADMONITION AND LEARNING

Jeroboam is a prime example of the fact that a good, valiant, industrious man can misuse or abuse his advancements, fall into the trap of "political ambition" and "religious chicanery," and be destroyed by his own stubborn disobedience!

No man can become so popular, so prominent, so revered—yea, so holy, or so Spirit-filled, that his opinions of worldly wisdom are to be accepted ahead of the Word of God! We may be tested and tried through an "old prophet's lies" (1 Kings 13:18), but "the roaring lion" will await us "just down the road" (13:24, 25) if we fall for the cunning deception rather than checking it against God's infallible, never-changing Word! We should not "go home with" or "eat with" people whom God has warned us to have no fellowship with!

—Lesson Seven—

NADAB: SECOND KING OF ISRAEL

Required Scripture Readings: 1 Kings 14:20; 15:25-31.

Pronunciation Helps: Gibbethon—GIB-eth-on; Baasha—bay-ASH-a.

RELEVANT FACTS
Chief character: Nadab.
Time span: 2 years; about 953-951 B.C.
Seat of government: Probably Shechem; but possibly Tirzah.
Contemporary personalities: Asa, king of Judah.
Lineage: Son of Jeroboam; of the tribe of Ephraim. Mother not named.
Death: Assassinated by Baasha, who succeeded him (1 Kings 15:28).

THE HISTORICAL SITUATION
As far as we know, Nadab was the only surviving son of Jeroboam. Israel had just lost 500,000 men in the battle with Judah. The city of Gibbethon was a Levite city in Dan, but the Levites had deserted it in their exodus to Judah. Since it bordered Philistine territory, the Philistines apparently had occupied it.

We are told that the city of Bethel was taken by Judah (2 Chronicles 13:19), but nothing is said of the golden calf idol that was worshipped there. Some have suggested that the people of Israel removed it to a place of safety when they saw the city threatened. It seems to have still been in existence some one hundred years later (2 Kings 10:29).

All in all, it was a difficult time for a new (and possibly young) king to take the throne.

NADAB THE KING
Little is known of Nadab, either before he became king or during his reign. It appears that he simply became king as a matter of inheritance from his father, Jeroboam. We are told

immediately that "he did evil in the sight of the Lord, and walked in the way of his father, and in his sin wherewith he made Israel to sin" (1 Kings 15:26).

The untimely death of his brother Abijah, whom the prophet had indicated was the only one in the house of Jeroboam in whom "some good thing toward the Lord God of Israel" could be found, had in no way inspired Nadab to be like that deceased one.

Near the end of his reign, "Nadab and all Israel laid seige to Gibbethon" (15:27), which meant war with the Philistines, who now claimed that it belonged to them. During this war, a conspiracy against the king developed—"Baasha...conspired against him." Conspiracy supposes the involvement of more than one person; however, no details are given in this instance.

At least one commentator suggests that Baasha was Nadab's captain of the host and took advantage of his position. *Josephus* states positively that Nadab "was conspired against while he was there by *a friend of his,* whose name was Baasha."

At any rate, "Baasha smote him...," or assassinated him, "and reigned in his stead" (15:27, 28). *Matthew Henry* makes the presumption that "so little interest had he in the affections of his people that his army did not only not avenge his death, but chose his murderer for his successor."

Be that as it may, Nadab had gained nothing by following in his wicked father's footsteps; and in the immediate subsequent history we will find that his brief two-year reign also brought Jeroboam's dynasty to its end, fulfilling Ahijah's prophecy (1 Kings 14:10-14).

FOR OUR ADMONITION AND LEARNING

Consider Jeroboam's two sons. It seems that Abijah was (as is sometimes said) "too good to live in this world," while Nadab was too wicked! It was probably the very goodness of God that He took Abijah to Himself. With a father such as Jeroboam and a brother of the same wicked caliber, what might Abijah have become?

Evil men seem not to care that their children may follow in their footsteps; in fact, they seem to desire that it be so! Still, Nadab, as an individual, was responsible for his own conduct.

And so are we all!

BAASHA: THIRD KING OF ISRAEL

Required Scripture Readings: 1 Kings 15:16, 17; 15:27-34; 16:1-6; 2 Chronicles 16:1-6.

Pronunciation Helps: Ben-hadad—ben-HAY-dad; Ijon—I-JON; Abel-beth-maachah—A-bel-beth-MAY-a-cah; Cinneroth—KIN-er-oth; Jehu—JAY-hew.

RELEVANT FACTS
Chief characters: Baasha and Asa.
Time span: 24 years, beginning around 950 B.C.
Seat of government: Tirzah (1 Kings 15:33).
Contemporary personalities: Asa, king of Judah; the prophets Azariah, Jehu, and Hanani.
Lineage and family: Son of Ahijah, of Issachar. Son: Elah.
Death: (1 Kings 16:6) Cause not given.

THE HISTORICAL SITUATION
At the time of Baasha's accession, Israel was trying to regain territory lost to Judah near the end of Jeroboam's reign (2 Chronicles 13:15-19), as well as Gibbethon, which the Philistines had taken over when the Levites had left it (1 Kings 15:28). Asa was king of Judah, "And there was war between Asa and Baasha king of Israel all their days" (1 Kings 15:16, 32).

The chronological order of the record (especially of Asa) both in 1 Kings and 2 Chronicles tends to confuse the student who endeavors to follow the orderly succession of events. For instance, Asa's death is recorded relative to his own reign, but he continues to be mentioned later in connection with other kings of Israel. This must not be allowed to cause undue concern as we follow each individual's history.

BAASHA THE KING
When Baasha and his fellow-conspirators had removed Nadab, Baasha became king. The conspiracy may have included the understanding that Baasha should be enthroned. At any rate, there seems to have been no opposition.

His first official act was to smite all the house of Jeroboam (1 Kings 15:29). "Any that breathed" would indicate that both men and women, aged and youth, were included. We are told so little of Jeroboam's family that it seems Baasha had little to fear from them; but apparently he was running no risk. Besides, the prophecy of Ahijah was coming to pass (1 Kings 14:7-11), even though Baasha may have taken that matter into his own hands, as we shall see momentarily.

War with Judah is about all that remains of Baasha's history. It must have been with some success, for he penetrated the territory of Judah as far south as Ramah, only a few miles from Jerusalem (2 Chronicles 16:1; 1 Kings 15:17). It is safe to assume that Bethel also was regained for Israel. In saying that Baasha "built Ramah," historians claim that he aimed to make it something of a fortress by which to check the defection of his own people to Jerusalem.

Although the Bible record gives no details of it, it does hint that King Ben-hadad of Syria made leagues with Judah and Israel by turns, probably with whichever was most to his advantage at a given time. Asa appealed to him to make a league with him, such as had at one time existed between their fathers; but in order to do this, it would be necessary to break a league which was then in effect between Syria and Israel (1 Kings 15:18-20; 2 Chronicles 16:2-4).

It is apparent, then, that Ben-hadad and his army had first aided Israel in their advances into Judah's territory. Now he "hearkened unto king Asa, and sent the captains of his armies against the cities of Israel . . . " (2 Chronicles 16:4). Undoubtedly "the silver and gold" offered him by Asa was too attractive to turn down.

Strangely, the cities and territory which Ben-hadad smote— "Ijon, and Dan, and Abel-beth-maachah, and all Cinneroth, with all the land of Naphtali" (1 Kings 15:20)—were all in the extreme northern end of Israel, near Syria, and far removed from Judah. This seems to have been purely a matter of distracting Baasha's interest from his Ramah project. No mention is made of troops from Judah joining the Syrian invaders, nor of Israel's troops offering resistance.

When Baasha heard what had taken place in Naphtali, "he left off building of Ramah, and let his work cease" (2 Chronicles 16:5). This is taken by some commentators to indicate a weakness in the mighty ten-tribe Israel with relation to the two-tribe Judah. He retired to Tirzah to live out the rest of his days.

There remains only the sentence of God against Baasha (1 Kings 16:1-4). This judgment has puzzled commentators, in that Baasha was so greatly condemned for doing against the house of Jeroboam that which God had ordained. But God is *just,* as well as *sovereign;* and His ways are past finding out (Romans 11:33, 34).

In God's reproving judgment through His prophet Jehu, something surfaces about Baasha that we have not been aware of before. God had "exalted [him] out of the dust" (1 Kings 16:2). *The Pulpit Commentary* says, "These words assuredly point to a lowly origin. He may well have risen from the ranks." The same commentator suggests that his being "of the house of Issachar" (1 Kings 15:27) may have been mentioned to recall "the significance of this tribe (Genesis 49:14, 15); then goes on to say, "Baasha owed his elevation to his own abilities or to his unscrupulous daring."

However that may have been, God had exalted him from the dust to the throne; yet, instead of honoring the Lord, he had followed Jeroboam's example, and had made the people of God to sin. Now he must suffer like judgment with Jeroboam. His posterity, and that of his house, would be taken away. Those of his family who would die would be eaten by the dogs and the fowls.

If we would ask why Baasha was punished for fulfilling prophecy, we must also ask: *Who was Baasha, that he should exterminate a man's house, then live just as wickedly?* Besides, his judgment was also for his own sinful reign.

After twenty-four years of nothing but evil, Baasha died, and his son Elah succeeded him.

FOR OUR ADMONITION AND LEARNING

Attainments made as the result of conspiracy will come to no good end. In order to pull a man down, one must be lower than he whom he pulls down. Baasha may have gloried for a few years in his execution of Nadab and all of Jeroboam's house; but the wicked all fall into one pit. And that pit is hell!

How oft has our loving God found men and women *in the dust of nothingness,* seen in them some potential for good, and exalted them to where that potential could develop! Israel herself is the most glaring example of this, as Ezekiel reminded her some three hundred fifty years later. (See Ezekiel 16. Though written of Jerusalem and Judah, all Israel was of the same root.) In fact, as Paul has said, "There is no difference: for all have sinned, and come short of the glory of God" (Romans 3:22, 23). But, thank God, not all have been as ungrateful as was Baasha. It will be profitable for us all, from time to time, to remember where God found us!

—Lesson Eight—

ELAH: FOURTH KING OF ISRAEL

Required Scripture Reading: 1 Kings 16:6, 8-14.

Pronunciation Helps: Elah—EE-lah; Arza—AR-za; Zimri—ZIM-RI.

RELEVANT FACTS
Chief characters: Elah and Zimri.
Time span: 2 years, about 930 B.C.; actually less than two full years, as can be seen by comparing 1 Kings 16, verses 8 and 10.
Seat of government: Tirzah.
Contemporary personalities: Asa, king of Judah, and Jehu the prophet (1 Kings 16:1-14).
Lineage and family: Son of Baasha; tribe of Issachar.
Death: Slain by Zimri (16:10).

THE HISTORICAL SITUATION
The once-Levite city of Gibbethon was still (or again?) in Philistine hands, and Israel was attempting to recover it. Though this is not mentioned in the few verses specifically pertaining to Elah, it is mentioned in connection with the seven-day reign of his successor, Zimri (1 Kings 16:15).

ELAH THE KING
As seen above, the events concerning Elah and Zimri are so interwoven that the brief history of Elah must draw on facts involving others.

We are not told how long the conflict over Gibbethon lasted (16:15), but it seems clear that it began after Elah came to the throne. At any rate, it figured in the only event recorded about Elah, which was at the end of his less than two-year reign.

Commentators parallel his history with that of Nadab, with the notable exception that Nadab went to battle with his army, but Elah stayed at home, sending his men to face the Philistine foe. He is criticized for this, as being cowardly, or irresponsible, or unconcerned. *Matthew Henry* judges him as having "loved his own ease and safety better than his honor or duty, or the public good." While this *seems* a reasonable assumption, of course we do not know why he remained at Tirzah.

He can hardly be excused for "drinking himself drunk" in his steward's house; but here again we are dealing with a conspiracy. It is not at all unlikely that the steward, Arza, was one of Zimri's co-conspirators. If so, the drinking bout may have been planned. And it seems suspicious that Zimri, being captain of half of Elah's chariots, should also have been in Tirzah instead of at Gibbethon.

All conjectures aside, the fact remains that Zimri went into Arza's house while the king was drinking there, and assassinated him. Was Arza at home? Was Elah a habitual drunkard? Should he have been elsewhere? We do not have positive answers. Since he was a follower in his father's steps (16:13), we might be unduly prone not to credit him with *any* good thing.

FOR OUR ADMONITION AND LEARNING

When we do not have all the facts, it is not amiss to give even a sinful person "the benefit of the doubt." It is not unusual to find "a soft spot" in the hardest of hearts. Elah may have had a poor chance to become an upright man. Apparently he had at least two generations of evil examples behind him!

ZIMRI: FIFTH KING OF ISRAEL

Required Scripture Readings: 1 Kings 16:9-20.
Pronunciation Helps: Omri—OM-RI; Jehoadah—jee-HO-a-dah; Moza—MO-za.

RELEVANT FACTS

Chief characters: Zimri, Omni, and Elah.
Time span: 7 days (1 Kings 16:15).
Seat of government: Tirzah.
Contemporary personalities: Asa, king of Judah; Jehu, the prophet.

Lineage and family: Servant of Elah (1 Kings 16:9). Apparently he was a Benjamite, a descendant of Jonathan; his father's name was Jehoadah (1 Chronicles 8:16). If so, he had a son named Moza.

Death: Suicide (1 Kings 16:18).

ZIMRI THE KING

(The "Historical Situation" was the same as for Elah's reign.)

We have seen, under Elah's history, that Zimri was the chief conspirator against Elah; also his murderer. Since "as soon as he sat on the throne ... he slew all the house of Baasha," including his kinsfolks and friends (16:11), it appears that this deed was his passion and purpose for desiring to be king.

It is not said that the people made him king. He may have usurped the throne while attention was on the war. *Josephus* says "he took the kingdom himself." But when the people who were encamped at Gibbethon heard what he had done, he seems to have been rejected, for "all Israel made Omri, the captain of the host, king over Israel that day in the camp" (16:16).

When Omri and "all Israel" returned from Gibbethon, they besieged Tirzah. We may suppose that there was at least a small element there that supported Zimri; but when he saw that the city was taken, "he went into the palace of the king's house, and burnt the king's house over him ... and died" (16:18).

Zimri had become his own instrument in bringing the judgment of God upon himself for his sins and his treason against Elah. As with Baasha, so with Zimri; he was ill-qualified to purge another's house when his own was equally evil.

What an eternal price to pay for seven days on a stolen throne!

FOR OUR ADMONITION AND LEARNING

Those other than kings have been known to lay treacherous schemes against others, for nothing more than the egotistical satisfaction of proving that they can unseat a brother and take his chair. And some have possibly committed *spiritual suicide* rather than repent or be brought to justice!

OMRI: SIXTH KING OF ISRAEL

Required Scripture Readings: 1 Kings 16:16-29.

Pronunciation Helps: Tibni—TIB-NI; Shemer—SHEE-mer; Ahab—A-HAB; Ginath—GI-nath.

RELEVANT FACTS
Chief characters: Omni and Tibni.
Time span: 12 years, beginning about 929 B.C. (1 Kings 16:23).
Seat of government: Tirzah, six years; Samaria, six years (16:23, 24).
Contemporary personalities: Asa, king of Judah; Jehu, the prophet.
Lineage and family: Tribe not known. There are Omris listed in 1 Chronicles 7:8 (a Benjamite), and 9:4 (of Judah), but there is no reason to think they were the same as King Omri. He was "captain of the host" under Elah (1 Kings 16:16). Son: Ahab.
Death: Apparently of natural causes (16:28).

THE HISTORICAL SITUATION
The short span of time covered between the end of Baasha's reign and the beginning of Omri's gives room for little change in the historical conditions. However, Zimri's burning of the palace at Tirzah left Omri with something of an inconvenience. Secular history records the name of Omri (*Humri* in the Assyrian language), and his name was found on the famous Moabite Stone. *Zondervan's Bible Dictionary* states: "It is a fact that Omri subdued Moab."

OMRI THE KING
We have seen that Omri, as captain of the host under Elah, was at Gibbethon when Zimri assassinated Elah and took the throne. But when the army made Omri king, a brief contest ensued; but Zimri's suicide brought that to a quick conclusion.

However, not everybody was happy with the army's selection of Omri. He had another contender, Tibni, the son of Ginath, about whom nothing but their names are recorded. Half of the people of Israel followed Tibni, but those who favored Omri prevailed. Comparing 1 Kings, verses eight and twenty-three, it seems possible that this contention may have lasted three or four years; but Tibni is not numbered as one of Israel's official kings. His death is said (by historians) to have been at the hands of "the conqueror," possibly Omri; but the Bible simply says, "so Tibni died, and Omri reigned" (16:22).

After six years in Tirzah, probably with only a temporary "palace" from which to administer his royal affairs, "he bought the hill of Samaria," and built (evidently a new king's palace) on that hill. The word "Samaria" is a variation of the name "Shemer," from whom the purchase was made.

This move has been lauded as a wise relocation of Israel's capital, for its beautiful situation, its impregnable position of safety from enemy attack, and its convenient location on the main road from southern to northern Israel. It remained the capital until the exile in 721 B.C.

Omri's overall reign was characterized as of the evil pattern set by Jeroboam (16:25, 26), which included the worship of the golden calves. *Josephus* gives a fitting summation:

"Now Omri was no different from those kings that reigned before him, but that he grew worse than they, for they all sought how they might turn the people away from God by their daily wicked practices; and on that account it was that God made one of them to be slain by another, and that no one person of their families should remain."

Josephus' last statement must be qualified somewhat, since Omri actually began a dynasty which continued around thirty-five years through the reigns of Ahab, Ahaziah, and Jehoram.

FOR OUR ADMONITION AND LEARNING

Evil tends to beget worse and worse evils. The prophet Micah wrote of "the statues of Omri" (Micah 6:16) as having had a part in making Israel "a desolation." Since Omri "did worse than all that were before him," Micah passes over the notorious "sin of Jeroboam, who made Israel to sin," showing that the devil is never at a loss to bring forth something more wicked than ever before.

Often those who see their sin, and resolve to reform, find themselves impelled to commit even greater ones, and helpless in the enemy's hands! Only by fleeing to the Saviour and casting themselves at His feet, confessing their utter lostness in Adam, may they enjoy the miraculous deliverance out of the power of Adam's successful tempter!

But there *is* deliverance! Thank God!

—Lesson Nine—

AHAB: SEVENTH KING OF ISRAEL

Required Scripture Readings: 1 Kings 16:28 to 22:40; 2 Chronicles 18:1-34.

Pronunciation Helps: Jehoshaphat—jee-HOSH-a-fat; Hiel—HI-el; Ahaziah—A-ha-ZI-ah; Micaiah—mi-KAY-ah; Joram—JO-ram; Jehoram—je-HO-ram; Cherith—KEH-rith; Zaraphath—ZARA-fath; Obadiah—O-ba-DI-ah; Ramoth-gilead—RAY-moth-GIL-e-ad.

RELEVANT FACTS

Chief characters: Ahab; the prophet Elijah and Micaiah; Jezebel; Jehoshaphat.

Time span: 22 years (1 Kings 16:28-34); beginning about 920 or 919 B.C. (*Thompson's Chain-Reference* chronology).

Seat of government: Samaria; a second palace at Jezreel.

Contemporary personalities: Asa and Jehoshaphat, kings of Judah; the prophets Elijah and Micaiah.

Lineage and family: Son of Omri; tribe not known. Wife: Jezebel; perhaps others. (Jezebel was princess of Tyre and daughter of Ethbaal, king of the Zidonians.) Sons: Ahaziah and Joram (Jehoram); "seventy sons" (2 Kings 10:1).

Death: Slain in battle (1 Kings 22:34-40).

THE HISTORICAL SITUATION

A Preview

In certain respects a new era for Israel was ushered in with the reign of Ahab. In fact, his father Omri should be included in one phase of it—that of building cities. Omri had made a principal city out of Samaria. Ahab had other cities built, enlarged, or restored (1 Kings 22:39). Jezreel was perhaps the most important one—and Jericho the most infamous.

Material prosperity marked the new era; but, though God often allows this, it is seldom for the lasting good of a nation—or even a church (consider the Laodicean church).

Wealth tends to foster pride and vanity, and a dependence on the arm of flesh.

The era also was marked by a terrifying plunge into idolatry, with not only a disregard for the Second Commandment (as with Jeroboam) but an open defiance of the First Commandment, as we shall see. With this came a flagrant disobedience regarding intermarriage with the Canaanites (Exodus 34:16).

Along with the pathetic spiritual declension came the counteracting ministry of the greatest prophet since Moses—the prophet Elijah. In fact, this was the beginning of what one commentator has called "a great extension of the prophetic order and mission," with an unparalleled frequency of miracles and a spectacular demonstration of God's power.

During this period Israel and Syria were in almost constant conflict, waging three distinctive wars. At the other extreme was a sort of alliance between Israel and Judah, at least for a short period of time.

AHAB THE KING

1 Kings 16:28-34 gives a brief preview of Ahab's twenty-two year reign which immediately characterizes him: "And Ahab the son of Omri did evil in the sight of the Lord above all that were before him" (verse 30). The same was said of his father (verse 25), but now Ahab has outdone Omri in evil.

Then we are given a glimpse of the chief instigation for this affluence of wickedness: Ahab deliberately defied the law of God and married a Canaanite woman—Jezebel, a Baal worshipper of the worst sort, who led her husband into that heathen, idol service and worship. In God's eyes, this was a sin so horrible that, by comparison, the sins of Jeroboam were "a light thing" (1 Kings 16:31).

Next we see another open violation of a specific order of God given in Joshua's day: The rebuilding of the wicked city of Jericho (Joshua 6:26). Though Hiel the Bethelite was in charge, Ahab was king. True to the earlier warning, Hiel's firstborn died when the foundation was laid, and his youngest son died when the work was completed (1 Kings 16:34). (NOTE: Such expressions as "in the firstborn" and "in the youngest" in early passages of Scripture had reference to the price of a thing. In this case, the "price" to Hiel for the rebuilding of Jericho was the life of two of his sons.)

Enter the Prophet

We cannot be sure just how long Ahab had been king before God confronted him with his terrible sinfulness through the prophet Elijah. The *Thompson Chain-Reference* chronology fixes the date for 1 Kings 17 at about 910 B.C., or perhaps ten years into Ahab's reign. At any rate, his pattern of exceeding sin was so evident to God that He sent Elijah to warn him.

Their first confrontation was brief: "As the Lord God of Israel liveth, before whom I stand, there shall not be dew nor rain these years, but according to my word (1 Kings 17:1). In other words, an extensive drouth would immediately begin, and there would be no more rain—nor even dew—until God should send Elijah again to announce it.

The Lord had His plans for the care of His prophet. First, He directed him to a hiding place by the brook Cherith, near Jordan, not far north of the Dead Sea. There he had water to drink for a season, and God commanded the ravens to bring him bread and meat (1 Kings 17:2-7). Then, when the brook dried up, the Lord sent him to Zaraphath, south of Zidon, in Phoenicia—a distance of some one hundred fifteen miles north from the brook Cherith. There he was sustained by a widow woman until the drouth ended (17:8-16). This widow's son fell ill, and "his sickness was so sore, that there was no breath left in him" (17:17). God used Elijah wonderfully in the restoring of the child.

At the end of three and a half years (18:1; James 5:17), the Lord said to Elijah, "Go, shew thyself unto Ahab; and I will send rain upon the earth." *As God would have it,* about that time Ahab and Obadiah, the governor of his house, went in search of water and grassland, for "there was a sore famine in Samaria" (18:2). Ahab went one way and Obadiah another.

Now Obadiah (not the prophet Obadiah) was a God-fearing man. Jezebel had had God's prophets "cut off," or slain (18:4, 13), but Obadiah had hid one hundred of them in two caves, and had fed them during the drouth. *As God would have it,* Elijah met Obadiah, probably near Mount Carmel, about fifty miles south of Zaraphath. He told Obadiah to go and tell Ahab, "Behold, Elijah is here."

A great fear fell on Obadiah, for he knew his master well. He had sent many others in search of the prophet, and it had not gone well with them, because they had not found him.

Now Obadiah feared that Elijah would go into hiding again while he was bringing Ahab, and that the king, in anger, would slay him. But Elijah assured him that he would show himself unto Ahab that day; so Obadiah delivered the message, and Ahab went to meet Elijah (18:16).

Ahab's first insolent words were, "Art thou he that troubleth Israel?" Elijah turned the trouble-maker role on Ahab: "I have not troubled Israel; but thou, and thy father's house, in that ye have forsaken the commandments of the Lord, and thou hast followed Baalim" (18:18).

Perhaps Elijah did not give Ahab opportunity to refute the charge. Quickly he challenged the king to a showdown. Ahab should gather all Israel, along with his four hundred fifty prophets of Baal, and the four hundred prophets of the groves (seemingly Jezebel's particular variety), and meet him on Mount Carmel, where it was to be made known who was "God." In due time, the session convened.

As is so often the case when despots are in power, the people seemed uncertain. Elijah spoke to them first, pressing them to make a firm decision either for God or Baal. "And the people answered him not a word" (18:21). So he set forth his proposition. It would be Elijah ("I, even I only"—18:22) against the four hundred fifty prophets of Baal. Each side would offer a sacrifice without putting the usual fire under it, and "the God that answereth by fire, let him be God." The people agreed.

The prophets of Baal were extended the courtesy of being first. They laid their bullock on their altar and began to call on Baal to hear them. They leaped upon the altar, but at noon Baal hadn't answered. Elijah mocked them, and goaded them to greater fervency; perhaps Baal slept (18:27)! So they worked themselves into a mad frenzy, even cutting their flesh with knives and lancets till the blood gushed out. Evening came; no fire! It was Elijah's time—*and God's!*

He called the people to come near. He "repaired the altar of the Lord that was broken down," evidently by taking twelve stones and building it "in the name of the Lord" (18:30, 32). He made a trench around the altar; then he put the wood in place and laid the bullock on the wood. Take note that this *type of John the Baptist* "prepared the way" up to this point. No man was asked to contribute a single thing, nor to do any work.

Only then did he give *the people* opportunity—not to help the Lord, but to hinder the only true evidence—*the fire of God!* "Fill four barrels with water, and pour it on the burnt sacrifice, and on the wood" (18:33). Twelve barrels of water drenched the sacrifice and filled the trench. Then God's man stood before Him and prayed:

"Lord God of Abraham, Isaac, and of Israel, let it be known this day that thou art God in Israel, and that I am thy servant, and that I have done all these things at thy word.

"Hear me, O Lord, hear me, that this people may know that thou art the Lord God, and that thou hast turned their heart back again" (1 Kings 18:36, 37).

Without any leaping on the altar, without any loud crying, without either self-punishment or self-righteousness, he prayed a prayer two sentences and twenty seconds long. "Then the fire of the Lord fell and consumed the burnt sacrifice, and the wood, and the stones, and the dust, and licked up the water that was in the trench.

"And when all *the people* saw it, they fell on their faces: and they said, The Lord, he is the God; the Lord, he is the God."

Then Elijah commanded *the people* to "take" the prophets of Baal, and he slew every single one of them. And this was done, with Ahab looking on—in silence. He must have looked pitiful and pathetic as the prophet turned to him and said, "Get thee up, eat and drink; for there is a sound of abundance of rain."

Whether "fasting" had been a part of the Baal ritual we are not told. Maybe Ahab had been too "excited" with *hopeful anticipation* to take time out for lunch. But even though his side had suffered *hopeless disappointment,* it was time to get on with the *affairs of State.*

While Ahab was having dinner, Elijah and his servant went to the top of Carmel. The *fire* had fallen, but not the *rain,* as yet. Elijah prayed (James 5:18) while the servant watched the sky for clouds. Six trips he made from the place of prayer to where he could look out over the old Mediterranean, each time reporting, "There is nothing." But the seventh time was different: "Behold, there ariseth a little cloud out of the sea, like a man's hand."

If Ahab was still eating, his dinner was interrupted when Elijah's servant stood at his side with the message: "Prepare thy chariot, and get thee down, that the rain stop thee not."

Ahab may have thought to finish his "lamb chop" and have one more drink, but "in the mean while the heaven grew black with clouds and wind." Surely Ahab must have accelerated his travel plans at that point. The Bible says, "And Ahab rode, and went to Jezreel" (18:45). Under the circumstances, we must assume that he *rode fast,* for "there was a great rain"! If his chariot stayed ahead of the rainstorm, there was no time to lose.

While they were hurriedly loading the chariot, *God laid His hand on Elijah* (18:46), and he tightened the girdle of his loins. This procedure is hardly done for a leisurely stroll, but for a footrace. When the old chariot rolled down from Mount Carmel, perhaps drawn by the king's swiftest steeds, Elijah took the lead on foot, "and ran before Ahab to the entrance of Jezreel"—about twenty-five miles!

Enter Jezebel

When Ahab recapped the day's events to Jezebel, and she learned that all the prophets of Baal had been slain (*Josephus* says "her prophets"—the prophets of the groves—probably besides the prophets of Baal), she swore by her gods that Elijah too would be slain by the next day at that time. When her messenger told this to Elijah, "he arose, and went for his life . . . " (19:3)—to Beer-sheba, to Mount Horeb, then to Syria, and back into Israel (19:3-16).

Enter Syria

According to the chronology, about five years after the contest on Mount Carmel, the Syrians, under King Ben-hadad, along with twenty-five other kings (probably vassals), beseiged or surrounded Samaria (20:1). Then he sent his terms to Ahab, demanding the surrender of his personal wealth, and also his wives and children.

Ahab's ready concession could have meant that he saw that Israel's forces were no match for Syria's. Despite *the people's* confession on Mount Carmel, Ahab at this point seemed not to consider looking to God for help. Some contend that he was simply leading Ben-hadad on, so to speak, never intending to meet his demands.

Ben-hadad next was emboldened to spoil all Israel, supposing that "house" included the whole house of Israel (20:6).

He set the time for the next day. But Ahab, though possibly willing to meet the personal terms, was less so to surrender the whole nation. He sought the advice of the elders, and they said, "Hearken not unto him, nor consent." Ahab sent that message to the Syrian king.

Ben-hadad returned a boastful threat of war, and Ahab sent him a timely retort: "Let not him that girdeth on his harness boast himself as he that putteth it off" (20:11). Further emboldened by drink, Ben-hadad set his army in array.

But God was watching! He sent a prophet to tell Ahab that, regardless of Syria's great multitude, He would deliver them into Israel's hands, by "the young men of the princes of the provinces," two hundred thirty-two in number; and Ahab would order the battle. God stipulated His purpose in this apparently one-sided fight as being that Ahab should know that He was the Lord.

A meager army of seven thousand was mustered to back up the young men, and they went out at noon to face the foe. Ben-hadad sent "a drunken order" for his great army to take Israel's host alive, even if they had come out peaceably.

The battle was surprisingly short. *Josephus* indicates that Ben-hadad and the Syrians were so cocksure that they had no idea that Ahab would attack. His army did not even have on their armor. Israel's young men, by God's power, began slaying the Syrians, and they fled in confusion. Ben-hadad and his horsemen escaped on horses, and Ahab "smote the horses and chariots, and slew the Syrians with a great slaughter" (20:21).

The unnamed prophet visited Ahab again and told him to strengthen his forces and be prepared, for "at the return of the year" the Syrians would strike again.

In Syria, Ben-hadad was planning a new strategy. In his spiritual ignorance, he reasoned that Israel's "gods" did better in the hills, so he would fight them in the plains. At the appointed time the battle was pitched at Aphek. The Syrians "filled the country," while Israel was "like two little flocks of kids" (20:27).

"A man of God" came to Ahab promising that God would give Israel a great victory. After seven days the battle was joined, and Israel slew one hundred thousand Syrians in one day. The rest fled to Aphek, where a wall fell on twenty-seven thousand more! Again Ben-hadad fled. *Josephus* says that he and some of his most faithful servants hid themselves in a cellar for fear of Ahab. The servants suggested that they appeal to Ahab to spare Ben-hadad's life, which they did; and Ahab seemded more than glad to oblige.

But God was displeased with this "covenant" arrangement (20:34), and sent a prophet to Ahab with a message. In a manner similar to that used by Nathan in confronting David with his sin, the prophet made Ahab to understand that he had allowed his enemy to "escape." Because of his having done so, the time would come when Ahab's life would be taken instead of Ben-hadad's, and that Israel would suffer a defeat at Syria's hands (20:42).

Enter Infamy!

Ahab apparently was stubborn about owning God as the Lord. We now find him involving himself in an act of terrible infamy. Next to his palace in Jezreel, a man named Naboth owned a vineyard which he cherished as an inheritance from his ancestors. Ahab wanted to buy it, but Naboth wouldn't sell.

Ahab probably was not accustomed to having his will opposed, so he went home displeased and acting like a spoiled child (1 Kings 21:4). But Jezebel reminded him that he was king; and she promised that she would obtain the vineyard for him. So she framed a lie against Naboth and sent letters in the king's name to the elders and nobles of the city, instructing them to proclaim a fast, and to set Naboth before the court. Two sons of Belial were to witness against him, saying that he had blasphemed God and the king.

Jezebel's treacherous scheme was carried out, and Naboth was stoned to death under a false accusation. Ahab then took possession of the coveted vineyard; *but he was not to enjoy it.* Apparently the Lord had the prophet Elijah there, perhaps on the occasion of Ahab's having "gone down to possess it" (21:18)! Imagine the "greeting":

"In the place where dogs licked the blood of Naboth shall dogs lick thy blood, even thine" (21:19).

Ahab still counted Elijah as his enemy. But Ahab was the enemy of God, having completely *sold himself to work evil!* Elijah pronounced God's judgment against Ahab—and Jezebel.

God would take away his posterity and cut off his entire family in due time. As for Jezebel, "The dogs shall eat Jezebel by the wall of Jezreel" (21:23; see 2 Kings 9:30-37).

At last God's conviction touched the wicked monarch of Israel (21:27). Did he *repent?* God said he was *humbled* (verse 29); and because he humbled himself, God postponed His pronouncement against him until the days when his sons would reign.

Re-enter Syria

After three years of at least a strained peace, God began to bring to pass His word concerning the matter of Ahab and Ben-hadad (20:42).

Jehoshaphat was now the king of Judah, and there was an affinity between him and Ahab, because Jehoram (Joram), Jehoshaphat's son, had married Ahab and Jezebel's daughter, Athaliah (2 Kings 8:18, 25-27). So Jehoshaphat was visiting Ahab, and it came about, at Ahab's suggestion, that Jehoshaphat agreed to go with him to war against Syria. Ahab rather smoothly presented the matter as a joint-claim of Israel and Judah against Syria, saying that Ramoth-gilead "is ours," and that "they" should repossess it (22:3, 4).

Jehoshaphat readily agreed, but wanted to inquire of the Lord about the matter. Ahab called in about four hundred "prophets," who all agreed that the Lord would deliver Ramoth-gilead into their hands. However, Jehoshaphat wanted to inquire of "a prophet of the Lord" (22:7).

Ahab mentioned the prophet Micaiah, who always prophesied evil against him. Nevertheless Micaiah was sent for.

In the meantime, Ahab's "prophets" continued urging the venture (22:1-12). But finally Micaiah arrived. That he spoke words of irony at first (22:15) is evident from his final prophecy (22:19-23). Ahab recognized the sarcasm (verse 16).

Then Micaiah told of a vision God had given him (22:17, 19-22)—the meaning of which was that Ahab would be killed, and "every man" (perhaps the people of both Israel and Syria) would go home in peace. He had also seen a spirit standing before God that had volunteered to be "a lying spirit in the mouth of all his [Ahab's] prophets." And God had permitted it to be so, possibly because Ahab was deliberately choosing to believe a lie.

Zedekiah arrogantly smote Micaiah, and challenged him to prove whose prophecy was from the Spirit of the Lord—his and the four hundred, or Micaiah's. Micaiah merely indicated that all would be clear when it was fulfilled (22:25).

Ahab had Micaiah imprisoned (verses 26, 27); but the prophet made one final prediction—Ahab's death—and pled with the people to hearken.

Enter Death!
Much as though no inquiry had been made of God, the two kings returned to their battle strategy. Ahab would disguise himself, since Ben-hadad's troops would be looking for him on the field. Jehoshaphat would wear his royal robes. So the battle began.

Ben-hadad had instructed his captains of the chariots to direct their weapons only against the king of Israel (22:31). When the captains saw only one king, Jehoshaphat, they mistook him for the king of Israel. He "cried out," and the captains perceived that it was not Ahab. Jehoshaphat had had a narrow escape! *But Ahab's disguise did not hide him from God!*

"And a certain man drew a bow at a venture, and smote the king of Israel between the joints of the harness," or his armor (22:34). he was mortally wounded, and requested to be carried from among the warring hosts. But it was an impossible request. The battle was only increased; and the charioteers held Ahab up in the chariot so the Syrians would not learn what had happened. *His life-blood drained out into the chariot!*

At sundown, there was a proclamation made throughout the host: "Every man to his *city,* and every man to his own *country.*" Did this mean that Ben-hadad had learned of Ahab's death, and that the war was ended? After all, Ben-hadad had no quarrel with Israel; Ahab had initiated the war, and now he was dead.

Ahab's body was taken to Samaria, where he would be buried.

"And one washed the chariot in the pool of Samaria; and the dogs licked up his blood . . . according unto the word of the Lord which he spake" (22:38; 21:19).

FOR OUR ADMONITION AND LEARNING

The pronouncements of God against sin are not cancelled out by the passing of time. Hiel rebuilt Jericho some five hundred twenty-five years after Joshua's warning against it, yet the predicted judgment was carried out to the letter. Ahab, too, was guilty for allowing (or ordering) the project; but his day would come later! Sin was sin in Eden; and it is sin today. *And the soul that sins shall die!*

It is amazing—appalling—the trust that cultists put in their false "idols"! They seem not to know the difference between "god" and "God" until matters reach a crisis. Some have heard the gospel a hundred times and have disregarded or rejected it; yet they readily respond to the wooing of that "spirit of antichrist," and serve it with a dedication that should put most Christians to shame!

Consider the *sacrificial suffering* of the prophets of Baal on Mount Carmel; then be admonished. Even "good Christians" may be misled to "feel" they can "buy" God's answers or solutions to their problems by *personal sacrifices*—as though Christ's was an insufficient one! The need of all needs, if we would hear from heaven, is to put FULL FAITH and IMPLICIT TRUST in the once-for-all Sacrifice, which provided *all things!*

It is frustrating to encounter conflicting interpretations or predictions, such as those made by Micaiah and the "lying prophets." But when there is uncertainty, it is safer to "wait" than to be "carried away." In the meantime, there is need for patience. God has no need to hurry. If we will hold His hand, we will never get ahead of Him, nor lag behind.

—Lesson Ten—

AHAZIAH: EIGHTH KING OF ISRAEL

Required Scripture Readings: 1 Kings 22:40, 51-53; 2 Chronicles 20:35-37; 1 Kings 22:48, 49; 2 Kings 1:1-18; 2 Kings 3:4, 5.

Pronunciation Helps: Baal-zebub—BAY-al-ZEE-bub; Jehoram—je-HO-ram; Ophir—O-fir; Tarshish—TAR-shish, or Tharshish—THAR-shish; Ezion-geber—EE-zi-on-GE-ber; Eliezer—EL-i-EE-zer.

RELEVANT FACTS
Chief characters: Ahaziah; Elijah.
Time span: 2 years, or less, beginning about 897 B.C. (1 Kings 22:51).
Seat of government: Samaria.
Contemporary personalities: Jehoshaphat, king of Judah; Elijah the prophet.
Lineage and family: Son of Ahab and Jezebel. He had no son (2 Kings 1:17). Sister: Athaliah, who married Jehoram (Joram), son of Judah's king Jehoshaphat, who later became king of Judah.
Death: From an injury received in a fall (2 Kings 1:2, 4, 16, 17).

THE HISTORICAL SITUATION
Ahaziah inherited a "fallen kingdom"—that is, fallen from God. Israel had gone to great sinful depths under his father's rule. In fairness to the new king, he had known nothing but the wickedness of his predecessors, from Jeroboam until his father's excelling idolatry. However, he was aware of Elijah's work of reformation on Mount Carmel, so he was without excuse, as we shall see.

It has been observed that everything relating to his short reign was unfortunate. Even a renewed alliance with Judah's king Jehoshaphat ended in disaster. Lands and people that were under tribute were lost. A personal accident and illness brought his reign and life to a conclusion.

AHAZIAH THE KING

We are introduced to Ahaziah through a concise and ugly description of his reign:

"And he did evil in the sight of the Lord, and walked in the way of his father, and in the way of his mother, and in the way of Jeroboam the son of Nebat, who made Israel to sin.

"For he served Baal, and worshiped him, and provoked to anger the Lord God of Israel, according to all that his father had done" (1 Kings 22:52, 53).

Somewhat out of consecutive order, it seems, the first event of his reign is given. This is the result of a belated introduction of Jehoshaphat's accession to the throne of Judah, after having read of the alliance between him and Ahab. Now we find that Jehoshaphat was in his seventeenth year when Ahaziah suddenly inherited Israel's throne.

This first recorded event had to do with a marine project (1 Kings 22:48, 49; 2 Chronicles 20:35-37). It is difficult to understand which of the two kings initiated the project. At any rate, they joined their efforts to make "ships of Tharshish to go to Ophir for gold," apparently manned by sailors from both Israel and Judah (1 Kings 22:48, 49). "Ships of Tharshish" are thought to refer to a particular type of vessel, since they were built, not at Tharshish, but at Ezion-geber in Edom, at the north extremity of the Gulf of Aqaba between the Sinai Peninsula and the Land of Midian. The proposed destination was Ophir, at the southern tip of Arabia.

The ships did not fulfill their mission. They were "broken," or destroyed, perhaps by a storm. A prophet named Eliezer revealed to Jehoshaphat that the disaster was from the Lord because He was displeased with his alliance with Ahaziah (2 Chronicles 20:37).

Next we read that the Moabites rebelled against Israel (2 Kings 1:1), to whom they had been paying tribute as subjects since the days of David (2 Samuel 8:2). They seemed to see their long-hoped-for opportunity upon the death of Ahab. Secular history says they gained a brief period of independence at one time, but were again brought under tribute by Omri. This same secular history indicates that they easily regained independence during their rebellion against Ahaziah.

In the second year of his reign, Ahaziah suffered a fall "through a lattice," or a latticed window or railing which he probably thought was more secure than it was. His injury was so great that he was deeply concerned about his recovery; so he sent messengers to inquire of Baal-zebub, one of the gods of the Baalim system. On their way, they met the prophet Elijah, to whom "the angel of the Lord" had given a message for Ahaziah—"Is it not because there is not a God in Israel, that ye go to inquire of Baal-zebub the god of Ekron?" (2 Kings 1:3).

The messengers did not continue their journey, but returned to Ahaziah with Elijah's message, including God's declaration of judgment: "Now therefore thus saith the Lord, Thou shalt not come down from that bed on which thou art gone up, but shalt surely die."

Ahaziah immediately recognized Elijah as having been the man whom his messengers described to him (2 Kings 1:8). Commentators observe that the king considered Elijah to be his enemy, as had Ahab before him. Some contend that he sent the "captain of fifty and his fifty" men to capture and imprison Elijah. The Bible gives no indication of such an intention, unless it is assumed from God's words to Elijah in verse fifteen—"be not afraid of him"; or unless it be supposed that the destruction of the pursuers should confirm an evil purpose in Ahaziah. If there had been any reason to fear imprisonment, the Lord gave the prophet assurance that now he would be safe.

The first captain and his fifty were consumed by fire from heaven (1:10), proving that Elijah was a "man of God," as the captain had addressed him. A second captain and his fifty met with the same consumption. But Ahaziah was persistent, for whatever reason, so he sent a third captain and his fifty. This third captain proceeded more tactfully—perhaps in fear, or in wisdom, or in an awesome respect for a man who had such power with his God! He fell on his knees before Elijah and begged that their lives would be spared (1:13, 14).

The angel of the Lord (who may not have left Elijah's side from the time of God's first directive—verses 3 and 4) now bade him go down unto the king. Upon arrival at Ahaziah's palace, he repeated the original message (1:10).

Josephus says, "Accordingly the king in a very little time died, as Elijah had foretold."

FOR OUR ADMONITION AND LEARNING
Matthew Henry comments: "Some sinners God makes quick work with.... Miserable are the children that not only derive a stock of corruption from their parents, but are thus taught by them to trade with it...." Yet we know that each individual is responsible to order, or reorder, his own life, no matter what kind of hindrances his ancestral background may try to impose upon him.

"For it is written, As I live, saith the Lord, every knee [individually] shall bow to me, and every tongue shall confess to God.

"So then every one of us shall give account of himself [personally] to God" (Romans 14:11, 12).

God knows the whereabouts of every wicked individual. All false security will utterly fail in due time. Ahab's disguise did not hide him from the arrow shot "at a venture." Neither did Ahaziah's latticed abode prevent his falling through it to his mortal injury.

"The way of the wicked is as darkness: they know not at what they stumble" (Proverbs 4:19).

We may not be guilty of seeking counsel of Baal-zebub, but let us never forget that Satan is the prince of this world and the enemy of God. When we make the arm of flesh our trust, and seek counsel from this wicked world, "Is it not because there is no God in Israel," or in Christendom—yea, in the Church?

JEHORAM: NINTH KING OF ISRAEL
Required Scripture Readings: 2 Kings 1:17; 3:1-27; 5:1-9; 6:8-33; 7:1-20; 8:1-6, 28, 29; 9:1-26; 2 Chronicles 22:5-8.

Pronunciation Helps: Mesha—MESH-a; Elisha—ee-LI-sha; Naaman—NA-a-man; Gehazi—ge-HAY-zi; Shunamite—SHOO-na-mite; Hazael—HAY-za-el; Jehu—JAY-hu; Nimshi—NIM-SHI; Dothan—DO-than.

RELEVANT FACTS
Chief characters: Jehoram; Elisha the prophet; Ahaziah (king of Judah); Jehu.

Time span: 12 years (2 King 3:1), beginning about 896 B.C.

Seat of government: Samaria.

Contemporary personalities: Jehoshaphat, Jehoram, and Ahaziah, kings of Judah; Elisha the prophet.
Lineage and family: Son of Ahab and Jezebel (2 Kings 1:17).
Death: Slain by Jehu, his successor (2 Kings 9:14-26).

THE HISTORICAL SITUATION

Ahaziah's untimely death left the Moabite rebellion unresolved, as far as Israel was concerned. Repossessing this territory was first on Jehoram's agenda.

In reading about this period from the Bible, it will be necessary to pay close attention to several names in order to avoid confusing the histories of Israel and Judah. Ahaziah and Jehoram (sometimes called Joram) were brothers, sons of Ahab and Jezebel. Both were kings of Israel.

But another Jehoram, a king of Judah, appears in the record during the reign of Israel's Jehoram. Judah's Jehoram was succeeded by a son named Ahaziah. Also there appears another Jehoshaphat, son of Nimshi, whose son, Jehu, became king of Israel. This Jehoshaphat must not be confused with Judah's king Jehoshaphat who reigned twenty-five years.

All of these personalities occupied positions of historical note within a period of twelve years, most of them living at the same time. We present the following for convenience:

Ahaziah, son of Ahab; king of Israel less than two years, about 897 and 896 B.C.

Ahaziah, son of Jehoram (son of Jehoshaphat); king of Judah one year, about 885 B.C.

Jehoram, son of Ahab; king of Israel twelve years, about 896 to 885 B.C.

Jehoram, son of Jehoshaphat (son of Asa); king of Judah eight years; began to co-reign with his father about 885 B.C.

Jehoshaphat, son of Asa; king of Judah twenty-five years, beginning about 914 B.C.

Jehoshaphat (not a king), son of Nimshi; father of Jehu, king of Israel twenty-eight years, beginning about 884 B.C.

JEHORAM THE KING

Jehoram is introduced to us as one practicing a somewhat "tempered evil":

"And he wrought evil in the sight of the Lord; but not like his father, and like his mother: for he put away the image of Baal that his father had made.

"Nevertheless he cleaved unto the sins of Jeroboam . . . he departed not therefrom" (2 Kings 3:2, 3).

One commentator, *Philip Smith*, has written: "He maintained a close alliance with Judah, and it was perhaps by the influence of Jehoshaphat that he was a shade better than his father and his brother." Remember that his sister Athaliah had married Jehoshaphat's son Jehoram; thus the motive for the almost constant alliance between Israel and Judah for the past several years. However, the *spiritual ties* did not match the *blood ties*.

Three-King Alliance

But we find Jehoram seeking Jehoshaphat's help in bringing the Moabites back under Israel's dominion (2 Kings 3:7). Together they marched their armies through Edom, south and east of Judah, where they gained the help of the king of Edom and his troops. It was a long journey around the south of the Dead Sea to the border of Moab on its east side. After seven days they came into an area where there was no water for the soldiers and cattle (perhaps "baggage animals").

We see one of Jehoram's character traits as he faces this problem. Though he had not sought God before launching the expedition, he now blamed God because it seemed that He had "called these three kings together, to deliver them into the hand of Moab" (3:10). Jehoshaphat was a man of faith and not of despair. His first thought was to seek God's guidance through a prophet. One of Jehoram's servants had knowledge that the prophet Elisha was there. He had probably accompanied the troops at God's direction (perhaps for Judah's sake), without making his presence known to the kings.

Jehoshaphat said, "The word of the Lord is with him," so the three kings approached Elisha. The prophet ironically suggested that Jehoram seek the idol prophets instead of a prophet of God. After all, he had made only a half-reformation, and was still encouraging the worship of the golden calves. Besides, it would be Jehoram (Ahab's son) who would see the judgment on Ahab's house fulfilled.

But Jehoram insisted that Elisha give them aid, for he was in desperation. So Elisha consented, making it clear that it was because of Jehoshaphat's presence. He ordered that the valley be made full of ditches to hold the water which the

Lord would provide, and by which the Moabites would be delivered into their hands (3:16-18).

Josephus says: "... Before the sun-rising, a great torrent ran strongly; for God had caused it to rain very plentifully at a distance of three days' journey into Edom, so that the army and the cattle found water to drink in abundance...." The Bible stresses the miraculous effect of the early morning sun shining on the water, making it appear as blood. The Moabites wrongly concluded that the armies of Israel, Judah, and Edom had slain one another; so they moved in to take the spoil. But they were surprised when the Israelites rose up and smote them. The victory was great, as Elisha had predicted (3:19, 24-27).

The King Snubs a Syrian Captain

The merciless disposition of Jehoram is evidenced in his brief connection with the healing of the leprous Syrian, Naaman. Naaman was captain of the host under the king of Syria. He was a great and honorable man. His wife had a little Israelite maid who had been taken captive. She knew about Elisha's power with God, and she was instrumental in getting Naaman into his presence.

Not knowing how to get in touch with a roving prophet, the king of Syria assumed that the king of Israel would give his assistance. Appropriate gifts and a letter were sent with Naaman to Jehoram, who jumped to the conclusion that the Syrian king was making him personally responsible for Naaman's recovery (2 Kings 5:6). In anger and frustration, he said, "Am I God, to kill and to make alive, that this man doth send unto me to recover a man of his leprosy?" He accused the king of Syria of agitating a quarrel with him.

Elisha heard of Jehoram's dilemma, so he sent him word—"Wherefore hast thou rent thy clothes? let him [Naaman] come now to me, and he shall know that there is a prophet in Israel" (5:8). Jehoram's involvement ended there, with Elisha's withering insinuation that he, too, should have known that there was a prophet of God in his kingdom.

Syria's Warmongering

Perhaps a year later, Syria's old festering enmity toward Israel flared up again. Ben-hadad the king laid an ambush of his servants in a certain place where Jehoram would be slain by them in passing. Elisha sent a warning not to pass that way. Apparently, the king had his servants to scout the area, and, finding Elisha's words true, his life was spared a number of times.

When Ben-hadad learned that it was Elisha who was alerting Jehoram, he sent a whole army to Dothan (where spies had found him) to capture the lone prophet (6:13, 14). Elisha smote them with blindness (probably a mental blindness of confusion and bewilderment), and led them to Samaria, where "the Lord opened their eyes." Jehoram seemed as shaken as the Syrians must have been! In fact, he was so shaken that he actually "stooped" to address Elisha respectfully—"My father, shall I smite them? shall I smite them?" (6:21).

Elisha reminded him that the Syrian army was the same as captured, and that, as captives, he should feed them—then send them back to their king. The Syrians respected this kindness and returned home without further agitation.

But the old enmity was not dead. Perhaps within a year Ben-hadad and all his host besieged Samaria until a great famine resulted within the city's walls (6:24-29). It became so dire that they were eating their young children. (NOTE: See God's prophecy in Deuteronomy 28:52-57, of conditions Israel would bring upon herself for her sins.)

Jehoram beheld this horrifying state of things as he walked upon Samaria's walls; and he put on sackcloth and vowed to have Elisha beheaded. Undoubtedly he was angered because the prophet had not besought God for a miracle of deliverance from the Syrian siege. So he sent a messenger to Elisha with his threat; but Elisha knew Jehoram himself would follow, so he ordered his servant not to admit the messenger.

It is generally assumed that the king did come, and that the words in 1 Kings 6:33 are his. From that difficult passage, some commentators think Elisha earlier had advised Jehoram to wait—not to surrender to the Syrians; but that now he would wait no longer to surrender, though his head had cooled enough to spare the prophet's life. Others think he was saying he would wait no longer to have Elisha's head!

Miracle of Deliverance

Now that the siege and its devastation had climaxed, Elisha was ready to speak. It was not merely to save his life, for he promised a miracle, and God alone works miracles. It was apparent that the siege would be lifted, or else the promise of flour and barley—and at so low a price—could not have been possible. In fact, one of Jehoram's men clearly doubted that even the opening of the windows of heaven could work such quick results; and he would pay for his doubts later on! (2 Kings 7:1, 2).

The lifting of the siege was the first miracle. Four lepers, sitting outside Samaria's gate as outcasts, decided to go to the Syrian camp, hoping for mercy and food. They were starving, so they had nothing to lose. But when they arrived, the miracle had already taken place; "there was no man there" (7:5).

"For the Lord had made the host of the Syrians to hear a noise of chariots, and a noise of horses, even the noise of a great host . . . . "

They had fled at twilight, thinking Jehoram had somehow hired other kings to come to Israel's aid. And the second miracle was that they had left everything behind in order to escape more rapidly. When the lepers gave their report later that night, Jehoram was skeptical. He thought the Syrians were enticing them out for food, then would fall upon them and take the city. But upon investigation, the truth was confirmed. The people spoiled the Syrian tents, and Elisha's prophecy came to pass word for word (7:16), even to the trampling of the man who had dared to doubt the prophet's words; he saw the food, but did not get to eat thereof (17:2, 17-20).

An Act of Kindness

It is noteworthy that Jehoram had a heart that could be touched. We saw this in the case of the famine during the Syrian siege, and now again in an interesting coincidence, also resulting from a famine (8:1-6).

A seven-year famine had just ended in Israel, but where it fits chronologically is uncertain; it may have ended in about 891 B.C. At the beginning, Elisha had counselled a Shunamite woman to take her son and sojourn elsewhere until the famine should end. She had gone to Philistia. This woman had befriended the prophet before, and he had prayed that she and her husband would have a child. The prayer was answered; but after several years, the child fell ill and died. Elisha was sent for, and, through him, God restored the child's life (2 Kings 4:8-37).

Now, apparently the woman was a widow. When she returned from Philistia, it seems that others had taken over her property. Coincidentally—yea, providentially—on this certain day, Jehoram was questioning Elisha's servant Gehazi about all of his master's great works. Just as he was relating the story of the restoration of the Shunamite's son to life, the woman appeared, with her son, crying unto the king concerning her house and land. Gehazi said, "My lord, O king, this is the woman, and this is her son, whom Elisha restored to life."

The woman confirmed Gehazi's testimony, and Jehoram was moved to order her property restored to her, and a recompense made of all the fruits of the field for the years she was away (8:3-6).

Another Conflict with Syria

Syria had a new king, Hazael; and Judah's Ahaziah had come to the throne. The city of Ramoth-gilead was still under dispute, so possibly the new king Hazael was wanting to distinguish himself by securing the city (2 Kings 8:28, 29; 2 Chronicles 22:5, 6). Judah's king Ahaziah went with Israel's King Jehoram (Joram) to the battle. Jehoram was wounded, so he retired to Jezreel to recover. *Josephus* says he had already taken the city by force; however, he left his army at Ramoth-gilead, perhaps lest Syria should try to take advantage of his absence. Ahaziah went to visit him in Jezreel.

A Successor Anointed

Then Elisha sent one of the sons of the prophets to Ramoth-gilead to anoint Jehu to succeed Jehoram as king of Israel. Jehu was an army captain at the time. The young prophet spoke the Lord's message privately with him, saying that God had anointed him king over the people of the Lord in Israel, and that he would smite the house of Ahab as the Lord's vengeance for the blood of His prophets and all of His servants whom Jezebel had slain; and Jezebel herself would be eaten by the dogs (9:6-10). When the message had been delivered, he fled, as Elisha had commanded, without waiting for Jehu's reply.

Jehu must have understood that he was to have accession at once, for he immediately formed a conspiracy against Jehoram, telling his fellow-captains what the young prophet had done and said. *Josephus* describes the occasion thus:

"When he [Jehu] had said this, every one of them put off his garment, and strewed them under him, and blew their trumpets, and gave notice that Jehu was king."

Jehu, and a company with him, set out for Jezreel immediately, lest another should break the news first, and there be opposition. Jehoram had set a watchman on duty, in case there should be any word from the army he had left at Ramoth-gilead. When the watchman saw the company approaching from a considerable distance, he sent a horseman to inquire if there was peace. Jehu only told the horseman to follow him. Jehoram had the watchman send out another horseman, but Jehu gave him the same order.

The watchman then reported to Jehoram that the company appeared to be led by Jehu, who apparently had a name for *driving furiously*. At this word, Jehoram had his chariot made ready and, accompanied by Ahaziah, went to meet Jehu, himself inquiring if he had brought tidings of peace. Jehu hurled back the answer:

"What peace, so long as the whoredoms of thy mother Jezebel and her witchcrafts are so many?" (2 Kings 9:22).

Jehoram had the charioteers turn about and flee, saying, "There is treachery, O Ahaziah!" But Jehu smote him with an arrow. *Josephus* says "through his heart," and that he "fell down immediately on his knee, and gave up the ghost."

Jehu then bade his captain cast Jehoram's body in the field where Jezebel had had Naboth slain. he called to remembrance the word of the Lord against the house of Ahab, and that, because of Ahab's momentary repentance, his judgment was reserved to be executed against his son (9:25, 26). Now it was done!

FOR OUR ADMONITION AND LEARNING

Jehoram's limited-reformation may have its antitype in the *professing Christian* who may have been motivated more by *the fear of hell* than *the love of God*. It is a *self-righteousness* tailored to suit the individual's pleasure. In God's sight, it is "as filthy rags" (Isaiah 64:6; Romans 10:3). It is hypocritical, and has the curse of God upon it (Matthew 23:33)!

It is commendable to lend a helping hand, but it is expedient that the cause be just. Jehoram wanted Jehoshaphat's help, never seeming to give a thought to seeking God's will in his venture. Worse yet, the righteous Jehoshaphat knew Jehoram's character. How good God is, many times, to sinners, because He recognizes their godly associates. But as a rule, it is risky to be "traveling with law-breakers"!

Wicked men are not above laying the blame for their sins on the righteous. Jehoram seemed tender-hearted when he saw the awful toll the famine in Samaria was taking in the lives of innocent children, but instead of *taking the blame*, he wanted to place it on Elisha. *Matthew Henry* says, "Instead of vowing to pull down the calves at Dan and Bethel, or letting the law have its course against the prophets of Baal and of the groves, he swears the death of Elisha." But God takes care of His own, as He did the prophet.

—Lesson Eleven—

JEHU: TENTH KING OF ISRAEL

Required Scripture Readings: 1 Kings 19:16, 17; 2 Kings chapters 9 and 10; 2 Chronicles 22:8, 9; Hosea 1:4; Jeremiah 35:2-19.

Pronunciation Helps: Jehonadab—jee-HON-a-dab; Rechab—REE-cab.

RELEVANT FACTS

Chief characters: Jehu; and "a son of the prophets," not named (2 Kings 9:1-10).

Time span: 28 years, beginning about 884 B.C.

Seat of government: Samaria.

Contemporary personalities: Athaliah, "queen" of Judah; Joash (Jehoash), king of Judah; Elisha the prophet; and Elijah the prophet (1 Kings 19:16, 17).

Lineage and family: Son of Jehoshaphat (son of Nimshi, 2 Kings 9:14); a captain of the host under Jehoram; Son: Jehoahaz (2 Kings 10:35), the only one named.

Death: Of natural causes, apparently (2 Kings 10:35).

THE HISTORICAL SITUATION

The first biblical mention of Jehu, son of Jehoshaphat (son of Nimshi) is found in 1 Kings 19:16, 17. The prophet Elijah was on Mount Horeb, where he had fled from Jezebel's threat on his life. The prophet had been discouraged, but the Lord visited him and showed him the work to be done by him, including the anointing of Jehu to be king over Israel. (Elijah's successor, Elisha, would do this anointing at the proper time.)

We have seen the circumstances by which he came to the throne. His anointing was from God; outwardly he appeared to have been made king by the army (2 Kings 9:11-13). It seems evident that he anticipated some opposition, since he immediately formed the conspiracy against king Jehoram, and made particular and speedy plans to get to Jezreel before anyone else should "escape out of the city" of Ramoth-gilead and reach Jezreel (where Jehoram was recovering) before he did (9:15, 16). Though he was *king in fact*, he was not *king enthroned* while Jehoram lived. As it turned out, Jehoram came forth to his death. Technically, Jehu became king with full authority when Jehoram fell in his chariot. And the God-given responsibilities, though gory, fell on him at the same moment (9:6-10). Not only was he responsible to rule the kingdom, but also to be God's instrument of judgment on the house of Ahab, in a sweeping annihilation, as it were. He seemed ready—perhaps eager—to begin.

JEHU THE KING

First Orders of Business

His first act was hardly on the agenda; but he mortally wounded Judah's king Ahaziah as he fled the death-scene of Jehoram (verse 27). Commentators suppose he did this because Ahaziah had been on such close terms with Jehoram's predecessor; also because of the affinity through the marriage of Ahab's daughter Athaliah into Judah's royal line. (Athaliah was Ahaziah's mother.)

Virtually the first face he saw upon his arrival in Jezreel was that of Jezebel. Opinions very as to why she had *painted her face* and *tired her head* after receiving word that her son Jehoram had been slain, and why she stationed herself in public view when she might have been in mourning.

Some conjecture that she hoped to entice Jehu—for she had now been a widow for about three years. This view seems ridiculous when we note her first scathing words to him as he entered the gate to the palace—"Had Zimri peace, who slew his master?" (2 Kings 9:31; 1 Kings 16:8-10).

It is more probable that she reasoned that her time had run out, and that she arrogantly purposed to defy Israel's God and die as she had lived! Since she seemed to be aware of the events just past, it is likely that she had been told what Jehu had said of her to her son only moments before his death. She could hardly have hoped for, nor desired, any favorable attentions from this new, avenging monarch.

At any rate, Jehu did not relay her case "to the grand jury," so to speak. He considered that he had a mandate from a

Higher Court, and he carried it out on the spot. He did not ask that the infamous "queen mother" be escorted down to him in royal style. *"Throw her down!"* was the new king's order.

As ruthless and heartless as Jehu's actions may appear, bear in mind that all was done "under the law." Stoning would have been her sentence many times if Israel had been functioning by God's law instead of Baal's. Now, God's longsuffering was filled up. It is said that the "stoning" of the Law was sometimes done by throwing the offender from a height upon stones or stonework. If so, Jezebel was stoned to death.

Be that as it may, Elijah's prophecy concerning her was fulfilled to the letter (1 Kings 21:23), as well as that of Elisha's (2 Kings 9:10). Jehu went into the palace for some nourishment "after a hard day's work." While he was eating, it came to him that "this cursed woman" should be buried; so he ordered it to be done. But God and the dogs were there first! In so short a time, nothing was left of her wicked person but "the skull, and the feet, and the palms of her hands" (9:35)!

God's mercy is great, and He suffers long; but His judgments are sure!

Next on Jehu's schedule was the purging of the house of Ahab. The tactics he used are interesting indeed (2 Kings 10:1-12). Instead of "storming the throne," he sent letters to the authorities in Samaria, the capital city, and *to whom it might concern* in Jezreel, challenging any who might choose to put an "Ahabite" on that throne. This did not mean that he would step aside if a descendant of Ahab were preferred, as is seen from his words, "and fight for your father's house" (10:3).

The rulers and elders "were exceedingly afraid" when they had read the challenge. This man Jehu was bold and straightforward. He was daring and sure of himself. He had just slain two kings—Jehoram and Ahaziah. He had made a quick and thorough work of slaying Jezebel. He had the army behind him. "How then shall *we* stand?" the rulers and their associates asked themselves.

So it appears that the officer who was in charge of the palace, the governor of Samaria and his council of elders, and the tutors of the younger "Ahabites," came to a conclusion, and sent their reply to Jehu: "We are thy servants, and will do all that thou shalt bid us; we will not make any king: do thou that which is good in thine eyes."

Jehu's diplomacy was working well; probably better than he had expected. A firm commitment had been made to further the business at hand, the nature of which those wisest heads in Israel must have anticipated. So Jehu handed them his first mandate. It being a bloody one would make them prove whether or not they were *his* and would hearken to *his authority* (10:6).

Simply stated, they were to behead the "seventy sons" of Ahab—generally thought to have been, or to have included, his grandsons, the sons of Jehoram—and, as veritable proof, to send their heads to Jehu in baskets. Reading the record, we get the impression that the mandate was carried forward without so much as a cringe on the part of the executioners (10:7)! And Jehu seems to have been equally untouched when the heads were delivered to him in Jezreel. No more would be done or said "until the morning" (10:8, 9).

And morning came. "Unfinished business" was taken up first. Jehu commended the people as being "righteous," using a rather quirky turn of reasoning (10:9, 10), somewhat paraphrased by *Matthew Henry* (and others concur) as follows: "I slew but one; they have slain all these: I did it by conspiracy and with design; they have done this merely in compliance and with an implicit obedience. Let not the people of Samaria, nor any of the friends of the house of Ahab, ever reproach me for what I have done, when their own elders, and the very guardians of the orphans, have done this."

Then, as if to offer relief to himself and all to whom he spoke, Jehu offered a justifying conclusion: "Know now that there shall fall unto the earth nothing of the word of the Lord, which the Lord spake concerning the house of Ahab: for the Lord hath done that which he spake by his servant Elijah" (10:10).

So, as though the Lord's word was not yet quite fulfilled, "Jehu slew all that remained of the house of Ahab in Jezreel, and all his great men, and his kinsfolks, and his priests, until he left none remaining" (10:11).

He was then ready to proceed to Samaria and occupy the royal palace. But on the way he "met with the brethren of

Ahaziah king of Judah," who said that they had come to visit "the children of the king" (Jehoram?) and "the children of the queen" (Jezebel?).

Since there were forty-two of them (10:14), some have questioned the truth of their reply to Jehu when he inquired who they were. It is true that their own king had been visiting Jehoram before both were killed by Jehu; and it is probable that they had not had time or opportunity to learn of their deaths, and of Jezebel's. However, Jehu immediately assumed that they had heard earlier "of disturbances in the kingdom of the ten tribes," as one commentator states it, and that Athaliah had sent them to see if they could lend their influence in strengthening the house of Ahab. (We must remember the affinity which existed through intermarriage.)

All conjectures aside, they were there at an opportune time for Jehu, while he was unsparingly purging the house of Ahab of everyone who pertained to it in the least. So, without further inquisition, he had all forty-two of them slain on the spot!

Jehu Makes An Ally

Still traveling toward Samaria, Jehu met a man who was a descendant of Rechab (2 Samuel 4:2; 1 Chronicles 2:55). *Josephus* offers some information from Jewish history about him, as follows:

"... There met him [Jehu] a good and righteous man, whose name was Jehonadab, and who had been his friend of old. He saluted Jehu, and began to commend him, because he had done every thing according to the will of God, in extirpating the house of Ahab. So Jehu desired him to come up into his chariot, and make his entry with him into Samaria."

History portrays Jehonadab (and the Rechabites) as prescribing a strict, ascetic rule of life. (See Jeremiah 35:2-19.) This would agree with the Scripture, in that *his heart was as Jehu's heart*; however, his motives may have been purer than Jehu's. As bold as the new king would have himself to appear, it is likely that he faced the final aspect of his purging work at Samaria—an "Ahabite" stronghold—with some trepidation. If so, having a man like Jehonadab as his ally was something of a godsend.

With the invitation, "Come with me, and see my zeal for the Lord," the journey was resumed. No words are wasted in Scripture concerning the quick work the new king did in Samaria. "All that remained unto Ahab" was destroyed (10:17).

One Step More

The *Thompson Chain-Reference* chronology gives only one date—884 B.C. for all the events of Jehu's reign. However, dates are given only at the beginning of chapters (with an occasional exception, but none here). Since Jehu reigned twenty-eight years (10:36), and since there seems to have been no cessation of his purging work until it was finished, we can only assume that his final work of note should be included in his first few days or weeks.

This work was done with great subtilty (10:19). In fact, it must have been with such "clever sincerity" that the Baal worshippers were totally gullible; they obeyed his every order with unbelieveable dedication. They must have been fascinated with imaginations of what the Baal ceremonies would be like, led by a king whose zeal to date had been unmatched. If this orgiastic worship under Ahab and Ahaziah had been "little," what would "much" be like!

Reading the account carefully (10:19-28), we see that Jehu's strategy was a well-kept secret among "the servants of the Lord" (verses 23, 24), who did their part as though Jehu's zeal had been highly contagious!

With "a packed house," the Baalim rites were ready to be begun; but the burnt offering to Baal had to be made first (verse 25). Before the orgies could begin, eighty men of God were signalled to go into the house of Baal and slay every one! And it was done! Then the images were burned, and "the house of Baal" was broken down, and its site was made "a draught house"—the city's "sewer," or "dunghill."

The Reformation Ended

Now we come to a sad *"Howbeit..."* (10:29). "Howbeit from the sins of Jeroboam... Jehu departed not from after them, to wit, the golden calves that were in Bethel, and that were in Dan." Seemingly the most of Jehu's twenty-eight-year reign was spent, otherwise uneventfully, under this evil practice (10:30, 31).

Of course, God was not pleased; however, He was gracious in promising Jehu a four-generation dynasty as a reward for that portion of his reign which he had spent in carrying out His will. But God, being *just* as well as *gracious*, would not prosper the nation while no heed was taken to walk in His law.

The context of verses thirty-one through thirty-three indicates that Israel's having been *cut short* had to do with their losses to Syria, and perhaps to other foreign powers. God had suffered long with His people—who had virtually resented being His people!

Matthew Henry concludes: "Notice is taken, in general, of his [Jehu's] might; but, because he took no heed to serve God, the memorials of his mighty enterprises and achievements are justly buried in oblivion."

FOR OUR ADMONITION AND LEARNING

And *act* "for God" may be good and right, but the *motive* wrong— as with Jehu (and Baasha). "Doing God's commandments" either by *reluctant obedience* or an *egotistic zeal* does not merit the pleasure of God. When our service is motivated by God's love for us in Christ on Calvary, God is pleased, even though the volume of accomplishment may be less—as men see it!

Like Jezebel, the wife of Ahab, the Jezebel at Thyatira (Revelation 2:2-24) was given "space to repent of her fornication; and she repented not." The church was not in the favor of God because it allowed that wicked person to continue spreading her putrid influence and "this doctrine" (verse 24). She *called herself* a "prophetess," no doubt in order to so impress the people that they would be afraid to put their hands on her devilish doctrine! Remember, those letters were written with the admonition: "He that hath an ear, let him hear what the Spirit [not the self-anointed Jezebel] saith to the churches."

Jehu's bloody, relentless, unsparing purgation may be seen as typical of *the final day*, when the last "day of grace" has been squandered by the unbelievers, and nothing remains but wrath and judgment for the ungodly (Romans 2:2-11)!

Jehu apparently had a warped view of serving God, seen in his *difference in idols*. Images worshipped "in the name of" Baal were to be destroyed, but the golden calves worshipped "in the name of" the Lord God of Israel were tolerated—yea, encouraged! God alone knows the empty worship—the crying of "Lord, Lord" (Matthew 7:21, 22)—the *professed* prophesying, and casting out devils, and the wonderful works—that goes on "in His name"! Yes—*God knows!*

—Lesson Twelve—

JEHOAHAZ: ELEVENTH KING OF ISRAEL

Required Scripture Readings: 2 Kings 10:35; 13:1-9, 22.

Pronunciation Helps: Jehoahaz—je-HO-a-HAZ.

RELEVANT FACTS
Chief characters: Jehoahaz; Hazael and Ben-hadad.
Time span: 17 years, beginning about 856 B.C.
Seat of government: Samaria.
Contemporary personalities: Jehoash (Joash), king of Judah; the prophet Elisha.
Lineage and family: Son of Jehu (2 Kings 10:35). Son: Joash, only one named (13:9).
Death: Of natural causes (13:9).

THE HISTORICAL SITUATION
Despite the purging of Baal-worship and worshippers by Jehu, the past twenty-eight years had been spent in continuing idolatry—for such was the worship of the calves of Jeroboam, regardless of Israel's lipservice to God. So, spiritually, the nation was living under God's anger (2 Kings 13:3).

We do not know what losses of territory were suffered during Jehu's reign (10:32, 33), but Syria, with Hazael as king, seems to have been the chief invader, and continued to be during this new reign. The *Ben-hadad* of this period is not the same as we have encountered in earlier lessons.

JEHOAHAZ THE KING
Jehoahaz took up where his father left off, with "the sins of Jeroboam" still provoking the Lord to anger. And God, seeing that the new king gave no indication of bettering the situation, allowed a Syrian oppression to come upon Israel (2 Kings 13:2, 3). The sword of this foreign foe became God's instrument of chastisement.

Though briefly stated, the fact is that the people of Israel became subjects under Syria. "All the days" (13:3) pertains to the days under discussion, or the seventeen years that Jehoahaz was king of Israel, but subject to Hazael and Ben-hadad.

One commentator had remarked, "Oppression is always hateful to God, even when He is using it as His instrument for chastizing or punishing a guilty people." But it is usually effective, in varying degrees, though its "mill grinds slowly." It moved king Jehoahaz to beseech the Lord for relief (13:4).

Holy Writ inserts a *parenthesis* here (verses 5 and 6), relative to the king's prayer. But the context shows that the "saviour" whom God gave was not given immediately, but during the reigns of his successors. Because the prayer was not one of repentance, but only for relief, the immediate answer was given accordingly. Israel was permitted to dwell "in their tents" more quietly, perhaps, but very much subdued. If it ever occurred to Jehoahaz that God was angry because of the worship of the calves, he must have thrust the thought aside either as unimportant or as too great a revolution to undertake, with one hundred thirty-five years or more of the practice having made it a much-loved tradition.

So their power of resistance was diminished by the Syrians, who limited them to "fifty horsemen, and ten chariots, and ten thousand footmen" (13:7). *Matthew Henry* pertinently states, "The debauching of a nation will certainly be the debasing of it." Israel continued their debauched lifestyle and brought themselves to a condition of debasement. The puny forces left to them was only a mockery, considering the hordes of Syria's troops.

But God is "touched with the feeling of our infirmities." He did not ignore the prayers of Jehoahaz altogether. They opened the way for greater favor later on.

FOR OUR ADMONITION AND LEARNING

Men, as a depraved race, seem so satisfied spiritually with just enough favor with God to keep life flowing along over the concealed bed of treacherous rocks that will eventually destroy their frail raft! In times when all hope seems gone, they may cry, "O God! deliver us from this that threatens our comfort!" All other times they may use His name in vain and spurn His wooings! *True repentance* is indeed a rare commodity! When men count the cost, they deem it too great; so they keep bowing to "the calves," with only an occasional "aside" to God when in trouble!

God's "first message" in every time of reformation and spiritual awakening has been, "REPENT YE!" And He always knows if men desire true, cross-bearing discipleship, or merely the "escape hatch"!

JEHOASH: TWELFTH KING OF ISRAEL

Required Scripture Readings: 2 Kings 13:9-25; 14:8-16; 2 Chronicles 25:17-24.

Pronunciation Helps: Jehoash—jee-HO-ASH, or Joash—JO-ASH; Amaziah—am-a-ZI-ah; Beth-shemesh—beth-SHEE-mesh.

RELEVANT FACTS
Chief characters: Jehoash; Amaziah; Elisha the prophet.
Time span: 16 years, beginning about 839 B.C.
Seat of government: Samaria.
Contemporary personalities: Jehoash (Joash) and Amaziah, kings of Judah; Elisha the prophet.
Lineage and family: Son of Jehoahaz (2 Kings 13:9, 10). Son: Jeroboam II, only one named.
Death: Of natural causes (2 Kings 13:13; 14:16).

THE HISTORICAL SITUATION
Israel was in subjection to Syria when Jehoash came to the throne, but he gained some favor with God that may have resulted from his father's prayers. Some territory was regained from Syria. The "calf worship" continued, however.

A mark of Israel's weakness may be noted in 2 Kings 13:20. This surprise invasion by the Moabites went uncontested.

Apparently in the second or third year of his reign, there was a victorious conquest of Judah, particularly Jerusalem, provoked by Amaziah, king of Judah (14:8-14).

(NOTE: Care must be taken while reading these chapters, not to confuse Jehoash (Joash), king of Israel, with another Joash, king of Judah, both ruling at the same time.)

JEHOASH THE KING
One's first impression of Jehoash ("Joash" being used interchangeably) might be that he was as "his father living

on." (Compare 2 Kings 13, verses 2 and 11.) If his history ended there, we could "write him off" as unworthy of further comment. But, though the biblical historian next records his death, he then returns with two incidents which tend to change our impression somewhat.

The prophet Elisha, now aged, fell sick. King Jehoash (Joash) went to visit him (13:14). *The Pulpit Commentary* gives a thought-provoking appraisal of this visit, as follows:

"The visit of a king to a prophet, in the way of sympathy and compliment, would be a very unusual occurrence at any period of the world's history. In the East, and at the period of which the historian is treating, it was probably unprecedented. Prophets wait upon kings, not kings upon prophets. If a king came to a prophet's house, it was likely to be on an errand of vengeance [2 Kings 6:32, e.g.], not on one of kindness and sympathy. The act of Joash certainly implies a degree of tenderness and consideration on his part very uncommon at the time, and is a fact to which much weight should be attached in any estimate that we form of his character. He was, at any rate, a prince of an amiable disposition."

Jehoash seemed so moved at the prophet's near-death condition that he wept and repeated the words which Elisha had first said when he had seen his master Elijah ascending in the chariot of fire by a whirlwind (2 Kings 2:12).

History says the Northern Kingdom, Israel, had no good kings. Spiritually speaking, this seems true. But *Josephus* speaks of Jehoash as "a good man, and in his disposition was not at all like his father." He goes on to relate that Joash expressed a desire to die with Elisha rather than to be left to face the Syrians without his wise counsel; but that Elisha then encouraged him through the demonstration of the arrows, as the Scriptures elaborate on (13:15-19).

The shooting of the arrow, and the smiting of the ground, had to do with Israel's victory over Syria. Though the prophet somewhat angrily reproved the compassionate king for his lack of faith and zeal, Jehoash could take courage from the prophecy that he would smite Syria successfully three times—which he did (13:25).

Amaziah Provokes Israel

His last recorded feat was a military clash with Judah, where Amaziah was the new king (14:8-14). Amaziah provoked the confrontation unnecessarily. Jehoash tried to reason with him, but he insisted. *Josephus* says it was an attempt to bring all Israel under his rule, as Jehoash reflected in his parable of the thistle and the cedar, seeking the "marriage" of Judah and Israel (14:9).

In the battle at Beth-shemesh in Judah, some fifteen miles west of Jerusalem, "Judah was put to the worse before Israel" (14:12). Jehoash captured Amaziah, and upon the threat of his life (says *Josephus*), he let Jehoash and his army into Jerusalem. Apparently to assert their power and to put Amaziah in his place, they broke down about six hundred feet of the city's wall, took all the gold and silver and all the vessels that were found in the house of the Lord, and the treasures of the king's palace, along with hostages (2 Kings 14:13, 14; 2 Chronicles 25:23, 24). Then, as though Amaziah were "a spanked child," he released him and returned to Samaria.

If the events of Jehoash's reign have been given in consecutive order, the chronology would indicate that at least three-fourths of his years as king were spent uneventfully. Jeroboam's calves continued to be worshipped, thus making Jehoash's rule "evil in the sight of the Lord," despite any "goodness" which may have cried out for expression.

FOR OUR ADMONITION AND LEARNING

Men at the peak of their strength and anointing are often "too busy" for reflection. In their "mad rush" of being "busy here and there," they may give no thought to those who have only recently "thrown them the torch." There was a long period in Elisha's life when it seemed that others paid small heed to his very existence. It was only when he was on his deathbed that Jehoash realized how much the great and good prophet would be missed. While the king was mostly "evil," many who think themselves "good" might well be humbled by his example on that occasion!

JEROBOAM II: THIRTEENTH KING OF ISRAEL

Required Scripture Readings: 2 Kings 13:13; 14:16, 23-29; Amos 1:1 and 7:9-11 (whole book is applicable); Hosea 1:1.

Pronunciation Helps: Hamath—HAY-math; Amittai—a-MIT-i; Gath-hepher—gath-HEEF-er.

RELEVANT FACTS
Chief characters: Jeroboam II; the prophets.
Time span: 41 years (2 Kings 14:23), beginning about 823 B.C.
Seat of government: Samaria.
Contemporary personalities: Amaziah and Uzziah (Azariah), kings of Judah; the prophets Jonah, Joel, Hosea, and Amos.
Lineage and family: Son of Jehoash (2 Kings 14:16). Son: Zachariah, only one named.
Death: Cause not sure; probably a natural death (2 Kings 14:29). See Amos 7:9-11. This is thought by some to have been a false report by the priest, and that Amos had not so prophesied.

THE HISTORICAL SITUATION
Israel's territorial holdings had been greatly "cut short," or diminished, during the reigns of Jehu and Jehoahaz. Syria especially had made invasions, finally bringing Israel under subjection to them. God had given Jehoash some favor, but as a whole, the nation was in distress.

It is of special note that the Minor Prophets have a significant role beginning with the reign of Jeroboam II. Until now, the numerous prophets had left no written records. The biblical authors wrote of them historically, of course. So, though the Scriptural account of Jeroboam's reign is very brief, much can be learned about the Israel of his time by reading the books of the prophets named above.

JEROBOAM II THE KING

The Bible Record
The writer of 2 Kings introduces Jeroboam somewhat as "just another evil monarch" (14:24) who continued the calf-worship of the earlier one whose name he bore. Two verses (25 and 28) make brief mention of the wars he engaged in with notable success.

Two verses (25 and 26) speak of the prophet Jonah, the son of Amittai of Gath-hepher, as having directed the king concerning the restoration of Hamath, on the northern boundary of the original Holy Land. Jonah's intervention was because "the Lord saw the affliction of Israel, that it was very bitter" (14:26), and there was no one but God to help them.

The Lord's mercy shines through in verse twenty-seven. Despite their just deserts, He would not "blot out the name of Israel from under heaven," but He would make Jeroboam the "saviour" He had spoken of during the reign of Jehoahaz (Jeroboam's grandfather), which work He had begun under Jehoash (his father).

In conclusion, the successful military conquest for Damascus in Syria is only mentioned. Then, the death of Israel's longest-reigning king is noted in the usual manner. So we gather that this limited account is sufficient for the strictly historical acts of a king who was personally "evil in the sight of the Lord."

The Prophets Speak

As stated above, the prophets of this era began writing, as God directed. Insofar as chronology can be trusted, we gather that Jeroboam ruled from about 823 to 782 B.C. Jonah's book is said to have been written about 862 B.C., probably in the earlier years of his ministry; but 2 Kings 14:25 involves him with Jeroboam II much later. Joel's book was written in about 800 B.C., near the middle of Jeroboam's reign. Amos wrote in about 787 B.C., near the end of the reign. Hosea's written prophecy is said to cover the years 785 to 725 B.C. Of course, their ministry span may have covered many years.

Jeroboam's name is mentioned in the prophetic books only in Hosea 1:1 and Amos 1:1 and 7:9-11; but the plight of Israel (and Judah, in some instances) is clearly seen as God saw it, and the nation's condition reflected its head. As a student, you will be enriched by reading the four books cited here.

Take, for instance, a few references in Hosea. Israel's idolatrous adultery is rebuked by illustration of a symbolic marriage (1:2-6). Their wilful ignorance is mentioned as having contributed to their destruction (4:6-11). Chapters six, verse four through thirteen, verse eight give God's response to their condition.

Amos begins with God's angry "roar" (1:2). Israel's discrimination against the poor comes under judgment (2:6,

7). Their luxurious ease, with its feasting and banqueting, reveals the economic prosperity of the times, along with the Lord's abhorrence of it all (6:1-8). The reference in chapter seven, verses seven through thirteen appears to relate a false accusation by Amaziah the priest of Bethel against Amos to Jeroboam, perhaps in the hope that the king would kill the prophet, or at least expel him from Israel.

The pending exile is prominent in many of the prophecies, as is the coming "day of the Lord" and the future restoration of Israel. King Jeroboam apparently gave no heed to the prophecies, except that of Jonah.

The Offerings of History

As a rule, the additional contributions by historians and commentators can be trusted for accuracy. One, *Philip Smith*, states: "His [Jeroboam's] reign is by far the most prosperous in the annals of Israel [the Northern Kingdom]... He not only recovered from Syria the whole district east of the Jordan from Hamath to the Dead Sea, and reconquered Ammon and Moab, but he attacked Damascus itself.... The apparent ease of these conquests may be explained by the sufferings of Syria from the constant attacks of the great Assyrian Empire, now at the height of its power."

Aside from all the prosperity, *Josephus* characterizes Jeroboam II as a king "guilty of *contumely* [haughty and contemptuous rudeness; scornful insolence or insult] against God, and became very wicked in worshipping of idols, and in many undertakings that were absurd and foreign. He was also the cause of ten thousand misfortunes to the people of Israel."

FOR OUR ADMONITION AND LEARNING

Material prosperity is often mistakenly thought to be a mark of God's special favor upon nations and individuals—or churches. Perhaps more often they are *permitted* of God. When we consider that God knows the *end* of a thing from its *beginning*, it is doubtful that He would deliberately bestow an abundance of something, the end of which would be the destruction of the nation, individual—or church. The prosperity in Jeroboam's time turned into a stench in the nostrils of God! It did not have to be so, of course—but all too often—!

ZACHARIAH: FOURTEENTH KING OF ISRAEL

Required Scripture Readings: 2 Kings 14:29; 15:8-12.

Pronunciation Helps: Zachariah—ZACK-a-RI-ah.

RELEVANT FACTS
Chief characters: Zachariah.
Time span: 6 months, beginning about 762 B.C. (**NOTE CAREFULLY**: A chronological time-variance of from 11 to 22 years is held by some historians to represent a lapse between the reigns of Jeroboam II and Zachariah, assuming that there was no king during that time. While there is disagreement about this, in this course we will allow 20 years, which will make the beginning date of the exile [721 B.C.] fall where it should be.)
Seat of government: Samaria.
Contemporary personalities: Uzziah (Azariah), king of Judah; the prophets Jonah, Joel, Hosea, and Amos.
Lineage and family: Son of Jeroboam II.
Death: Slain by Shallum, who succeeded him.

ZACHARIAH THE KING
(*"The Historical Situation"* had not changed in the short six months' reign.)

It would appear that the only purpose for Zachariah occupying the throne at all was to fulfill God's promise to Jehu that his dynasty would continue unto the fourth generation. "And so it came to pass" (2 Kings 15:12).

Nothing changed. Zachariah kept up the abominable sin of Jeroboam I, doing "evil in the sight of the Lord."

A man named Shallum (*Josephus* calls him a "friend") conspired against Zachariah and killed him publicly, it seems, without any remonstration from the people.

FOR OUR ADMONITION AND LEARNING
If we would ask why God allowed the wicked dynasty of Jehu to continue a hundred years or more, we might answer with another question: Why is the return of Christ delayed today after almost twenty centuries of mankind's provocation? Peter has given us the answer:

"The Lord is not slack concerning his promise, as some men count slackness; but is longsuffering to us-ward, not willing that any should perish, but that all should come to repentance" (2 Peter 3:9).

Then Peter solemnly reminds us, "But the day of the Lord *will come . . .* "!

—Lesson Thirteen—

SHALLUM: FIFTEENTH KING OF ISRAEL

Required Scripture Reading: 2 Kings 15:10-15.

Pronunciation Helps: Shallum—SHALL-um; Jabesh—JAY-besh; Menahem—men-AH-hem; Jehizkiah—JEE-hiz-KI-ah.

RELEVANT FACTS
Chief character: Shallum.
Time span: 1 month, in the year 762 B.C.
Seat of government: Samaria.
Contemporary personalities: Uzziah (Azariah), king of Judah; the prophets Jonah, Hosea, Joel, and Amos.
Lineage and family: Son of Jabesh (2 Kings 15:10). (See 2 Chronicles 28:12—Jehizkiah, the son of Shallum; not sure if this is the same Shallum.)
Death: Slain by Menahem, who succeeded him.

THE HISTORICAL SITUATION
Jeroboam II had regained much territory for Israel. No mention is made of any gains or losses during Zachariah's six-month reign. So, economically, Israel was prosperous, but under the frown of God.

SHALLUM THE KING
Shallum is an "unknown" so far as his ancestry is concerned. Mention is made of a "Shallum" of Ephraim, who had a son named Jehizkiah (2 Chronicles 28:12), but we cannot be sure that this was the Shallum under study here. If so, from the context, his son would seem to have been a better man than his father.

If *Josephus* was right is stating that Shallum was a "friend" of Zachariah, he was either a deceitful person or something came between the two to sever their friendship. Shallum formed a conspiracy, the details of which are not given. At any rate, he publicly slew Zachariah (2 Kings 15:10).

He may have usurped the authority of the throne, but nothing is said of any opposition from the people who looked on. His being made king was probably a condition of the conspiracy. But in his case, only "a full month" passed before it happened as Jesus said much later, "They that take the sword shall perish with the sword" (Matthew 26:52).

Following is *Josephus'* amplification of the account of Shallum's death: "... Menahem, the general of his [Shallum's] army, who was at that time in the city of Tirzah, and heard of what had befallen Zachariah, returned thereupon with all his forces to Samaria, and joining battle with Shallum, slew him...."

The Bible says simply that Menahem "smote Shallum the son of Jabesh in Samaria, and slew him..." (15:14). So, whether in battle, or a man-to-man confrontation, we cannot be certain; but in either case, Menahem was responsible for his death.

FOR OUR ADMONITION AND LEARNING

Envy—covetousness—conspiracy! All that they represent is evil. Usually they are "undercover operations." Their victim may be totally in the dark as to what is going on in the mind of the one who envies his abilities, covets his position or possessions, or secretly plots his ruin. The Lord has not held it necessary that we know the details of Shallum's conspiracy against his king—yes, possibly his "friend." But the details do not alter *the principle.* It is selfish; hypocritical; merciless; despicable. If given free rein, it will destroy not only its innocent victim, but the very soul of the one who wields its ruthless sword!

MENAHEM: SIXTEENTH KING OF ISRAEL

Required Scripture Reading: 2 Kings 15:13-22.

Pronunciation Helps: Menahem—men-AH-hem; Pul—POOL; Tiglath-pileser—TIG-lath-pi-LEE-ser; Tiphsah—TIFF-sah; Gadi—GAY-di.

RELEVANT FACTS
Chief character: Menahem.

Time span: 10 years, beginning about 762 B.C.
Seat of government: Samaria.
Contemporary personalities: Uzziah (Azariah), king of Judah; the prophets Hosea and Isaiah.
Lineage and family: Son of Gadi (2 Kings 15:14, 17). Son: Pekahiah, only one named.
Death: Of natural causes (2 Kings 15:22).

MENAHEM THE KING

(*"The Historical Situation"* had not changed from the time of Zachariah and Shallum.)

Menahem became king after he had slain Shallum, as we saw in Lesson Twelve. He was the third king to occupy the throne within a year. *Josephus* says he "made himself king." It seems that he had no competitors or objectors, since he reigned ten years. It is possible that the people counted him brave and noble for avenging Zachariah's death. However, as time went on, he proved to be a very cruel ruler.

The conquest of Tiphsah (15:16) probably was made immediately after he took the throne. One commentator, *J. F. Keil* (with others concurring), views it as follows: Zachariah had intended to extend his father's expansion efforts unto Tiphsah, and had gathered a large army and stationed it at Tirzah, about ten miles east of Samaria, with Menahem over it as captain of the host. When Shallum killed Zachariah, Menahem avenged him, took the power of the throne, and returned with the army to Tirzah, and thence to Tiphsah to carry out Zachariah's battle plan.

Tiphsah was in Syrian territory, far to the northeast on the Euphrates River. Jeroboam II had been successful in re-subjecting Syria to Israeli rule, since Assyria had already weakened the Syrians. Menahem's character showed its darkest side in that invasion (15:16).

Josephus describes the slaughter as cruel and barbaric. He says the inhabitants of the city barred the gates against Menahem, and this infuriated him so that "he burnt the country round about it, and took the city by force, upon a siege; and being very much displeased at what the inhabitants of Tiphsah had done, he slew them all, and spared not so much as the infants . . . ."

His naturally cruel disposition, along with the continuance of the sinful practices of Jeroboam I, made him a tyrant.

115

Sometime later in his reign, Pul, the king of Assyria (also known in history as Tiglath-pileser II) came against Israel. This was the beginning of the threat of an eventual Assyrian take-over, as the prophets had been predicting without getting Israel's ear!

Evidently Menahem was wise enough to know Israel was no match for Pul's host, but not wise enough to humble himself and turn to God. He managed, "at a vast expense, to purchase a peace with him," as *Matthew Henry* states it. We must give credit where it is due, and recognize in him a consideration for the poor, exacting the tribute money (for such it was, in fact) from "all the mighty men of wealth" (15:20).

Today we would say it was a "pay-off," which usually is only temporarily satisfactory. But Pul and his army took the money and went home. It is doubtful that Menahem really believed that the kingdom was confirmed in his hand (15:19). Perhaps he was too near the end of his reign to see how temporal the arrangement really was.

FOR OUR ADMONITION AND LEARNING

It is a terrible thing for a man to "sell out" to the enemy of his soul; yet the "sale" never ceases, day or night! However, God has granted man "free moral agency"—the power to make his own choices. Menahem had the freedom to sell *his own future* to Assyria, but simply to "keep up appearances" that Israel was secure with the kingdom in his hands, *he sold the nation*, without the people's consent—yea, without their knowledge at the time!

What a pity it is when men—in government or church—in whom we place our confidence, "Sell us down the river"!

PEKAHIAH: SEVENTEENTH KING OF ISRAEL

Required Scripture Reading: 2 Kings 15:22-26.

Pronunciation Helps: Pekahiah—PECK-a-HI-ah; Pekah—PEEK-ah; Remaliah—REM-a-LI-ah; Argob—AR-GOB; Arieh—a-RI-eh.

RELEVANT FACTS
Chief character: Pekahiah.
Time span: 2 years, beginning about 752 B.C.
Seat of government: Samaria.
Contemporary personalities: Jotham, king of Judah; the prophets Hosea, Isaiah, and Micah.
Lineage and family: Son of Menahem (2 Kings 15:22).
Death: Slain by Pekah's conspiracy (2 Kings 15:25).

THE HISTORICAL SITUATION
Pekahiah inherited a kingdom that was unconfessedly under tribute to the great Assyrian Empire. Pul, or Tiglath-pileser, was "being nice" for the moment, for it was to his advantage in the long run. One wonders if the people of Israel really understood the situation. It was something of "a deal"—Pul would not *occupy* the land, but would let Menahem remain on as king "for pay" (15:19). But Menahem soon passed off the stage of action. Others would feel the brunt of Menahem's "arrangement."

PEKAHIAH THE KING
Pekahiah's short reign was uneventful. He was just another one of Israel's succession of evil "calf worshippers" (15:24). He was probably not well-liked, so a move to dethrone him got under way. One of his captains, by the name of Pekah, formed a conspiracy to kill him. This they did "in the palace of the king's house, with Argob and Arieh."

Argob and Arieh are variously held to have been Pekahiah's friends, or guards, who were slain with him while defending him, or two of Pekah's chief conspirators, who, along with the "fifty men of the Gileadites," carried out the assassination (15:25). Some might also contend that the Gileadites were slain "with" Pekahiah rather than that they were "with" Pekah in the conspiracy.

Regardless of the conjectures, Pekah's object was attained—"he killed him, and reigned in his room."

FOR OUR ADMONITION AND LEARNING
Retribution inevitably follows the flagrant disregard for God's Word. Men often take it upon themselves to manipulate "the powers that be." Such as these are lesser men than those they attempt to "use," or "influence," or "displace."

It is apparent that God either "caused" or "allowed" retribution in Israel because of the continued idolatrous practices. They often made elaborate "offerings," even "calves of a year old" (Micah 6:6), as God's law had specified, yet at the center of it all were those other "calves" made of gold!

Micah pushes aside all the hypocritical elaboration—"thousands of rams, or ten thousand rivers of oil"—and declares what God requires; (1) to do justly, (2) to love mercy, and (3) to walk humbly with God (Micah 6:7, 8). All else is unacceptable substitution.

Illustrious leaders may come and go, in the political arena and in the Church, yet "The Lord's voice crieth unto the city, and the man of wisdom shall see thy name: hear ye the rod, and who hath appointed it" (Micah 6:9).

Generations pass one after the other, with their efforts of *sowing much but reaping little*—

"For the statutes of Omri are kept, and all the works of the house of Ahab, and ye walk in their counsels; that I should make thee a desolation, and the inhabitants thereof an hissing: therefore ye shall bear the reproach of my people." (Read Micah 6:11-16.)

—Lesson Fourteen—

PEKAH: EIGHTEENTH KING OF ISRAEL

Required Scripture Readings: 2 Kings 15:25-31, 37; 16:5; 2 Chronicles 28:6-15; Isaiah 7:1-9.

Pronunciation Helps: Azariah—az-a-RI-ah; Ijon—I-JON; Abel-beth-maachah—A-bel-beth-MAY-a-cah; Janoah—Ja-NO-ah; Hoshea—ho-SHEE-a; Elah—EE-lah; Rezin—REE-zin; Ahaz—A-HAZ; Shear-jashub—SHEE-ar-JAH-shub; Ben-Tabeal—BEN-TAB-e-al.

RELEVANT FACTS
Chief characters: Pekah; Rezin; Isaiah.
Time span: 20 years, beginning about 750 B.C.
Seat of government: Samaria.
Contemporary personalities: Uzziah (Azariah), Jotham, and Ahaz, kings of Judah; the prophets Isaiah, Hosea, Micah, and Oded.
Lineage and family: Son of Remaliah.
Death: Slain by Hoshea, who succeeded him.

THE HISTORICAL SITUATION
Menahem's arrangement with Assyria continued through Pekahiah's two years, and on into the reign of Pekah. But Pekah was not one to voluntarily submit to a state of tribute, as we shall see. It is likely that he had in mind to change that situation when he conspired to get Pekahiah out of the way. Assyria had risen to become a formidable foe in the eyes of many nations.

PEKAH THE KING
The inspired Word tells us that Pekah was another evil king who followed in the way of his forefathers (2 Kings 15:28). But his era was one of shaky diplomatic relations among the surrounding nations, and we see the hand of God moving in the affairs of men.

Menahem had subdued Syria once again, but the Assyrians had done practically the same to Israel, though with a hypocritical diplomacy. Now, Pekah saw that some alliance would be needed if any resistance was to be put forth against the mighty foe to their east, for Assyria was taking over the cities of northern Israel—Ijon, Abel-beth-maachah, Janoah, Kedesh and Hazor—all cities of Naphtali. They were doing likewise in Galilee farther south, and in Gilead east of the Jordan (15:29).

The kings of Judah—Jotham, and later Ahaz—did not seem interested at the moment, so Pekah made an alliance with Rezin, king of Syria, whose land lay in a dangerous position adjoining Assyria. The Scriptures are brief on this period, but historical data offers several details.

Pekah and Rezin schemed to bring Judah into their alliance by trying to dethrone Ahaz, king of Judah, aiming to put a certain Ben-Tabeal (son of Tabeal) in his stead (Isaiah 7:1-9). Although Ahaz was one of Judah's evil kings, Judah was "the apple of God's eye," and He would give her some assistance. So He sent Isaiah to warn Ahaz of the plot Pekah and Rezin had under way. But there were words of assurance: "It shall not stand, neither shall it come to pass" (Isaiah 7:7). However, if Ahaz would not "believe" (Isaiah 7:9), Assyria would eventually be their undoing.

Ahaz did not believe, even after a second offer of help (Isaiah 7:11-13). It appears that it was at this point that Pekah and Rezin made their advance. There is some vagueness in the passages in 2 Kings 16:5 and 2 Chronicles 28:5-8. The advance on Jerusalem seems to have been mostly ineffective because of the strength of its walls (so says *Josephus*).

The account in 2 Chronicles is thought to be a different confrontation. *Josephus* says that Syria continued on into Edom and drove the Jews out of the city of Elath, at the northern end of the Gulf of Aqaba. He says that the Syrian army returned to Damascus, and Ahaz thought his army was a match for Pekah's army alone.

The Bible account, however, is clear in the fact that Syria was involved in this second confrontation; perhaps even first (2 Chronicles 28:5, 6). Then Pekah took a heavy toll of 120,000 men of Judah, and captured and carried away 200,000 men, women, and children (2 Chronicles 28:9).

Perhaps it was because of the *unbelief* of Ahaz, and even more because of his *wickedness*, that God allowed Israel this victory over Judah (2 Chronicles 28:4, 5, 9). But God sent the prophet Oded to Pekah, directing him to release his captives (28:11). "Then certain of the heads of the children of Ephraim" (Israel) considered Oded's words and decided to obey them (28:12-15).

It is difficult to determine the order of events during Pekah's reign, but this seems not to be important. His twenty-year reign came to an end when "Hoshea the son of Elah made a conspiracy" against him and slew him (2 Kings 15:30). *Josephus* says that Hoshea was—or had been—a "friend" of Pekah, but he offers no motive for the assassination by conspiracy. Possibly it was the lust for the power of the throne, since Hoshea was "his friend's" successor.

FOR OUR ADMONITION AND LEARNING

Treachery knows no decorum; plays no favorites. "Friends" turn into "enemies" when such better suits their ends. David once lamented this fact: "Yea, mine own familiar friend, in whom I trusted, which did eat my bread, hath lifted up his heel against me" (Psalms 41:9). This psalm is classified among the Messianic Psalms, and the verse above is considered a prophecy of the treacherous, despicable betrayal of Jesus by His disciple, Judas Iscariot.

On another occasion, during one of David's particularly trying hours, he wrote of the "deceit and guile" of a supposed-friend:

"For it was not an enemy that reproached me; then I could have borne it: neither was it he that hated me that did magnify himself against me; then I would have hid myself from him:

"But it was thou, a man mine equal, my guide, and mine acquaintance.

"We took sweet counsel together, and walked unto the house of God in company" (Psalms 55:12-14).

Pekah slew Pekahiah; Hoshea slew Pekah. But it was nothing new. It was a vicious cycle. Even in Christendom, all too often it happens. Not in physical murders, of course; but in the eyes of God, is "character assassination" or "killing a brother's influence" any better?

HOSHEA: NINETEENTH KING OF ISRAEL

Required Scripture Readings: 2 Kings 15:30; 17:1-23; 18:9-12.

Pronunciation Helps: Shal-maneser—SHALL-man-EE-ser; Halah—HAY-lah; Habor—HAY-bor; Gozan—GO-ZAN; Hezekiah—HEZ-a-KI-ah; Sargon—SAR-gon.

RELEVANT FACTS
Chief character: Hoshea.
Time span: 9 years, about 730 to 721 B. C.
Seat of government: Samaria.
Contemporary personalities: Ahaz and Hezekiah, kings of Judah; the prophets Isaiah, Hosea, and Micah.
Lineage and family: Son of Elah (2 Kings 15:30).
Death: Not known. He was carried away to Assyria—the beginning of the 70 years of exile.

THE HISTORICAL SITUATION
Much Israeli territory had been lost to Assyria during Pekah's reign (2 Kings 15:29). Enmity between Israel and Judah had become very bitter. A change in Assyrian monarchs hastened the end for Israel, but largely through their own revolt.

History relates that one of Jeroboam's golden calves had been carried away by the Assyrians during Pekah's reign; but there is disagreement as to whether it was the one at Dan or the one at Bethel. It is more reasonable to think it was the one at Dan, since one of the Assyrian invasions was in that area (2 Kings 15:29). It is noted that Hoshea did not replace it.

HOSHEA THE KING
Although *Josephus* characterizes Hoshea as "a wicked man, and a despiser of the Divine worship," he was not as evil as the kings that were before him (2 Kings 17:2). Possibly the loss of one of the golden calves had somewhat dampened the manner of worship.

In 2 Chronicles, chapter thirty, concerning worship in Judah, the king had sent letters "to Ephraim and Manasseh" (verse 1), and "throughout all Israel" (verse 5), welcoming the people to the feast of the passover. According to chronology, this was during Hoshea's reign over Israel, and there is no indication that he objected; and the record shows that some attended (2 Chronicles 30:11, 18).

It appears from secular history that Hoshea became king while Tiglath-pileser was still king of Assyria. In fact, it may have been with his permission that Hoshea was allowed to succeed Pekah. Israel was paying some measure of tribute, as in the days of Menahem.

But a new ruler came to power in Assyria—King Shalmaneser. Hoshea may have thought this a good time to revolt; but he would need help.

"And the king of Assyria found conspiracy in Hoshea: for he had sent messengers to So, king of Egypt, and brought no present to the king of Assyria, as he had done year by year: therefore the king of Assyria shut him up, and bound him in prison" (2 Kings 17:4).

It was then Shal-maneser's turn to take advantage of the situation. With Israel's king in hand, with an army that virtually covered the land he came up and laid siege to the capital city of Samaria. The king of Egypt evidently did not respond in Hoshea's behalf. The siege continued three years. History bears record that possibly there was some sort of revolution in Nineveh of Assyria about that time, which may have delayed the immediate take-over of Samaria, though the siege was maintained. In the meantime, the reign of Shalmaneser came to an end, and Sargon took his place. In chapter eighteen, where part of the history is repeated relative to Judah, Shal-maneser is designated as the king laying the siege (18:9); then, after three years, "the king of Assyria" is said to have led the captivity, but the king's name is not given there (verses 10 and 11).

This brings the Northern Kingdom of Israel to an end in the year 721 B.C.

"In the ninth year of Hoshea, the king of Assyria [Sargon] took Samaria, and carried Israel away into Assyria, and placed them in Halah and in Habor by the river of Gozan, and in the cities of the Medes" (17:6).

The region in which Halah, Habor, and Gozan were located was perhaps some five hundred miles northeast of Samaria, and perhaps one hundred miles or less east of the Haran of Abraham's history. The cities of the Medes must have been much further east. Apparently, the captives of Israel were scattered over a very large area.

The Conclusion of the Matter

The sins for which Israel was carried into captivity are enumerated in 2 Kings 17:7-23 (which read). *Josephus* summarizes the situation in one sentence: "And such a conclusion overtook the Israelites, when they had transgressed the laws, and would not hearken to the prophets, who foretold that this calamity would come upon them, if they would not leave off their evil doings...."

It may seem strange that Israel should go into captivity at the time they had their best—or least wicked—king. But there was no repentance; it was more of a surrender to existing circumstances. The Lord beckoned to them through Hezekiah's invitation of Jerusalem on that particular feast of the passover (2 Chronicles 30). Perhaps Hoshea would have allowed a nation-wide response; but only a few went to the feast. Actually, Hoshea did not encourage them, nor did he show a hunger for the true God.

A little later, instead of going to *God* for help and deliverance from the threatening Assyrian take-over, they appealed to *Egypt*; the very thing which God had warned them against through His prophets: "Ephraim also is like a silly dove without heart: they call to Egypt, they go to Assyria" (Hosea 7:11; see also 2 Kings 18:21, 24).

Israel was ripe for judgment. Now it had come!

FOR OUR ADMONITION AND LEARNING

A conclusion by *Matthew Henry* seems appropriate by way of warning and instruction:

"... Rather shall heaven and earth pass than one tittle of God's word fall to the ground. When God's word and His works are compared, it will be found not only that they agree, but that they illustrate each other. But why would God ruin a people that were raised and incorporated, as Israel was, by miracles and oracles? Why would He undo that which He Himself had done at so vast an expense? Was it purely an act of sovereignty? No, it was an act of *necessary justice*. For they *provoked Him* to do this by their wickedness. Was it *God's* doing? Nay, it was *their own*; by their way and their doings they procured all this to themselves, and it was *their own wickedness* that did correct them . . . . "

—Lesson Fifteen—

THE KINGS OF JUDAH
REHOBOAM: FIRST KING OF JUDAH

Required Scripture Readings: 1 Kings 11:43; 12:1-24; 14:21-31; 15:6; 2 Chronicles 9:31 through 12:16; 13:7.

Pronunciation Helps: Rehoboam—REE-ho-BO-am; Adoram— a-DO-ram, or Hadoram—ha-DO-ram; Shemaiah—she-MAY-ah; Naamah—NAY-a-mah; Mahalath—MAH-a-lath; Abihail—a-BI-hail; Maachah—MAY-a-cah; Abijah—a-BI-jah; Shishak—SHI-SHAK; Iddo—ID-do; Jerimoth—JER-i-moth; Eliab—e-LI-ab; Jeush—JEE-ush; Shamariah—sham-a-RI-ah; Zaham—ZAY-ham; Attai—AY-ti; Ziza—ZI-zah; Shelomith—SHELL-o-mith.

RELEVANT FACTS
Chief character: Rehoboam; Jeroboam.
Time span: 17 years, beginning in 975 B.C.
Seat of government: Jerusalem.
Contemporary personalities: Jeroboam, king of Israel; the prophets Ahijah, Shemaiah, and Iddo.
Lineage and family: Son of Solomon. Tribe of Judah. Mother: Naamah, an Ammonitess. Wives: (Eighteen, and threescore concubines, 2 Chr. 11:21); Mahalath (daughter of Jerimoth, son of David), Abihail (daughter of Eliab, son of Jesse), and Maachah (daughter of Absalom). Children: Jeush, Shamariah, Zaham, Abijah (Abijam, 1 Kings 14 and 15), Attai, Ziza, and Shelomith; *Josephus* says he had 28 sons and 60 daughters.
Accession to the throne: At age 41, in 975 B.C.
Death: Of natural causes (1 Kings 14:31).

THE HISTORICAL SITUATION
Review, under Lesson Six, the sub-topics entitled "The Divided Kingdom" and "The Historical Situation," and the first four paragraphs under "Jeroboam the King." The history of the division into two kingdoms is so interwoven that it is unnecessary to repeat it here.

A quotation from *Zondervan's Pictorial Bible Dictionary* under "Rehoboam," says much in a few words about the historical situation as Solomon had left it:

" . . . Solomon's wild extravagances and his vain ambition to make Israel the world power of his day led him to set up a tremendously expensive capital [at Jerusalem], and a very elaborate harem [wives, concubines, and women servants of the king]. The importation of so many pagan women for his harem resulted in a spiritual debacle in Israel. The luxuries of his palace and the expenses of his diplomatic corps and of his vast building program resulted in burdensome taxation . . . . An appeal was made to Rehoboam for easier taxes, [but he] heeding the advice of young men, refused to heed the appeal, with the result that Israel rebelled. When Adoram [who was over the tribute] was sent to collect the tribute, he was slain and Rehoboam fled to Jerusalem (1 Kings 12:16-19) . . . . "

We see, then, that Rehoboam had inherited some *problems* along with his *crown*; but, " . . . *the cause was from the Lord*, that he might perform his saying, which the Lord spake by Ahijah the Shilonite unto Jeroboam the son of Nebat" (1 Kings 12:15. Read also 1 Kings 11:29-37).

As to his family history, Rehoboam's mother, Naamah (1 Kings 14:31), was one of Solomon's foreign wives, from Ammon. No mention is made of any other son of Solomon. (For the names of his wives and children, see under "Lineage and family.")

REHOBOAM THE KING

Despite the economic unrest, it was assumed at the time of Solomon's death that his son Rehoboam would succeed him. Rehoboam selected the historic city of Shechem for his coronation and inauguration, and "all Israel" went there "to make him king" (1 Kings 12:1).

Although Jeroboam had a mandate from the Lord, apparently his earlier premature move in *lifting up his hand* against Solomon (1 Kings 11:25ff) had taught him to hold his peace. He had not been forgotten, however, for "they sent and called him" to return from Egypt (12:2, 3). But he was one with "all the congregation" who spoke to Rehoboam about reducing the tax burden. It seems clear that Rehoboam was, in fact, already crowned king at that point, and, as king, asked for the three days in which to consider their request.

There may be a tendency to be critical of Rehoboam about his seeming lack of wisdom in handling this matter, but this would be ungracious since we know that God was directing. *Matthew Henry* rather harshly charges him of being "a fool" who "did not inherit his father's wisdom," which "stood him in little stead to inherit his father's throne." The deeper truth is that, despite his earlier wisdom, *Solomon* played the fool in his later years, and it was because of his folly that *his son* was suffering as a victim of circumstances. If Rehoboam was "a fool," he was so by inheritance, and because of a certain loyalty to his illustrious father.

So, *as God would have it*, the new king sought counsel of "the old men, that stood before Solomon his father," and also of "the young men" of his own generation (12:6, 8). While the old men had respected Solomon, they recognized that the people were weary and overburdened, so they advised, "If thou wilt be a servant unto this people this day, and wilt serve them, and answer them, and speak good words to them, then they will be thy servants for ever" (12:7).

The young men had grown up accustomed to luxury. It is altogether likely that their fathers had borne the greater portion of the tax levy, so that they had not yet come to realize its pressure. Instead of a "tax cut," they envisioned an even more affluent lifestyle, so they advised the king to tell the people, "My little finger shall be thicker than my father's loins. And now whereas my father did lade you with a heavy yoke, I will add to your yoke: my father hath chastised you with whips, but I will chastise you with scorpions" (12:10, 11).

Though the words "yoke," "whips," and "scorpions" are largely only figurative, it must be remembered that "slave labor" was not uncommon in Israel's history. This was especially true of those heathen peoples who had become subjects, or vassals, of Israel. Therefore it is not improbable that some measure of physical goading was intended.

At any rate, Rehoboam was inclined to agree with his peers, so he turned a deaf ear to the people and the older counsellors, ans set forth the decree of the younger ones—*"for the cause was of God*" (2 Chronicles 10:15), not that God is the author of confusion and division, but because He would use it as His instrument of chastisement. The Omniscient Father knew the hearts of His people, that they were already "bent to backsliding," as the prophet Hosea later characterized them (Hosea 11:7).

Incensed by Rehoboam's words, the people confirmed the already impending division, declaring as the *Pulpit Commentary* paraphrases it, "Since we have no kindness or fairness from *David's seed*, what is *his house* to us? Why render homage to his son? We *receive* nought from him, why *yield* aught to him? His tribe is not ours; his interests are not ours."

Then all but David's tribe, Judah, along with the tribe of Benjamin (within whose inheritance a portion of the city of Jerusalem lay), rebelled and made Jeroboam their king, and Shechem his headquarters.

The King at Judah's Helm

Rehoboam was somewhat exasperated at the turn of events. Jeroboam at least had the prophet Ahijah's prediction to support him; but God Himself would never be far from his chosen tribe of Judah!

Rehoboam felt it his duty to try to prevent a permanent disruption, so he raised an army of 180,000 chosen men from the two tribes to fight against the Northern Kingdom in an effort to bring them back under him. But God sent a prophet named Shemaiah, saying, "Thus saith the Lord, Ye shall not go up, nor fight against your brethren the children of Israel: return every man to his house; for *this thing is from me*" (1 Kings 12:24). And Rehoboam obeyed the Lord.

One commentator observes: "Rehoboam did not sit repining, but set to work to make his realm strong." He built (and possibly rebuilt) several cities in Judah, and some in Benjamin (2 Chronicles 11:5-12), and thoroughly fortified them, with a strong defense in mind. His two-tribe kingdom must have seemed small and defenseless to the young king, who had grown up under the regime of a father whose twelve-tribe nation was awesome in the eyes of all others!

His kingdom was strengthened considerably by the Levites. Their cities were scattered throughout the Promised Land, as had been assigned to them by Joshua; but when Jeroboam made the golden calves and established his abominable system in Israel, the Levites defected to Judah and Jerusalem, where they could continue in the worship of God (2 Chronicles 11:13-16).

For three years all went well—"For three years they walked in the way of David and Solomon" (verse 17). Then we read, "And it came to pass, when Rehoboam had established the kingdom, and had strengthened himself, he forsook the law of the Lord, and all Israel with him" (2 Chronicles 12:1).

Josephus analyzes the situation well, as follows:

"Now I cannot but think that the greatness of a kingdom, and its change into prosperity, often become the occasion of mischief and of transgression to men; for when Rehoboam saw that his kingdom was so much increased, he went out of the right way unto unrighteous and irreligious practices, and he despised the worship of God, till the people themselves imitated his wicked actions: for so it usually happens, that the manners of subjects are corrupted at the same time with those of their governors, which subjects then lay aside their own sober way of living, as a reproof of their governors' intemperate courses, and follow their wickedness as if it were virtue; for it is not possible to show that men approve of the actions of their kings, unless they do the same actions with them. Agreeable whereto it now happened to the subjects of Rehoboam; for when he was grown impious, and a transgressor himself, they endeavored not to offend him by resolving still to be righteous. But God sent Shishak, king of Egypt, to punish them for their unjust behaviour towards him . . . ."

In the fifth year of this new Southern Kingdom, God's judgmental chastisement fell upon them for their transgressions. Shishak, the king of Egypt, came against them with twelve hundred chariots, sixty thousand horsemen, and soldiers without number—some from allied nations (2 Chronicles 12:2-4).

First, they took the cities Rehoboam had so carefully fortified. When they marched on Jerusalem, God sent Shemaiah to Rehoboam to tell him why; and he and the people humbled themselves. *Josephus* says, "When they [Israel] besought God to give them victory and deliverance, they could not persuade God to be on their side." But He sent the prophet again, saying that He would not pour out His wrath; however, He would allow them to become the servants of Shishak (12:5-8).

So Shishak spoiled the temple at Jerusalem, as well as the king's palace (12:9), seemingly with no resistance from Rehoboam, who took God at His word. For the golden treasures and shields Shishak had taken, Rehoboam made replacements of brass. (NOTE: It is said that *brass*, in the Scriptures, represents *judgment!*) After this, "in Judah things went well" (12:12). *Josephus* says, "So, instead of warlike expeditions, and that glory which results from public actions, [Rehoboam] reigned in great quietness, though not without fear, as being always an enemy to Jeroboam."

The meaning is not clear where it is stated that "there was war between Rehoboam and Jeroboam all their days" (1 Kings 14:30; 2 Chronicles 12:15). There is no record of open warfare. Some hold that it consisted only of a hostile attitude between the two kings personally.

Summarily, Rehoboam's reign was evil (1 Kings 14:22-24; 2 Chronicles 12:14). God could not wink at the high places and groves, nor the toleration of sodomy in the land, and other abominations of the heathen peoples who had formerly possessed the territory. Israel suffered much for their transgressions; but it seems that Rehoboam ended his reign with a better posture.

FOR OUR ADMONITION AND LEARNING

Excusing oneself because of "the circumstances" is a lame argument. Rehoboam could have done better than he did, even though he was "a victim of inherited circumstances." After all, he was forty-one years old when he took the throne—by no means a youth. God never puts upon us more than we are able to bear (1 Corinthians 10:13). Our failures result from our own bendings under pressure; or from our foolhardiness in leaning on our own understanding instead of seeking the will of God.

We may learn from our foolish mistakes, if we will. There is little indication that Rehoboam even tried to put into practice the unwise counsel of his peers. The fortifications he built were as nothing compared with his father's elaborate exploits. When we find that we have erred through personal boasting and vaunting our own abilities, the shortest route out of the consequences is repentance and making a "right about face."

There is no fleshly "fortification" strong enough to stand against the righteous judgment of God. We may "feather our nest" luxuriantly, and lay by a great store, but when we forsake God, He will find some instrument by which to reach all our "padlocked vaults." In Rehoboam's case, Shishak was the instrument; but the power was God's.

ABIJAM: SECOND KING OF JUDAH
(Abijah—2 Chronicles 13 and 14)

Required Scripture Readings: 1 Kings 14:31; 15:1-8; 2 Chronicles 12:16; 13:1-24; 14:1.

Pronunciation Helps: Abijam—a-BI-jam, or Abijah—a-BI-jah; Zemaraim—ZEM-a-RAY-im; Jeshanah—je-SHAN-ah; Ephrain—ef-RAY-in, Abishalom—a-BISH-a-lom; Uriel—u-RI-el.

RELEVANT FACTS
Chief characters: Abijam (Abijah); Jeroboam.
Time span: 3 years, beginning about 958 B.C.
Seat of government: Jerusalem.
Contemporary personalities: Jeroboam I, king of Israel; the prophets Ahijah and Iddo.
Lineage and family: Son of Rehoboam. Mother: Maachah. Wives: 14 (2 Chr. 13:21). Children: Asa, only one named; 22 sons and 16 daughters (2 Chr. 13:21).
Death: Natural causes (1 Kings 14:1).

THE HISTORICAL SITUATION
Judah was in subjection to Egypt, as under Rehoboam's reign. Nothing changed, except that Jeroboam made war against Judah during Abijam's short reign.

Abijam's family history requires some clarification on his mother's side. There is no doubt that Maachah was his mother (2 Chronicles 11:20, 22), but she is called Michaiah in 2 Chronicles 13:2. Also, in 1 Kings 15:2 she is said to have been the daughter of Abishalom, while in 2 Chronicles 11:20 she is said to have been the daughter of Absalom; but in 2

Chronicles 13:2 she is called the daughter of Uriel of Gibeah. It has been explained that Maachah was the daughter of Tamar, the daughter of Absalom (David's son) (2 Samuel 14:27), and that Tamar's husband was Uriel. She would therefore have been Absalom's granddaughter.

Some Bible scholars attribute these and other seeming discrepancies to erring transcribers and/or translators, but it is not uncommon for individuals in the Bible records to have gone by more than one name. Also, *grandsons* and *granddaughters* were sometimes referred to as "sons" and "daughters," fondly, perhaps. There is no reason to believe that the use of a different name, or a variation in spellings, represents an error *in fact*. A similar variance appears in Abijam being called Abijah in 2 Chronicles.

While these things may seem (or be) unimportant to us, lineage meant a great deal in Old Testament times.

ABIJAM THE KING

Abijam is characterized as walking in the sins of his father, with a heart that was not perfect with the Lord (1 Kings 15:3). But God had made a covenant, with David, and for David's sake, and His faithfulness to that covenant, He spared those in that lineage, though He often chastened them severely. Thus we read here:

"Nevertheless for David's sake did the Lord his God give him a lamp in Jerusalem, to set up his son after him, and to establish Jerusalem:

"Because David did that which was right in the eyes of the Lord . . . " (1 Kings 15:4, 5).

Only one event of note is recorded for Abijam's three-year reign—war with Israel under Jeroboam. It is not clear who agitated the fray (2 Chronicles 13:2, 3), or what it was about. *Josephus* charges Jeroboam with launching the expedition, with little motive other than that "he despised him [Abijam] because of his age." He portrays Abijam as not being afraid of Jeroboam, despite his army of some 800,000 against Judah's 400,000.

The two armies met at Mount Zemaraim, perhaps twelve miles north of Jerusalem and fifteen miles south of Shechem. Abijam stood upon the mount and called to "Jeroboam, and all Israel," then delivered an appeal for Israel not to oppose

God, because He had given "the kingdom over Israel to David for ever, even to him and to his sons [descendants] by a covenant of salt" (2 Chronicles 13:5). He accused Jeroboam of rebelling "against his lord [David], " and taking advantage of the occasion in the time of Solomon, and especially of Rehoboam when he was "young and tenderhearted," and could not withstand Jeroboam's "vain men, the children of Belial."

He further accused him of trying to withstand Israel, at a time of transition of kings, with a great multitude, trusting in their golden calves (13:8). He reproved Jeroboam for casting out the Levitical priesthood and allowing just about any man to be a priest.

Then he declared Judah's continuance in the worship of the Lord God, with the priests and Levites performing their God-ordained service (13:10, 11). He warned Israel not to fight "against the Lord God of your fathers," for they would not prosper in so doing.

But the hard-hearted, godless Jeroboam took advantage of the time Abijam was speaking to situate ambushments before and behind the army of Judah for what he thought would be a surprise attack.

The surprise, however, somehow "backfired." When Judah sensed what was happening, "they cried unto the Lord, and the priests sounded their trumpets. Then the men of Judah gave a shout: and as the men of Judah shouted, it came to pass, that God smote Jeroboam and all Israel before Abijah and Judah. And the children of Israel fled before Judah: and God delivered them into their hand" (13:14-16).

But not all fled, for 500,000 of Israel's 800,000 "fell down slain." "The children of Judah prevailed, because they relied upon the Lord God of their fathers" (13:18). They pursued after Jeroboam and took a number of cities, including Bethel, where one of Israel's golden calves was worshipped.

From this point, Jeroboam's reign was weakened, "But Ahijah waxed mighty . . . " (13:21).

FOR OUR ADMONITION AND LEARNING

The apostle Paul predicts a state of apostasy when men will have *a form of godliness*, but will deny *the power* (authority or strength) of true godliness (2 Timothy 3:5). *Matthew Henry* likens Abijam to such a state (1 Kings 15:2). His "walk," or conduct of life, was not consistent with godliness because of his imperfect heart.

There are multitudes who have a restrained respect for religion, but they are ashamed of its power. The grace of God extends His longsuffering for the sake of the New Covenant; but unless they respond positively to the chastening rod, they will be lost when finally "the door is shut"!

Abijam's wisdom is noteworthy in his effort to persuade the aggressor to put aside his aggressive spirit and listen to truth (2 Chronicles 13:4-12). The Saviour of the world has admonished His Church to do likewise. Brethren are to exhaust all means of reconciliation before resorting to church discipline (Matthew 18:15-17). But, as with Jeroboam, in the end the offender must be delivered "unto Satan for the destruction of the flesh, that the spirit may be saved in the day of the Lord Jesus" (1 Corinthians 5:5).

—Lesson Sixteen—

ASA: THIRD KING OF JUDAH

Required Scripture Readings: 1 Kings 15:8-24, 32; 2 Chronicles, Chapters 14 through 16.

Pronunciation Helps: Baasha—bay-ASH-a; Zerah—ZEE-rah; Mareshah—ma-RESH-ah; Zephathah—ze-FATH-ah; Gerar—JEE-RAR; Hanani—ha-NAY-ni; Cinneroth—KIN-er-oth.

RELEVANT FACTS
Chief characters: Asa; Baasha.
Time span: 41 years, beginning about 955 B.C.
Seat of government: Jerusalem.
Contemporary personalities: Jeroboam (briefly), Nadab, Baasha, Elah, Zimri, Omri, and Ahab (briefly), kings of Israel; the prophets Azariah, Jehu, Oded, Hanani, Elijah.
Lineage and family: Son of Abijam. Grandmother: Maachah. Son: Jehoshaphat, only one named.
Death: Apparently resulted from diseased feet (2 Chronicles 16:12, 13).

THE HISTORICAL SITUATION
Abijam's sweeping victory over Jeroboam's offensive was an asset to Asa, whose first ten years are said to have been "quiet" (2 Chronicles 14:1). Jeroboam soon passed off the stage of action in the Northern Kingdom, and the unstable state of affairs that followed (seven different kings during Asa's regime in Judah) left little time for trouble from that source until Asa's thirty-sixth year.

Asa's accession ushered in a spiritual atmosphere such as had not been experienced in many years. There were some weak spots, but on the whole it goes down in history as a good reign.

The inclusive history of *Israel* lists no "good king," with the possible exception of Jehu. It is noted that *Judah's* longer history saw both "good" and "evil" kings on the throne, but the reigns of the good kings were generally longer. Judah had not made so good a start, the first twenty years leaving much to be desired. But now with Asa comes a forty-one-year reign which, overall, pleased God.

ASA THE KING

Asa's introduction is good: "And Asa did that which was right in the eyes of the Lord, as did David his father.

"And he took away the sodomites out of the land, and removed all the idols that his fathers had made.

"And also Maachah his mother [actually his grandmother], even her he removed from being queen, because she had made an idol in a grove; and Asa destroyed her idol, and burnt it by the brook Kidron.

"But the high places were not removed: nevertheless Asa's heart was perfect with the Lord all his days.

"And he brought in the things which his father had dedicated, and things which himself had dedicated, into the house of the Lord, silver, and gold, and vessels" (1 Kings 15:11-15).

Commentator George Rawlinson says that "Maachah ... had been the leading spirit of the court during two reigns [Rehoboam's and Abijam's]. As his favorite wife, she had directed the religious policy of Rehoboam; and as his [Abijam's] mother, she had exercised a complete domination over ... Abijam. A devotee of the Syro-Phoenician religion, she had established her own shrine of Astarte worship in Jerusalem, probably of a sensual character."

But Asa's *perfect heart* would not "play favorites" even with his grandmother. What seems to be a contradiction concerning the "high places" in 2 Chronicles 14:3 and 15:17, and 1 Kings 15:14, may have derived from the destruction of Maachah's places of idol worship. One historian has offered the following exposition pertaining to the practice of worshipping on the "high places":

"The use of commanding elevations for altars seems to have been immemorial and universal. In itself the practice was not evil (Gen. 12:7, 8; 22:2-4; 31:54; Judges 6:25, 26; 13:16-23). After the establishment of Mount Moriah and the temple as the center of divine worship (Deut. 12:5 with 2 Chr. 7:12), the pentateuchal prohibition of the use of high places

(Deut. 12:11-14), which had looked forward to the setting up of such a center, came into effect, and high places became identified with idolatrous practices. The constant recurrence to the use of high places, even for Jehovistic worship, and after the building of the temple, proves how deeply rooted the custom was."

In other words, in some instances the faithful people built altars on elevated sites and worshipped the Lord God there. This was especially true in times of reformation and repentance, such as Asa was effecting. Undoubtedly the high places where idols were worshipped were no longer so used; but some, where sacrifices were offered to God, continued to be used. While it was not necessary, since the temple was in Judah's Jerusalem, it was tolerated in some measure because "Asa's heart was perfect with the Lord."

As stated earlier, Judah had rest from military conflicts the first ten years of Asa's reign. However, he knew from history that it would not always be so; therefore he used the time to fortify the cities and to train an army of five hundred eighty thousand men (2 Chronicles 14:6-8).

Evidently at the end of the ten quiet years, Zerah, king of Ethiopia, came against Judah with a million men and three hundred chariots. The two armies met at Mareshah in the valley of Zephathah, about twenty miles southwest of Jerusalem. Seeing the imposing army's host, Asa cried unto the Lord as his only help:

"Lord, it is nothing with thee to help, whether with many, or with them that have no power: help us, O Lord our God; for we rest on thee, and in thy name we go against this multitude. O Lord, thou art our God; let not *man* prevail against *thee*" (2 Chronicles 14:11).

Asa had put himself and all his defenses at God's disposal, and "the Lord smote the Ethiopians before Asa, and before Judah" (14:12). Whatever happened required no details on the record. God simply smote them, and they fled. Asa and his men pursued them to Gerar, about twenty miles southwest of the battle site.

The victory was great (14:13-15). After much slaying of the enemy host, they took an abundant spoil of cattle, sheep, and camels; and *Josephus* adds, "much gold, and much silver."

God had been good to Judah, and He wanted *conditions* to *continue* under which *His goodness could continue*. So He sent the prophet Azariah to meet Asa, as he was returning from the war, with a message for the king. The "keynote" of it was, "The Lord is with *you*, while ye be with *him*" (2 Chronicles 15:2). He reminded Asa of Israel's history before the division, with possibly some reference to the Northern Kingdom's strayings from God, from the priestly order, and from due respect for the Law. Yet God had been merciful in times of repentance. The message ended on a encouraging note: "Be ye strong therefore: and let not your hands be weak: for your work shall be rewarded" (15:7).

The good king Asa received the intended encouragement and continued the work of reformation (15:8-19). Even many of the people from Israel's tribes of Ephraim, Manasseh, and Simeon came under his leadership "when they saw that the Lord his God was with him" (verse 9). So, in Asa's fifteenth year as king, they had a great gathering and an abundant offering at Jerusalem, covenanting to seek the Lord diligently. Those who would not seek Him were to be put to death, without respect of persons.

The Lord was pleased with their spirit of dedication—for they had made it with all their hearts and their whole desire (verse 15)—and He gave them rest for possibly twenty years more. Then their history records a regrettable turn of events.

In Asa's thirty-sixth year, Baasha, king of Israel, made a move that was irritating to Judah's king. Perhaps it was done because of those from the Northern Kingdom who had come over to Judah's good regime. Baasha "came up against Judah, and built Ramah, to the intent that he might let none go out or come in to Asa king of Judah" (16:1). Ramah was "on the frontier of Judah," and on the main road from Jerusalem to Samaria. Some maps show it within Judah's border, only about five miles from Jerusalem. Baasha was making it a sort of "blockade station," or fortification. Some historians see this as a first step toward a future conquest of Judah.

One writer says, "It was then that the good king of Judah committed the one great error of his life. He not only resorted to the heathen king of Damascus [Syria], Ben-hadad I, but he took the treasures of the house of God to purchase the alliance" (1 Kings 15:18-20; 2 Chronicles 16:2-4).

It seems clear that Ben-hadad was more interested in the *bounty* than in Asa's *cause*, for he broke a league with Baasha in order to accept Asa's offer. Since Syria joined Israel on the north and east, Ben-hadad smote some of the Israeli cities in the inheritances of Naphtali and Dan—Ijon, Dan, Abel-bethmaachah, and Cinneroth.

Baasha perceived the straits he was in, so he gave up his Ramah project without a fight. Asa profited from Baasha's retreat. He called on the men of Judah to take the stones and timbers which Baasha had been using and move them to Geba and Mizpah, two sites not far apart, and not far from Ramah, where he built two forts.

Asa may have been basking in a glow of self-satisfaction—until Hanani the seer went to him with a word from God: "Because thou hast relied on the king of Syria, and not relied on the Lord thy God, therefore is the host of the king of Syria escaped out of thine hand" (2 Chronicles 16:7). Apparently God had in store a future victory for Judah over Syria, but Asa had foolishly let it slip through his fingers, even paying the Syrians to do the deed! The seer further reminded Asa of the great victory God had given him over the Ethiopians back in the days when he was relying on the Lord, concluding with the words, "Herein thou hast done foolishly: therefore from henceforth thou shalt have wars" (2 Chronicles 16:9).

Since there were no more wars in Asa's reign, Hanani surely had reference to the future of Judah, when they would have to suffer periodically at the hands of Syria (as time would tell) because of Asa's lapse of faith and trust.

Instead of standing corrected, Asa was in such an angry rage at the seer that he had him imprisoned. (We are not told if he was finally released, However, since his son Jehu figures in the reign of Asa's son, a good man, we would hope that Hanani was eventually set free.)

In the thirty-ninth year of his reign, Asa became exceedingly diseased in his feet. *Matthew Henry* rather *presumes* that it was gout, and that it was God's chastisement for his attitude when rebuked for turning away from God to Syria in his time of need. It could likewise be *presumed* that it was God's way of giving him opportunity to turn to Him again, for another sort of help.

Presumptions aside, we are told that "in his disease he sought not to the Lord, but to the physicians" (2 Chronicles 16:12). For what reasons—lack of faith, or an anger at God's reproof through Hanani—we are not told; but it seems clear that God stood ready to help him if he had only asked Him. but he died, probably as a result of his diseased feet, in the forty-first year of his reign.

FOR OUR ADMONITION AND LEARNING

Asa *fell short in one thing* in the early part of his reign by not completely doing away with the "high places," which meant that he failed to insist that the people worship God in the one place He had chosen. Though God accepted him as *perfect in heart* for his overall zeal in his reformation, we can't help wondering if his latter days would have turned out differently if he had not left a "loophole" in his faith in the beginning. In these last days, some scoff at what they call "fanatic conservatives," somehow inferring that it is much better to be a "fanatic liberal." Considering the risk, why should we quibble over "conservatism" versus "liberalism"— fanatic or otherwise? We would all do well to simply *follow the Book!*

Asa's prayer is significant (2 Chronicles 14:11)—"O Lord . . . let not man prevail against THEE." We are prone to pray, "Let no man prevail against ME [or US]." This asks God to share the glory, giving ME or US the greater portion. Our desire should be that no man prevail against GOD; that *we* do nothing to cause it to *seem* that *God* is not able to give us the victory. Because Asa prayed so unselfishly, God was fully glorified—and Asa and Judah were benefited.

We should make it a point NEVER TO FORGET what God has said to us. All too often we are moved only momentarily— then we forget. God's "combo" of *encouragement and warning* through the prophet Azariah (2 Chronicles 15:1-7) probably sprang from the foreknowledge of God, who was pondering circumstances that would develop some twenty-six years later (2 Chronicles 16:2, 3, 7). If Asa had remembered that God does not change, he might have faced a happier death.

And so might we!

―*Lesson Seventeen*―

JEHOSHAPHAT: FOURTH KING OF JUDAH

Required Scripture Readings: 1 Kings 15:24; 22:2-50; 2 Chronicles, chapters 17 through 21:1.

Pronunciation Helps: Jehoshaphat—je-HOSH-a-FAT; Micaiah—mi-KAY-ah; Chenaanah—ke-NAY-nah; Azubah—a-ZOO-bah; Shilhi—SHILL-HI; Jahaziel—ja-HAY-zi-el; Tekoa—te-KO-a.

RELEVANT FACTS
Chief characters: Jehoshaphat; Ahab; Micaiah.
Time span: 25 years, beginning about 914 B.C.
Seat of government: Jerusalem.
Contemporary personalities: Ahab, Ahaziah, and Jehoram, kings of Israel; the prophets Elijah, Elisha, Jahaziel, Micaiah, Zedekiah, and Jehu (son of Hanani).
Lineage and family: Son of Asa. Mother: Azubah (daughter of Shilhi). Sons: Jehoram, Azariah, Jehiel, Zechariah, Azariah, Michael, and Shephatiah (2 Chr. 21:2).
Accession to the throne: At age 35, about 914 B.C.
Death: Of natural causes (1 Kings 22:50).

THE HISTORICAL SITUATION
On the whole, Asa had left his son Jehoshaphat a peaceful heritage. Baasha, king of Israel, had not been friendly with Judah, but he had died, and three short-term kings followed; but internal problems kept them at home. Shortly after Ahab became Israel's king, Jehoshaphat ascended the throne in Judah. Jehoshaphat's son, Jehoram had married Ahab's daughter Athaliah, so a friendly affinity existed between the two kings and their kingdoms.

The reforms Asa had begun were continued by Jehoshaphat. His reign was not without its problems, but it was an exceedingly good regime.

JEHOSHAPHAT THE KING

Jehoshaphat's peaceful accession made it possible for him to begin immediately doing those things which were beneficial to his people. Because of past conflicts with Israel, he wisely strengthened the frontier between the two kingdoms (2 Chronicles 17:1).

By walking uprightly, he pleased the Lord. Also, he gained favor with the people under him, who brought him gifts in appreciation. By this favor with God and men, "he had riches and honour in abundance" (17:5).

He is credited with instituting a highly acceptable educational system. He authorized certain "princes" to see that this was done. With them he sent Levites and priests, "And they taught in Judah, and had the book of the law of the Lord with them, and went about throughout all the cities of Judah, and taught the people" (17:9).

The knowledge of the Lord caused His fear to fall upon all the surrounding kingdoms so that they tended to be peaceable. Even the long-time enemy Philistines brought presents to Jehoshaphat, and the Arabians gave him of their flocks (17:10, 11).

He placed capable captains over an imposing army, both at Jerusalem and in other cities (17:13-19).

Because of the family ties with Israel through his son's marriage to Ahab's daughter, Jehoshaphat was friendly with the notorious Ahab. "And after certain years he went down to Ahab to Samaria" (2 Chronicles 13:2). Since the incident related here marked Ahab's last year of life, it must have been about the seventeenth or eighteenth year of Jehoshaphat's reign. (See 1 Kings 22:51 and 2 Kings 3:1.)

It appears that Ahab thought to turn the family affinity to his own advantage, for he first feasted Jehoshaphat (2 Chronicles 18:1), then approached him about going with Israel to war against Syria to regain Ramoth-gilead (18:2, 3). It has been noted that, though Jehoshaphat was a righteous man, he was lacking in spiritual discernment; otherwise he would not have allowed himself and the armies of Judah to become involved with a man whom he must have known to be very wicked and conniving.

(NOTE: A review of Lesson Nine, sub-topics "Re-enter Syria" and "Enter Death," will make repetition unnecessary here.)

For many years Judah had been at peace with Syria, but now Ahab, for his own gain, asked Jehoshaphat to forfeit that peace. And, though Jehoshaphat was clearly unsure of himself—as is clearly seen from his insistence on a word from God through one of His prophets (2 Chronicles 18:6-27)—he quite readily consented to go with Ahab and the Israeli forces to Ramoth-gilead. Also, verse three indicates that Judah's host went with them to battle.

Ahab may have had an eye on Judah's peace-time defense build-up and hoped to turn its strength to Israel's good. Then, because he knew he was despised by Ben-hadad and would undoubtedly be his prime target, the "disguise strategy" (2 Chronicles 18:29) would make Jehoshaphat the "bull's eye" for Syria's arrows. There was at least a chance that they would win the war, and Ahab would escape—at Jehoshaphat's expense! Ahab was that kind of man!

But, despite Jehoshaphat's gullibility, or "lack of discernment," God directed the Syrian arrow! Ahab was slain—wearing his disguise—and Jehoshaphat was spared (2 Chronicles 18:31-33). "And Jehoshaphat the king of Judah returned to his house in peace to Jerusalem" (2 Chronicles 19:1). And, lest his faulty discernment had still not been activated, the Lord "went a little farther" and called him to "Attention!" Through the prophet Jehu, the son of Hanani, He rebuked the king for helping the ungodly and loving them that hated God, and pronounced wrath upon him—possibly through the pending invasion by the Moabites and the Ammonites (2 Chronicles 20:1). However, God let him know that He remembered the good things he had done, probably meaning that, though He would not spare him the invasion, He would see him through (19:3; 20:24).

That Jehoshaphat was grateful for the Lord's care of him is seen in his renewed effort in reforms (2 Chronicles 19:4-11). He persuaded those who had strayed from the right way to return to God. He set up judges in all the cities and instructed them to judge righteously (verses 5-7). Also, he strengthened his educational venture through the priests and Levites in order that the people would enjoy the blessings of serving according to God's law and commandments (verses 8-11).

A Time of Unrest

We saw earlier that the nations round about Judah liked Jehoshaphat and brought him presents and tribute (2 Chronicles 17:10, 11). But with the passing of the years, there was a change of attitude in some quarters. It is not unusual for a minority of agitators to provoke widespread unrest.

Two nations—Moab and Ammon—east of the Jordan came against Judah. There was "a great multitude, including the Edomites of Mount Seir and other allied nations. "And Jehoshaphat feared, and set himself to seek the Lord, and proclaimed a fast throughout all Judah. And Judah gathered themselves together, to ask help of the Lord: even out of all the cities of Judah they came to seek the Lord" (2 Chronicles 20:3, 4). (NOTE: It seems that the king's reforms and his teaching efforts had borne fruit.)

Jehoshaphat's earnest and humble prayer is worthy of ponderance (2 Chronicles 20:6-12). It shows that the king knew Israel's history, and he believed that the God of the past was eternal and unchanging. He recognized *God's uncontestable might* and *Judah's lack of might;* and very appropriately he closed his supplication on a note of submission:

"... We have no might against this great company that cometh against us; neither know we what to do: *but our eyes are upon thee*" (20:12).

At this, the Spirit of the Lord came upon Jahaziel, a Levitical prophet, and he spoke words of encouragement and assurance—"The battle is not yours, but God's." Then he delivered to them *God's battle plan* (20:16, 17). There was a time of intense worship and praise (verses 18, 19).

Early next morning they went forth into the wilderness of Tekoa. After bolstering the people's faith, Jehoshaphat appointed singers to "praise the beauty of holiness, as they went out before the army, and to say, Praise the Lord; for his mercy endureth for ever" (verse 21). As the melody rose, "the Lord set ambushments against the children of Ammon, Moab, and Mount Seir . . . and they were smitten." One commentator in *The Pulpit Commentary* aptly visualizes the incident as follows:

"Who the persons [ambushments] were, supernatural or not, or what their mode of operation, is not told, and is not plain. The *effects* are quite plain—that *first* the two confederates,

Moab and Ammon, thought they saw reason to fall on them 'of Mount Seir,' and *secondly,* having this done, to fall on one another to the end of mutual extermination" (2 Chronicles 20:22-25).

Truly the battle was God's! The spoil He left to the people of Judah.

After an assemblage for thanksgiving, they returned home with a great processional of victory (20:27, 28). God was glorified in that all the surrounding nations "heard that the Lord fought against the enemies of Israel."

A Trading Venture

Finally, Jehoshaphat's spiritual discernment failed him again. He joined with Israel's new and evil king, Ahaziah, in a ship-building venture, with a trading expedition in mind for gold from Ophir (2 Chronicles 20:35-37). Because God was displeased, He sent the prophet Eliezer to prophesy that the ships would be destroyed. And they were, apparently in a storm. (See also Lesson Ten, under "Ahaziah the King.")

Thus Jehoshaphat's twenty-five year reign was ended.

FOR OUR ADMONITION AND LEARNING

Educational efforts are good, and necessary. Samuel made valuable use of his "schools of the prophets," and in this lesson we can see how the people were benefited by the proper understanding of the law and worship of God. We must constantly beware of *Eden's serpent,* however. When education deteriorates to the low point of *making one wise in the flesh only* (Genesis 3:6), it is time to develop a holy curriculum!

The "affinity" brought about by the marriage of a godly man's son (Jehoshaphat's son Jehoram) and a wicked man's daughter (Ahab's daughter Athaliah) appeared on the surface to be a great "fence mender." All told, however, it was "no good"! And rarely is it acceptable for *believers* to be unequally yoked with *unbelievers* (2 Corinthians 6:14-18). It is unscriptural, and those who disobey should be prepared to reap the consequences, in one way or another, all the days of their lives!

While the gift of "discerning of spirits" is available, just plain *common sense* is helpful, too. To be "gullible" (easily cheated or tricked) usually means that the culprit is not "keeping his wits about him." He needs to keep his spiritual eyes and ears open, and to practice the art of perceptive sobriety!

JEHORAM: FIFTH KING OF JUDAH

Required Scripture Readings: 1 Kings 22:50; 2 Kings 8:16-24; 2 Chronicles 21:1-20.

Pronunciation Helps: Jehoram—jee-HO-ram; Zair—ZAY-ir; Libnah—LIB-nah; Azariah—AZ-a-RI-ah; Jehiel—je-HI-el; Shephatiah—SHEF-a-TI-ah; Jehoahaz—je-HO-a-HAZ.

RELEVANT FACTS
Chief characters: Jehoram; Elijah.
Time span: 8 years, beginning about 889 B.C.
Seat of government: Jerusalem.
Contemporary personalities: Jehoram (Joram), king of Israel; the prophet Elijah.
Lineage and family: son of Jehoshaphat. Wives: Athaliah, daughter of Ahab and Jezebel of Israel (2 Kings 8:18, 26), and others (2 Chr. 21:17). Brothers: Azariah, Jehiel, Zechariah, Azariah, Michael, and Shephatiah (2 Chr. 21:2). Son: Ahaziah (2 Chr. 22:1) or Jehoahaz (21:17). Since both references note that the "youngest son" succeeded Jehoram, he had two names, which was not uncommon.
Accession to the throne: At age 32, in about 889 B.C. (2 Kings 8:16, 17).
Death: From "an incurable disease" or "of sore diseases" (2 Chr. 21:18-20).

THE HISTORICAL SITUATION
The prevailing apostate spirit of the Northern Kingdom had "infected" Jehoram; therefore there was an alarming deterioration in Judah during these eight years. Besides the spiritual backsliding, Edom, which had been under tribute to Judah, successfully revolted. Also, the Philistines and the Arabians, who had been friendly with Jehoshaphat, turned on Jehoram.

Comparing verses 16 and 25 of 2 Kings 8, it appears that Jehoram co-reigned with his father Jehoshaphat about seven years, becoming king in his own right after Jehoshaphat's death. However, the chronology does not perfectly agree.

JEHORAM THE KING

We must wonder if Jehoshaphat's "discernment" proved defective again in the selection of his successor from among his seven sons (2 Chronicles 21:1, 2). The others could hardly have done worse than did Jehoram. The fact that he felt it necessary to slay all his brothers, along with other "princes," in order to *strengthen himself,* could indicate that he feared them because they were righteous (21:4, 13).

Both in 2 Kings 8:18 and 2 Chronicles 21:6, the word "for" shows that Jehoram's wicked ways were because of the evil influence of Ahab (and probably of Jezebel) through his wife Athaliah.

First we are told that he (personally) "walked in the way of the kings of Israel [all being evil], like as did the house of Ahab" (2 Chronicles 21:6). His administration would quite naturally reflect his character; so a little later we read that "he made high places in the mountains of Judah, and *caused* the inhabitants of Jerusalem to commit fornication, and *compelled* Judah thereto" (2 Chronicles 21:11).

The establishment of "high places" with all their idolatrous paraphernalia *caused* many who were not conscientious to respond to that evil system voluntarily. And, when power falls into the hands of wicked men, they will eventually use it to *compel* the compliance of those who oppose them.

Problems from Without

The Edomites, who with the Moabites and Ammonites had been stricken by the hand of God in Jehoshaphat's time, now revolted from Judean tribute. The wording concerning this incident leaves some uncertainty as to its outcome, but commentators generally agree that Jehoram could not subdue them. *Matthew Henry* says, "Though he chastised them (verse 9), yet he could not reduce them (verse 10)."

Then Libnah, a city of Judah some twenty-five miles southwest of Jerusalem, also revolted and set up a "free state," as it were—because Jehoram "had forsaken the Lord God of his fathers" (21:10).

Next, the Lord stirred up the Philistines and the Arabians, who plundered and ravaged the land and the king's house, carrying away even his wives, and all but the youngest of his sons.

God's Warning Spurned

God sent Jehoram a written message from Elijah the prophet. This seems inconsistent with the chronological record, since it appears that Elijah had already been translated as many as seven years earlier. However, if Jehoram co-reigned with his father for some time, his evil tendencies may have been known to Elijah, who may have written the prophetic warning for Elisha to deliver at the proper season. Then, Jehoram would hardly have slain his brothers before he was king in his own right. Elijah had known this; or perhaps he wrote it in advance by the inspiration of the Holy Ghost.

All conjectures are unimportant in the light of the weighty message (2 Chronicles 21:12-15). After spelling out the grounds for God's condemnation, the "great plague" of incurable sickness from the Lord was predicted. We cannot be sure at what point the message was delivered, but it came to pass in all of its consuming detail (2 Chronicles 21:18, 19).

Jehoram's house was judged furiously, but not the house (or lineage) of David, because of God's covenant by which He had promised David a light for ever (2 Chronicles 21:7).

Jehoram died a horrible death, the worst of it being that he lived so wickedly that he "departed without being desired"!

FOR OUR ADMONITION AND LEARNING

It is sad, but true, that evil influence spreads more readily than godly influence. Jehoram had a *very godly father,* Jehoshaphat; yet his life was influenced by a *very ungodly father-in-law,* Ahab, and his ungodly wife, Athaliah. We marvel at this circumstance, first seen in Eden, where our first representative, Adam, let us down. But we need not spend our lives in lamentation, for God has provided full redemption in our second Representative, Jesus Christ the righteous, by whose blood we are not only justified, but wholly sanctified! Now, to be influenced to sin is to return to Adam's fleshly "free choice," trampling the sanctifying blood beneath our feet in the doing! God forbid! And, O! the horrible disease that consumed the physical bowels of Jehoram is as nothing compared with the spiritually destructive power of SIN!

AHAZIAH: SIXTH KING OF JUDAH

Required Scripture Readings: 2 Kings 8:25-29; 9:16-28; 2 Chronicles 22:1-9.

Pronunciation Helps: Ahaziah—AY-ha-ZI-ah; Ebleam—IB-le-am; Megiddo—me-GID-do.

RELEVANT FACTS
Chief characters: Ahaziah; Jehu.
Time span: One year, in about 885 B.C.
Seat of government: Jerusalem.
Contemporary personalities: Jehoram (Joram) and Jehu, kings of Israel; the prophet Elisha.
Lineage and family: Son of Jehoram. Mother: Athaliah. Son: Joash, only one named. Wife: Zibiah (2 Chr. 24:1).
Accession to the throne: At age 22 (1 Kings 8:26): though 2 Chronicles 22:2 says age 42, this must be a transcriber's error, considering his father's age of no more than 40 at the time of his death; and Ahaziah was his youngest son. The year 885 B.C. allows for some overlapping years during which Jehoram and Jehoshaphat are said to have co-reigned.
Death: Slain by Jehu, king of Israel (2 Kings 9:27).

AHAZIAH THE KING
(*"The Historical Situation"* remained the same during this short reign.)

Ahaziah continued his father's corrupt practices (2 Kings 8:27). Young as he was (and possibly also immature), he either sought his mother Athaliah's counsel or she imposed it upon him (2 Chronicles 22:3, 4). The plurals "they were his counsellors" and "their counsel," of verses four and five, indicate that others of "the house of Ahab" were involved.

"There counsel" resulted in the one recorded event of his reign, which ended with his death. He "went with Jehoram [Joram] the son of Ahab king of Israel to war against Hazael king of Syria at Ramoth-gilead . . . " (2 Chronicles 22:5). Apparently early in the battle the Syrians wounded Jehoram and he had to withdraw and go to Jezreel to recuperate (2 Kings 8:28, 29; 2 Chronicles 22:5, 6).

Ahaziah went to visit Jehoram. In the meantime, the prophet Elisha anointed Jehu to be king of Israel, and he assumed that he was to take the throne at once (2 Kings 9:1-13). (NOTE: Review Lesson Ten, from the sub-topic "Another Conflict with Syria" to the end, where the details concerning Jehu's conspiracy and accession to the throne are given.)

When Jehu was approaching Jezreel, Jehoram and Ahaziah went forth to meet him, unaware of Jehu's intentions. But Jehu lost no time in slaying his predecessor. And "when Ahaziah the king of Judah saw this, he fled . . . . " But Jehu, apparently not wanting even one sympathizer with the house of Ahab to remain alive, had Ahaziah slain in flight—"And they did so at the going up to Gur, which is by Ibleam. And he fled to Megiddo, and died there. And his servants carried him in a chariot to Jerusalem, and buried him . . . " (2 Kings 9:27, 28; 2 Chronicles 22:8, 9).

We will not attempt to modify the apparent conflict in the two accounts in "Kings" and "Chronicles." Certain we are that the youthful king of Judah died by Israeli hands, and because of the unwise counsel of his own mother!

FOR OUR ADMONITION AND LEARNING

It is sad when young men and women bring sorrow and disaster upon themselves through rebellion against the wise counsel of godly parents. But one thing is sadder still: Sorrow and disaster befalling children because of the unwise counsel of ungodly parents! Our hearts bleed for the young king Ahaziah when we consider his disadvantages—ungodly parents (and grandparents on the maternal side); so heavy a weight upon his young shoulders; and the probable imposition of usurped counsel at a time when he most needed sane and sober guidance.

We should receive, and accept, both *admonition* and *learning* from this heart-rending ensample.

—Lesson Eighteen—

ATHALIAH: SEVENTH "RULER" OF JUDAH

Required Scripture Readings: 2 Kings 11:1-16, 21; 2 Chronicles 22:10-12; 23:1-15.

Pronunciation Helps: Athaliah—ATH-a-LI-ah; Jehosheba—je-HOSH-e-ba, or Jehoshabeath—je-HOSH-a-BE-ath; Jehoiada—je-HO-ya-da.

RELEVANT FACTS
Chief characters: Athaliah; Jehosheba or Jehoshabeath; Jehoida the priest.
Time span: 6 years (2 Chr. 22:12), beginning about 884 B.C.
Seat of government: Jerusalem.
Contemporary personalities: Jehu, king of Israel; the prophet Elisha.
Lineage and family: Daughter of Ahab and Jezebel; mother of Ahaziah, and of others that were slain.
Death: Slain by "the captains of the hundreds, the officers of the host" (2 Kings 11:13-16; 2 Chr. 23:12-15).

THE HISTORICAL SITUATION
This was a reign that never should have been, unless perchance it was somehow in the unrevealed will of God. Athaliah had no lineage of the house of David. Her father, Ahab, was not of the tribe of Judah. Her mother, Jezebel, was a Zidonian Baal-worshipper. Baal worship had been reinstituted by Jehoram, and had continued under Ahaziah. Athaliah's husband, Jehoram, and her brother, Joram (king of Israel), had been slain by order of Jehu, who had just come to the throne of Israel.

ATHALIAH THE "QUEEN"
Athaliah, true to character, saw her opportunity, as she thought, in the face of the circumstances. *Josephus* gives the following exposition, evidently with details from Jewish history:

"Now when Athaliah, the daughter of Ahab, heard of the death of her brother Joram, and of her son Ahaziah, and of the royal family [2 Chr. 22:10-12], she endeavored that none of the house of David might be left alive, but that the whole family might be exterminated, that no king might arise out of it afterward; and, as she *thought,* she had actually *done* it; but one of Ahaziah's sons was preserved, who escaped death after the manner following: Ahaziah had a sister . . . whose name was Jehosheba, and she was married to the high priest Jehoiada. She went into the king's palace, and found Jehoash [Joash], for that was the little child's name, who was not above a year old, among those that were slain, but concealed with his nurse; so she took him with her into a secret bed-chamber, and shut him up there, and she and her husband Jehoiada brought him up privately in the temple six years, during which time Athaliah reigned over Jerusalem and the two tribes."

It has been suggested that Athaliah had already been "in power"; that Ahaziah may have entrusted her with the government while he went to Israel (by her counsel!) to join Joram in the war against Syria. It possibly was known that the government was being run by her counsel during Ahaziah's reign as king. These may be the reasons that no remonstration was mentioned when she seized the throne, as though it were her right.

But it was generally known that the kingdom should have been in the hands of a descendant of David. However, in view of the *secret* preservation of the young Joash, there *seemed* to be no eligible Davidic successor.

Someone—somehow—would eventually have to divulge the secret and run some risks. So, when Joash was about seven years old, Jehoida the priest nerved himself for the task. A brief summation from 2 Kings 11:4-16 and 2 Chronicles 23:1-15 might go something as follows:

After six impatient years, during which the child had grown to where it was thought he was eligible to rule (with proper guidance), Jehoida ventured to let the captains of the host in on the secret, putting them under oath to keep the matter quiet as they moved step by cautious step. By and by, the Levites, then "all the congregation," were under the covenant of secrecy. All were assigned their roles in the proposed coronation of young king Joash.

We see in the people's loyalty the fact that it would be a relief to see Athaliah dethroned, even if a mere child must occupy the throne, for there is no hint that Athaliah had the least suspicion of the quiet proceedings.

Every precaution was taken to make the young monarch safe; units of guards were stationed at every strategic point. The temple was considered the safest locale for the crowning and anointing. Even there, trustworthy "hundreds" were ordered to slay anyone who might come "within the ranges," meaning any who might try to break through the guard.

Significantly, the captains were furnished with spears, shields, and bucklers that had belonged to the great King David. God had seen to it that one had been preserved to occupy David's throne, and now he was about to take his seat.

The "high moment" came at last. With all in their places, "... They brought out the king's [Azariah's] son, and put upon him the crown, and gave him the testimony [the book of the Law], and made him king. And Jehoida and his sons anointed him, and said, God save the king" (2 Chronicles 23:11).

Only "when Athaliah heard the noise of the people running and praising the king," and the sound of the musical instruments and singing, did she realize that anything unusual was under way. "... She came to the people into the house of the Lord" (2 Chronicles 23:12)—an area this Baal worshipper was not in the habit of entering. When she saw king Joash standing at his pillar (a raised pedestal or platform where kings stood when in the temple), she tore her clothes and cried, "Treason, Treason"! One historian says, "She cried out, 'Conspiracy! Conspiracy!' and turned away."

Jehoiada ordered the captains to remove her from the temple and to slay any who might follow her. The Scriptures are silent on the reason for ordering her killed. If *Josephus* can be trusted, it would appear that certain lives would not have been safe had she been allowed to live. He says: "... She rent her clothes, and cried out vehemently, and commanded [her guards] to kill him that had laid snares for her, and endeavored to deprive her of the government...."

"So they laid hands on her; and when she was come to the entering of the horse gate by the king's house, they slew her there" (2 Chronicles 23:15).

FOR OUR ADMONITION AND LEARNING
God's plans cannot be thwarted. He speaks, and it comes to pass—immediately, or after many generations. He had declared that there would always be a successor to David's throne. His enemies never ceased trying to annihilate his posterity. Athaliah must have smugly gloried in the supposition that she had succeeded. But NO! God had had the baby Joash's aunt and a nurse to rescue him secretly when all his kin were slain. God's promise had not failed!

In the gospel dispensation, the sons of God have even a safer hiding place—"For ye are dead [to sin, and with the Saviour], and your life is hid with Christ in God. When Christ, who is our life, shall appear, then shall ye also appear with him in glory" (Colossians 3:3, 4). Hallelujah!

Those who persistently defy God "run to their own destruction" by and by. It was so with Jezebel, who brazenly painted her face and sat at a window, from which she was thrown down to the dogs! And it was so with Athaliah, who irreverently rushed into the holy temple of the Lord, defying those who would restore God's order, only to be carried out to her execution!

Those who refuse to run to God's altar (the blessed Cross of Christ) are running swiftly toward "the second death" in the fire "prepared for the devil and his angels"!

JOASH: EIGHTH KING OF JUDAH

Required Scripture Readings: 2 Kings 11:2-12, 17-21; 12:1-21; 2 Chronicles 22:10-12; 23:1-11, 16-21; 24:1-27.

Pronunciation Helps: Joash—JO-ASH; Zibiah—ZI-bi-ah; Mattan—MAT-TAN.

RELEVANT FACTS
Chief characters: Joash (Jehoash, 2 Kings 12:1); Jehoida.
Time span: 40 years, beginning about 878 B.C.
Seat of government: Jerusalem.
Contemporary personalities: Jehu, Jehoahaz, and Jehoash, kings of Israel; the prophets Zechariah and Elisha.
Lineage and family: Son of Ahaziah. Mother: Zibiah of Beer-sheba. Son: Amaziah, only one named. (See 2 Chr. 24:3.)

Accession to the throne: At age 7, in about 878 B.C.
Death: Slain by a conspiracy of his servants.

THE HISTORICAL SITUATION

The nation as a whole was in idolatry, though it seems clear that the people had been pressed to conform to the pattern set by their rulers, Jehoram, Ahaziah, and Athaliah. Their loyal cooperation with Jehoida the priest in the matter of Athaliah's dethronement shows something of a hunger after the true God.

Jehoiada and Jehosheba were like a father and mother to the child-king. His mother, Zibiah, is named, but she was probably killed in Athaliah's wicked attempt to do away with David's posterity. So, even with the king on the throne, Jehoida remained his regent—acting in his place in matters too great for so young a mind and body.

We see this in 2 Kings 11:17-19 and 2 Chronicles 23:16-20, where the good priest used his godly influence and authority in effecting covenants of responsibility between the king and the people with the Lord. This resulted in the people breaking down the house, altars, and images of Baal, and slaying Mattan, the priest of Baal. Then he restored the Levitical priesthood and the burnt offerings, and appointed porters to keep all that was unclean out of the temple.

When all of these matters had been attended to, he organized a ceremonial processional, with the captains of hundreds, the nobles, the governors, and all the people of the land, to formally usher king Joash to his throne in the king's house. After this time of great rejoicing, there was peace and quietness in the city of Jerusalem.

JOASH THE KING

"And Joash did that which was right in the sight of the Lord all the days of Jehoiada the priest" (2 Chronicles 24:2).

He respected Jehoiada, and accepted his wise counsel and guidance. However, the high places were not taken away, but evidently they were used in the worship of God.

His One Important Work

It is not known at what age Joash instituted a financial plan by which to repair the house of the Lord. The priests and the Levites were to be in charge of the collections. The plan consisted of three parts, which are not particularly important to enlarge upon here. But the plan was to be taken to the people throughout the land, and the work was to be hastened.

For some reason, those charged with the responsibility neglected to carry it out. But Joash was patient, for in the twenty-third year of his reign (when he was age 30) the repairs had not been made, for the money had not been collected. Joash was no longer a child-king waiting on his aging uncle to tell him what to do. Jehoiada was chief of the priests (2 Chronicles 24:6), so Joash called him in for an accounting— "Why hast thou not required of the Levites to bring in out of Judah and out of Jerusalem the collection, according to the commandment of Moses the servant of the Lord, and of the congregation of Israel, for the tabernacle of witness?"

No answer was forthcoming, so Joash changed his plan. He had Jehoiada to make a chest with a hole in the lid, and the people were asked to drop their freewill offerings into the chest for this special work. The results were spectacular (2 Kings 12:9-14; 2 Chronicles 24:8-14). Not only was there money for the temple repairs, but also for the vessels used in the temple service.

A Sad Deterioration

Jehoiada grew feeble, and he died at the age of one hundred thirty years. He was so honored for his long life of faithful service that they buried him among the kings (2 Chronicles 24:16).

But a certain element of "the princes of Judah" had evidently had more respect for Jehoida's "grey hairs" than for his good and holy service and example. It was almost as though they had been waiting for him to die, so they could openly reveal their true feelings.

They came to Joash with the customary outward forms of "obeisance," and, as one historian says, "the worst species of flattery gained its disastrous ends." We are spared their hypocritical words, but "the king hearkened unto them" (2 Chronicles 24:17).

We are not spared, however, the substance of their pompous show: "And they left the house of the Lord God of their fathers, and served groves and idols...." And this, apparently, with Joash's "blessing"! But the resultant "curse" was not long delayed, for the same verse concludes with, "and wrath came upon Judah and Jerusalem for this their trespass" (verse 18).

Zechariah, the son of Jehoiada the priest, was now a prophet. He delivered God's rebuke, and the sentence that God had forsaken them. But instead of repenting, they conspired against the prophet and stoned him with stones—at the king's commandment! And "in the court of the house of the Lord"! So soon had Joash forgotten the kindness of his godly uncle and priest toward him! Zechariah died saying "The Lord look upon it, and require it" (2 Chronicles 24:22)!

God Required It!

"And it came to pass at the end of the year, that the host of Syria came up against him: and they came to Judah and Jerusalem, and destroyed all the princes of the people from among the people, and sent all the spoil of them unto the king of Damascus.

"For the army of the Syrians came with a small company of men, and the Lord delivered a very great host into their hand, because they had forsaken the Lord God of their fathers. So they executed judgment against Joash" (2 Chronicles 24:23, 24).

Joash seems to have been among the wounded, and the wounds resulted "in great diseases" (2 Chronicles 24:25). With the humiliated king on his bed, his servants conspired against him, lest he should recover and continue the evil way into which he had fallen.

So Joash was slain in infamy; and to the credit of the people (who had probably submitted to his apostate practices more or less unwillingly), they would not allow him to be buried in the sepulchres of the kings (2 Chronicles 25:25).

FOR OUR ADMONITION AND LEARNING

"Puppet righteousness" cannot maintain itself once the truly righteous man is no longer there to manipulate the strings. Joash only mimicked Jehoida's goodness, at the same time being on the receiving end of his kindness. Weak character—spineless conviction—such will not endure to the end. No man can take another to heaven. Somewhere on the journey, each must stand on his own two feet for God and the right!

Joash's second financial plan should speak to us today. On the whole, a "hit-and-miss," "from-here-a-little, from-there-a-little," "percentage hodge-podge" stimulates very little zeal. Honest people will be zealous for honest endeavors. They prefer one clear-cut objective at a time. When those Judeans dropped their offerings into the chest, they knew they were giving for the repair of the house of God. They did not have to give reluctantly, for none who gave had need to feel that most of his "shekel" would go for causes he did not care to support.

—*Lesson Nineteen*—

AMAZIAH: NINTH KING OF JUDAH

Required Scripture Readings: 2 Kings 14:1-22; 2 Chronicles 25:1-28.

Pronunciation Helps: Amaziah—am-a-ZI-ah; Jehoaddan—JEE-ho-ADD-an; Lachish—LAY-kish.

RELEVANT FACTS
Chief characters: Amaziah; Jehoash, king of Israel.
Time span: 29 years, beginning about 839 B.C.
Seat of government: Jerusalem.
Contemporary personalities: Jehoash and Jeroboam II, kings of Israel; the prophet, "a man of God," unnamed (2 Chronicles 25:7-9).
Lineage and family: Son of Joash. Mother: Jehoaddan. Son: Uzziah (Azariah), only one named.
Accession to the throne: At age 25, in about 839 B.C.
Death: Slain by a conspiracy.

THE HISTORICAL SITUATION
Before the death of Joash, God had used a small Syrian army to execute judgment against Joash (2 Chronicles 24:24) for tolerating the idolatry of certain "princes of Judah." For the sake of Judah as a nation, God had purged out "all the princes of the people from among the people" (24:23). This left a better atmosphere for the new king Amaziah.

AMAZIAH THE KING
"And he [Amaziah] did that which was right in the sight of the Lord, but not with a perfect heart" (2 Chronicles 25:2). The account in 2 Kings 14:3 explains that "he did according to all things as Joash his father did." This was literally true, for both began well, but failed to maintain their good start.

The high places which "the princes of Judah" had built for idol worship were not taken away. This situation always fostered a sort of compromised worship—a worship of God, but not in harmony with God's law.

Amaziah's first business of note was the slaying of his father's murderers. His carefulness at this early stage is seen in his having spared their children because it was according to the law of Moses (2 Chronicles 25:3, 4).

This done, he turned his thoughts toward his armed forces. He numbered those from age twenty and above, and found that there were 300,000 choice men from the two tribes who were able for war. He appointed captains over thousands and hundreds. Not quite satisfied, "He hired also an hundred thousand mighty men of valour out of Israel for an hundred talents of silver" (25:6).

He had in mind an expedition against the Edomites, who had revolted from Judah's tribute under Jehoram's reign some fifty years earlier. After they had gained their independence, they had been peaceful toward Judah. But now, Amaziah had decided to try to re-subjugate them.

While the plans were in the making, God sent a prophet to Amaziah, who said: "O king, let not the army of Israel go with thee; for the Lord is not with Israel .... But if thou wilt go ... God shall make thee fall before the enemy ... " (25:7, 8).

Amaziah was worried about the hire of the Israeli troops, for he had paid them in advance; but the prophet assured him that this was unimportant, considering the Lord's ability to compensate for that. So he dismissed the one hundred thousand men of Israel, who "returned home in great anger" (25:10). They felt that their capability or their fidelity had been held in question.

Amaziah proceeded to attack the Edomites, and God confirmed His word by giving them success. In the valley of salt, near the Dead Sea, they slew ten thousand of the children of Seir, and another ten thousand were thrown down to their deaths from the top of a great rock (25:11, 12).

But while Amaziah was warring with the Edomites, the rejected soldiers of Israel avenged Amaziah's affront by falling upon certain cities of Judah, killing three thousand people, and taking the spoil. When Amaziah returned, no mention is made of any immediate resentment over Israel's invasion and plunder. Perhaps he was too much taken up with the idol "gods" he had brought back from Seir! For he "set them up to be his gods, and bowed down himself before them, and burned incense unto them" (25:14).

Some commentators interpret both the Israeli invasion and Amaziah's turn to idolatry in the light of the prophet's statement in verse eight: "... God shall make thee fall before the enemy: for God hath power to help, and to cast down." They see this as predicted judgment against Amaziah's presumptuous attitude in turning to evil Israel for help; also possibly for his determination to raise war against Edom, who was at peace with Judah.

At any rate, the outcome was not all victory. Israel had struck back with some success; and although the events in Edom appeared as victory, Amaziah actually *fell* before the enemy in being carried away by their gods!

God's continued anger was expressed through the prophet once again: "Why hast thou sought after the gods of the people, which could not deliver their own people out of thine hand?" (2 Chronicles 25:15).

Amaziah was insolent toward the prophet, questioning his authority, and bidding him to be silent (25:16). The prophet withheld further counsel, but delivered God's sentence: "I know that God hath determined to destroy thee, because thou hast done this [set up idol gods], and hast not hearkened unto my counsel."

The prophecy did not even draw a response from the king, so unconcerned was he about it. He turned his head and hand to other matters. *Josephus* says, "but Amaziah was not able to contain himself under that prosperity which God had given him, although he had affronted God thereupon; but in a vein of insolence he wrote to Joash, the king of Israel, and commanded that he and his people should be obedient to him...."

(NOTE: Review Lesson Twelve, under JEHOASH, sub-topic, "Amaziah Provokes Israel.")

At this point, Amaziah had seemingly purposed to go his own way, ignoring any counsel from God or God's men. A somewhat belated vengeance on Israel seemed to satisfy his ego, so he pressed the provocation to the limit. But, as we saw in the lesson cited above, he came out "looking foolish." *The Pulpit Commentary* puts it thus: "Jehoash, ignominiously bringing Amaziah to Jerusalem (verse 23), contemptuously left him there, with a present of his life, though *less* his honour and much wealth."

A fifteen-year lapse of silence and apparent inactivity occur between the defeat by Israel and the next and last recorded event. Some think it was this inactivity which brought about the conspiracy of 2 Chronicles 25:27. Fifteen years seems a long time to allow Amaziah's idolatry to go unrequited, then to suddenly make it the object of a conspiracy; but perhaps it was more of *God's* doing than of those men who acted.

When Amaziah learned what was afoot, he fled Jerusalem and went to Lachish, a fortified city some twenty to thirty miles to the southwest; but the conspirators followed him and slew him there.

FOR OUR ADMONITION AND LEARNING

Doing "right" without one's heart in it will come to nought eventually, as a rule. Amaziah began well. *Josephus* says, "He was exceeding careful of doing what was right, and this when he was very young . . . ." In the Christian dispensation, high morals are actually abomination in God's sight when they are made a substitute for the changed heart at the foot of the Cross. Even if they are maintained to the day of death, they do not merit salvation. God sees them only as the filthy rags of self-righteousness.

A little success, when attributed to self-achievement, may be followed by great loss. Men seem unable to give God any credit for their human effort. They forget from where the "human" gets his strength. Like Amaziah, they do not consider that the gods of this world cannot defend even their own servants. The "visible god," no matter how puny, seems to have an appeal that overwhelms those whose spiritual eyesight is defective. May Elisha's prayer find its answer again and again—"Lord, I pray thee, open his eyes, that he may see" the encampments of God's host round about His own! (2 Kings 6:17).

UZZIAH: TENTH KING OF JUDAH
(Azariah—2 Kings 15:1)

Required Scripture Readings: 2 Kings 14:21, 22; 15:1-7; 2 Chronicles 26:1-23; Amos 1:1 and Zechariah 14:5, concerning an earthquake in his day.

Pronunciation Helps: Uzziah—uz-I-ah; Azariah—az-a-RI-ah; Eloth—EE-loth; Jecoliah—jek-o-LI-ah.

RELEVANT FACTS

Chief characters: Uzziah, Azariah the priest.
Time span: 52 years, beginning about 810 B.C.
Seat of government: Jerusalem.
Contemporary personalities: Jeroboam II, Zechariah, Shallum, Menahem, Pekahiah, and Pekah (briefly), kings of Israel; the prophets Amos, Zechariah, Isaiah, and Jonah.
Lineage and family: Son of Amaziah. Mother: Jecoliah (Jecholiah). Son: Jotham, only one named.
Accession to the throne: At age 16, about 810 B.C. The people made him king (2 Chr. 26:1).
Death: He was a leper (2 Chr. 26:21-23), which at least contributed to his death. *Josephus* says he died of grief and anxiety because of having been stricken with leprosy.

THE HISTORICAL SITUATION

In most ways, Uzziah's reign was good and prosperous—the most prosperous, purportedly, since the time of Solomon and Jehoshaphat. However, he came to the throne at a difficult time. Spiritually, the continuing "high places" had successfully tempted many to join their fickle kings in idolatry. Yet, there was an evident yearning for Jehovah-worship to be restored.

UZZIAH THE KING

Uzziah was made his father's successor by the people—"all the people of Judah" (2 Chronicles 26:1). Though only sixteen years old, he had the advantage of being liked and wanted.

"And he did that which was right in the sight of the Lord . . . " (2 Chronicles 26:4).

A certain prophet named Zechariah, about whom little is known, seems to have had a profound influence for good on the young king's life (26:5).

First mentioned of his accomplishments are his military achievements, including victories over such luminaries as the Philistines and the Arabians (26:6, 7). His army numbered 307,500, over whom were 2,600 mighty men of valor under Hananiah as captain (26:12, 13). And his army was not lacking in armor and weaponry. In verse fifteen is the first mention of any type of "sophisticated," mechanical weapons, called "engines." Fortification towers were built, not only at Jerusalem, but also "in the desert" areas. The Ammonites were friendly, and gave him gifts.

He loved husbandry (26:10), so "he had much cattle" and dug wells in order that they would have water. He also had well-kept vineyards in the mountains.

"When He Was Strong"

One writer remarks, "But he could not bear his prosperity...." It is probable also that his godly counsellor, Zechariah, died, and that he failed to seek the advice of other prophets. But "... As long as he sought the Lord, God made him to prosper" (26:5).

"... And his name spread far abroad; for he was marvellously helped, till he was strong.

"But when he was strong, his heart was lifted up to his destruction: for he transgressed against the Lord his God, and went into the temple of the Lord to burn incense upon the altar of incense" (2 Chronicles 26:15, 16).

Azariah, the chief priest, must have been surprised beyond the belief of his own eyes when he saw what the king proposed to do! What could the beloved monarch be thinking of? Was something driving him from within to be so presumptuous?

Scripture does not pointedly tell us the "why." But his already-long reign had been such that he may have reasoned that there was nothing in his kingdom that he could not do, if he so desired. The evil thought may have presented itself that only one thing—the priesthood—was yet above him. Why should that one exception remain? He decided that it shouldn't!

Azariah and eighty valiant priests withstood him; not in arrogance, but in their God-fearing responsibility, as well as out of a sense of respect and love for their king. They pled with him to leave the sanctuary, where he was already a trespasser, lest the Lord should greatly dishonor him!

But Uzziah's self-will was out of control! Who were these men, to withstand the king of Judah? He became angry, and he would have lighted the incense in the censor which he held in his hand; but God intervened!

" . . . While he was wroth with the priests, the leprosy even rose up in his forehead before the priests in the house of the Lord, from beside the incense altar.

"And Azariah the chief priest, and all the priests, looked upon him, and, behold, he was leprous in his forehead, and they thrust him out from thence; yea, himself hasted also to go out, *because the Lord had smitten him.*" (2 Chronicles 26:19, 20).

Mention is made in Amos 1:1 and Zechariah 14:5 of an earthquake in the days of Uzziah, king of Judah. While the authors of Kings and Chronicles make no such mention, the above references confirm that it happened. *Josephus* associates this quake with the leprous judgment of God on Uzziah. He says:

"In the meantime a great earthquake shook the ground, and a rent was made in the temple, and the bright rays of the sun shone through it, and fell upon the king's face, insomuch that the leprosy seized upon him immediately. And before the city, at a place called Eroge, half the mountain broke off from the rest on the west, and rolled itself four furlongs [half a mile], and stood still at the east mountain, till the roads, as well as the king's garden, were spoiled by the obstruction."

Regardless of the silence in Kings and Chronicles (or of any misgivings about Josephus' authenticity), and prophets Amos and Zechariah held it to be significant in relation to prophecy and judgment. The *Thompson Chain-Reference* chronology dates Amos 1:1 in 787 B.C., which would have been Uzziah's twenty-third year as king—less than half of his fifty-two years. However, the reference to his son Jotham being "over the house, judging the people of the land" (2 Kings 15:5), and Jotham having been twenty-five years old when he ascended the throne (in his own right, apparently), would seem to make the date 787 B.C. too early. This does not, however, refute the authenticity of the earthquake, which would have occurred in 785 B.C. if Amos began writing "two years before the earthquake."

If *Josephus'* description of the magnitude of the quake seems unreasonable, consider the words in Zechariah's reference—"as ye *fled from before the earthquake* in the days of Uzziah king of Judah." In other words, it was likened to the mighty earthquake which will divide the mountain when, upon Christ's return, His feet touch the Mount of Olives. Though we cannot be sure how near the end of Uzziah's reign this happened, be the years few or many, the leprosy remained; and because of its "uncleanness," he had to dwell in a house separate from others. He was "cut off from the house of the Lord" (26:21). God's judgments are "earth-shaking" for those who meddle in the office of the high priest—a type of our great High Priest, Jesus Christ!

FOR OUR ADMONITION AND LEARNING

It behooves every Christian to receive instruction from the ensample of Uzziah's life. We may think of the novice—the young and unstable—as being the one most apt to fail. But failures can be made at any stage or level of life. An inflated ego can result from a variety of causes—popularity (Uzziah had it!)—experience—seniority—education—office—"political" stature—parentage—yes, even from being acclaimed "meek and humble"!

Few, if any, will be smitten with *leprosy;* but leprosy is the most dreadful type of SIN known in the Bible! And, despite the flourishing (and damning) doctrine of "eternal security" (or "once in grace, always in grace"), it is possible to take our salvation into our own hands—and eternally lose it!!!

—Lesson Twenty—

JOTHAM: ELEVENTH KING OF JUDAH

Required Scripture Readings: 2 Kings 15:32-38; 2 Chronicles 27:1-9.

Pronunciation Helps: Jotham—JO-tham; Jerushah—je-ROO-shah; Zadok—ZAY-dok; Ophel—O-fel.

RELEVANT FACTS
Chief character: Jotham.
Time span: 16 years, beginning about 758 B.C.
Seat of government: Jerusalem.
Contemporary personalities: Pekah, king of Israel; the prophets Joel, Hosea, Micah, and Isaiah.
Lineage and family: Son of Uzziah (Azariah). Mother: Jerushah, daughter of Zadok. Son: Ahaz, only one named.
Accession to the throne: At age 25, in about 758 B.C.
Death: Of natural causes.

THE HISTORICAL SITUATION
Uzziah had been a good king until his last years, when he had become exalted. We do not know how effective his leadership was after he was stricken with leprosy and could not be among the people as in former years. He may have been somewhat despondent; but he seems not to have turned away from God. All in all, the kingdom was at peace and flourishing.

Jotham had been his father's regent in governmental affairs during those last years, so the experience was an advantage. The transition of the kingdom was probably made smoothly.

Isaiah the prophet had begun his ministry in the latter years of Uzziah's reign (about 760 B.C.), and since the burden of his prophecies largely concerned Judah and Jerusalem (Isaiah 1:1), it is probable that the young Jotham benefited from the prophet's counsel. If the chronology is dependable, chapter six of Isaiah covered the period of Jotham's reign, with the early chapters revealing the spiritual condition of the times. The prophet wrote as God moved him. As usual, things were not going as well as they may have appeared on the surface.

JOTHAM THE KING

Jotham had profited from the frightening experience of God's judgment upon his father. He respected Uzziah's earlier example, and recognized that as the desired pattern. So he did right according to all that his father had done, but he did not go into the temple presumptuously, as Uzziah did.

It is noted that *"the people* did yet corruptly" (2 Chronicles 27:2) by continuing to burn incense in the high places. We repeat that, although usually they did this in the name of the Lord, it was not pleasing in His sight, for they were privileged to live in the kingdom with Jerusalem as its capital and the temple of God available to them at all times.

Jotham's interest in the temple worship is seen in his continued repairs—"He built the high gate of the house of the Lord, and on the wall of Ophel he built much" (2 Chronicles 27:3). Comments by *Josephus* are of interest here:

"This king was not defective in any virtue, but was religious towards God, and righteous towards men, and careful of the good of the city (for what part soever wanted to be repaired or adorned, he magnificently repaired and adorned them). He also took care of the foundations of the cloisters in the temple, and repaired the walls that were fallen down, and built very great towers, and such as were almost impregnable; and if anything else in his kingdom had been neglected, he took great care of it."

Jotham was a builder. The wall of Ophel has been thought variously to have been either a retaining wall in the temple area, or a fortification. At any rate, it seemed important to the king. Then, he also built cities, castles, and towers, with the nation's progress and defense in mind.

In Uzziah's time, the Ammonites had been subdued, but apparently would not pay tribute to Judah. Jotham waged war with them and saw to it that the tribute, bought in money and in grain, was paid—at least for three years (2 Chronicles 27:5).

His Bible record closes on a highly complimentary note: "So Jotham became mighty, because he prepared his ways before the Lord his God" (27:6).

FOR OUR ADMONITION AND LEARNING

It is like a refreshing breeze to come upon an occasional testimony of a son following a godly father's example. The Adamic nature tries to insist that every generation assert itself in the freedom of the flesh. The leadership of nations has tended toward a similar pattern. It is doubtful, in our political systems, if we appreciate the efforts of a God-fearing ruler, who must cope with every imaginable sort of situation.

Jotham appeals to us as a godly king. However, not every subject of his kingdom was spiritually inclined. The evil element gets more attention, often overshadowing the better things that are promoted.

It would be better if we would heed the apostle Paul's advice:

"I exhort therefore, that, first of all, supplications, prayers, intercessions, and giving of thanks, be made for all men;

"For kings, and for all that are in authority; that we may lead a quiet and peaceable life in all godliness and honesty.

"For this is good and acceptable in the sight of God our Saviour" (1 Timothy 2:1-3).

AHAZ: TWELFTH KING OF JUDAH

Required Scripture Readings: 2 Kings 16:1-20; 2 Chronicles 28:1-27; Isaiah 7:1-16.

Pronunciation Helps: Ahaz—A-HAZ; Urijah—U-RI-jah; Maaseiah—MAY-a-SEE-ah; Zichri—ZICK-RI; Azrikam—az-RI-kam; Elkanah—el-KAN-ah.

RELEVANT FACTS

Chief characters: Ahaz; Urijah the priest; Pekah, king of Israel.

Time span: 16 years, beginning about 742 B.C.

Seat of government: Jerusalem.

Contemporary personalities: Pekah and Hoshea, kings of Israel; the prophets Oded, Isaiah, Hosea, and Micah.

Lineage and family: Son of Jotham. Sons: Hezekiah (2 Chr. 28:27) and Maaseiah (2 Chr. 28:7).

Accession to the throne: At age 20, in about 742 B.C.

Death: Of natural causes.

THE HISTORICAL SITUATION

It is doubtful that the people, nationally, had appreciated their good king Jotham. The warnings of the prophets indicated that for several years much of their "service to God" had been superficial and hypocritical. (See Isaiah 1:2-21; 2:6-11; 3:8, 9; 5:8-23; 7:1-16.) Jotham had set them a good example and had worked hard to advance the nation in righteousness and prosperity, but the outcroppings of evil persisted.

Now, as it were, the angry, lowering clouds of judgment were looming on every horizon! One writer says, "The moral darkness became thicker than ever during the sixteen years of his [Ahaz's] reign. Open apostasy was not the order of the day . . . ."

Therefore we may expect drastic changes in Judah's history as we proceed—and all of them for the worse!

AHAZ THE KING

The Bible introduces this young king as follows:

"Ahaz was twenty years old when he began to reign, and he reigned sixteen years in Jerusalem: but he did *not* that which was right in the sight of the Lord, like David his father:

"For he walked in the ways of the kings of Israel, and made also molten images to Baalim.

"Moreover he burnt incense in the valley of the son of Hinnom, and burnt his children in the fire, after the abominations of the heathen whom the Lord had cast out before the children of Israel.

"He sacrificed also and burnt incense in the high places, and on the hills, and under every green tree" (2 Chronicles 28:1-4).

This means, of course, that the king "set the pace" for his subjects. *Commentator George Rawlinson* characterizes him in a broad sweep, thus: "Ahaz, who succeeded his father, Jotham, upon the throne of Judah at the age of twenty, had neither courage, nor patriotism, nor energy, nor prudence, nor piety, nor even a decent regard for the traditions of his house and nation."

Henry Cowles, a Hebrew historian, says: "He made himself notorious for his wickedness, surpassing in crime and downright depravity all the kings of *Judah;* he was surpassed in sin by few, if any, of the most wicked kings of *Israel.*"

A thoughtful reading of the cited Scripture references makes us concur with these commentators. It was as though Ahaz actually sought to excel in the most wicked idolatry; for instance, the Satan-inspired practice of offering human sacrifices!!! This was "borrowed" from the various heathen religions of the Phoenicians, the Moabites, the Ammonites, and possibly others.

Judgment Begins To Fall!

(NOTE: Thoroughly review Lesson Fourteen, concerning Pekah, king of Israel, and Rezin, king of Syria, in order to make repetition unnecessary here.)

We observe from 2 Chronicles 28:5 that God Himself delivered Ahaz into the hand of the king of Syria, as well as into the hand of the king of Israel. This was His judgment upon Judah "because they had forsaken the Lord God of their fathers" (2 Chronicles 28:6). The *seige* against Jerusalem was not successful, but when the Syrians went on to Edom, God used Israel as His instrument of chastisement.

Judah's losses were heavy, despite the fact that the Lord offered them His aid if Ahaz would meet His conditions— which he did not (Isaiah 7:9-13). Besides the one hundred twenty thousand that were slain in one day, and the two hundred thousand that were taken captive, Zichri, of Ephraim, "slew Maaseiah the king's [Ahaz's] son, and Azrikam the governor of the house, and Elkanah that was next to the king" (2 Chronicles 28:7).

God's undeserved mercy toward Ahaz and Judah is seen in His sending the prophet Oded to negotiate the release of the captives (2 Chronicles 28:9-15). The crux of Oded's message to Israel was his question: "*. . . Are there not with you, even with you, sins against the Lord God?*" The answer was self-evident, so "the heads of the children of Ephraim" (verses 12 and 15) treated the Judeans kindly, and took them to Jericho, well within their home border.

It is noteworthy that neither Ahaz nor Pekah are mentioned as having been present at "the negotiating table." Both being evil men, we are made to wonder if God had purposely directed this matter in order to facilitate the showing of His favor to Judah.

It is difficult to put in order the events of the accounts in 2 Kings and 2 Chronicles, but it appears that Ahaz sought the help of Tiglath-pileser, King of Assyria, after his confrontation with Israel and Syria (2 Kings 16:7-9; 2 Chronicles 28:16-21). In 2 Kings it is stated that Tiglath-pileser hearkened to Ahaz and took Damascus in Syria, and slew Rezin. The Chronicles account states that Tiglath-pileser met with Ahaz, "but he helped him not."

The essence of the matter seems to be that Ahaz lost more than he gained. He had made Judah tributary to Assyria, in a sense paying him to do it (2 Kings 16:7, 8; 2 Chronicles 28:19-22). And what did it profit Ahaz that Assyria took Damascus? The irony of it was that when Ahaz went to Damascus to meet Tiglath-pileser, his typically idolatrous eye fell on an altar, which historians believe to have been an Assyrian altar. It suited his apostate fancy, so he sent the pattern and fashion of it ahead of him to Urijah the priest at Jerusalem, instructing him to build an altar like it.

When Ahaz returned to Jerusalem, Urijah had finished it, so he immediately offered God's ordained offering on an Assyrian altar!

One commentator says, "One sin leads to another. Having introduced his self-invented *quasi*-idolatrous altar into his temple... Ahab was not satisfied, but proceeded to another innovation." He had "the brazen altar, which was before the Lord" moved to a secondary location, and "the new altar" put in its place! He then instructed Urijah to alternate the use of the two altars between the morning and evening sacrifices (2 Kings 16:14-16).

From there, Ahaz's actions seem almost demonic. "For he sacrificed unto the gods of Damascus, which had smote him: and he said, Because the gods of the kings of Syria *help them*, therefore will I sacrifice to them, that they may *help me*. But they were the ruin of him, and of all Israel.

"And Ahaz gathered together the vessels of the house of God, and cut in pieces the vessels of the house of God, and shut up the doors of the house of the Lord, and he made him altars in every corner of Jerusalem.

"And in every several city of Judah he made high places to burn incense unto other gods, and provoked to anger the Lord God of his fathers" (2 Chronicles 28:23-25).

Secular history indicates that the Assyrians had home problems, which may have turned their attention away from Ahaz's "sell-out" to Tiglath-pileser. Then, a little later they were absorbed in the matter of the Northern Kingdom's captivity. Actually, *it was not God's time* for Judah's demise. Had it been, surely Ahaz had left nothing undone to have brought it to pass!

But better days were in store for Judah.

FOR OUR ADMONITION AND LEARNING

Laxness begets laxness. A little so-called "broadmindedness" on some Scriptural teaching will lead to the same on another, and then another. One's heart may be apprehensive about the "new interpretation" at first, but after ten years—twenty years—a generation—the conscience-pangs are gone. Those who then grow up on the "liberal" thought do not know the difference.

Sometimes these lenient views begin with just one—or a very few—boldly rebellious individuals. Left unrestrained, they influence a whole church organization. Ahaz was a *bold* rebel. His father and grandfather were godly men; but within sixteen years, Ahaz had "shut up the doors of the house of the Lord," and had established altars to his new belief "in every corner of Jerusalem"!!!

According to the Word of God, this should never be tolerated. The *boldness* should be on the side of TRUTH; the "modernists" should be the ones to cower—or to take their flight! "The *wicked* flee when no man pursueth: but the *righteous* are bold as a lion" (Proverbs 28:1). Satan bristles and roars *AS a lion;* but he is only bluffing those who will be bluffed. He is a great mimicker; a great counterfeiter! The real Lion is on the side of righteousness—"THE LION OF THE TRIBE OF JUDAH"!

—Lesson Twenty-one—

HEZEKIAH: THIRTEENTH KING OF JUDAH

Required Scripture Readings: 2 Kings, chapters 18 to 20; 2 Chronicles, chapters 29 to 32; Isaiah, chapters 36 to 39; Jeremiah 26:18, 19; Micah 3:12.

Pronunciation Helps: Hezekiah—HEZ-e-KI-ah; Abi—A-BI or Abijah—a-BI-jah; Shel-maneser—SHELL-man-EE-zer; Sennacharib—sen-AK-er-IB; Rabsaris—RAB-sa-ris; Rabshakeh—RAB-sha-keh; Eliakim—e-LI-a-kim; Shebna—SHEB-na; Berodach-baladan—BEE-ro-dak-BAL-a-dan.

RELEVANT FACTS
Chief characters: Hezekiah; Rab-shakeh; Eliakim; Shebna; Joah; Isaiah; Sennacherib.
Time span: 29 years, beginning about 726 B.C.
Seat of government: Jerusalem.
Contemporary personalities: Hoshea, king of Israel (about five years, until Israel went into exile to Assyria); the prophets Isaiah, Micah, Hosea, and Nahum.
Lineage and family: Son of Ahaz. Mother: Abi (2 Kings 18:2) or Abijah (2 Chr. 29:1), daughter of Zachariah. Wife: Hephzibah (2 Kings 21:1). Son: Manesseh, only one named. (See 2 Kings 20:18.)
Accession to the throne: At age 25, in about 726 B.C.
Death: Of natural causes.

THE HISTORICAL SITUATION
Hezekiah came to power in troublous and threatening times. The Northern Kingdom was no more than five years away from its predicted captivity and exile. This Assyrian take-over was bound to have repercussions in the Southern Kingdom. In fact, Ahaz had already made Judah tributary to Assyria, unnecessarily; and this situation spelled trouble for Hezekiah, as we shall see.

Israel was too involved with the Assyrian threat and encroachment to give her sister Judah trouble, as she had done in former years. So Hezekiah would have some time to establish himself in the kingdom, and in the hearts of his subjects.

Internal decay, spiritually, was the matter of greatest concern, for the Lord's favor had been lifted through the idolatrous and apostate doings of Ahaz, with altogether too much assent from the people.

The records for this period are fraught with uncertainties as to the chronology of some events, particularly in the first half of the regime. The 2 Kings account stresses certain matters, while the 2 Chronicles chapters emphasize other events, in varying degrees. The references in Isaiah are too important to bypass, but, because of the essential purpose of prophecy, time gaps tend to be confusing. For instance, historians suspect a time-lapse of uncertain length between verses one and two of Isaiah, chapter thirty-six.

Since our main purpose is to characterize the king of Judah, (with relation to his people, of course), chronology must take second place. Commentators through the centuries have struggled with this problem, so it is not ours to be dogmatic about consecutive dates here. The events themselves are clear enough—thanks to the infallible Word.

HEZEKIAH THE KING

"It would seem that a good mother had counteracted the evil influence of a bad father, in the formation of the character of Hezekiah," says *Commentator J. Glentworth Butler*. "In his character, Hezekiah stands with David and Josiah. These were counted the perfect kings, and furnished the standard models by which other kings were estimated. He did that which was right in the sight of Jehovah. He blended a thorough affection with a thorough devotion to Jehovah, and to the interests of His worship and His authority over the people."

The Right Beginning

"He in the first year of his reign, in the first month, opened the doors of the house of the Lord, and repaired them" (2 Chronicles 29:3).

Commenting on this undelayed forward move as that of first priority, *Josephus* says, "His nature was good, and righteous, and religious; for when he came to the kingdom, he thought that nothing was prior, or more necessary, or more advantageous to himself, and to his subjects, than to worship God. Accordingly, he called the people together, and the priests and the Levites, and made a speech to them . . . . "

Compare 2 Chronicles 29:4-11 with the "speech" as found in Jewish history and relayed by *Josephus:*

"You are not ignorant how, by the sins of my father, who transgressed that sacred honour which was due to God, you have had experience of many and great miseries, while you were corrupted in your mind by him, and were induced to worship those which he supposed to be gods; I exhort you, therefore, who have learned by sad experience how dangerous a thing impiety is, to put that immediately out of your memory, and to purify yourselves from your former pollutions, and to open the temple to these priests and Levites who are here convened, and to cleanse it with the accustomed sacrifices, and to recover all to the ancient honour which our fathers paid to it; for by this means we may render God favourable, and He will remit the anger He hath had to us."

There was instant and willing response to the new king's plea. They sanctified themselves, cleansed the house of the Lord, and put all the furniture and vessels in place in eight days (2 Chronicles 29:12-19). Then Hezekiah and the rulers of the city brought the proper beasts and commanded the priests to offer the sin offering and the burnt offering, to make reconciliation and atonement for all Israel (29:20-24).

Hezekiah seems to have overlooked nothing—the song of the Lord, trumpets and other musical instruments, as ordained by David more than three centuries earlier. After the offerings were ended, there was time for bowing and worshipping the Lord (29:25-29).

Since the sin offering and burnt offering were to be consumed in the fire, Hezekiah next allowed the people to bring sacrifices and thank offerings, to be eaten and enjoyed together, as well as additional burnt offerings according to their free hearts. The offerings were so many that the priests had to have the help of "their brethren the Levites" to flay the animals (29:30-35).

"So the service of the house of the Lord was set in order.

"And Hezekiah rejoiced, and all the people, that God had prepared the people: for the thing was done suddenly" (29:36);

that is, all were happy because the restoration had been made surprisingly soon, and without delay.

Further Restoration

By the time these first essentials were done, the time had passed for the observance of the Passover. (See Exodus 12:2, 6, 18.) But Hezekiah was reluctant to neglect it a full year. Undoubtedly the provision under the law in Numbers 9:10, 11 was deemed lawful for use under the circumstances; so after thorough counsel, it "pleased the king and all the congregation" to observe it in the second month (2 Chronicles 30:1-4).

Proclamation was made "throughout all Israel, from Beersheba even to Dan, that they should come to keep the passover unto the Lord God of Israel at Jerusalem" (30:5). After all, when it was first instituted, it was for all Israel. Hezekiah was a wise man, and he knew the spiritual plight of the Northern Kingdom. Without doubt he knew of the warnings of the prophets concerning the approaching Assyrian captivity. Perhaps he reasoned that God might be merciful if Israel could be persuaded to take advantage of this opportunity for revival and restoration.

So messengers were sent out to deliver the letters. (Read 2 Chronicles 30:6-9 for the word-by-word proclamation.) Sad to say, generally speaking, the messengers and their message were mocked, and laughed to scorn. However, some from Asher, Manasseh, and Zebulun "humbled themselves, and came to Jerusalem" to the feast (30:10, 11).

The contrast of attitude in Judah was remarkable. The people there, by the hand of God, were of one heart and one mind to obey Hezekiah's commandment (30:12). "A very great congregation" gathered. First they purged Jerusalem of the "altars"—probably those which Ahaz had set up when he had shut the doors of the temple (30:13, 14).

Faced with their sacred duties, and beholding the holy zeal of *the people,* the priests and Levites were put to shame. *Matthew Henry* expounds this as follows: " ... The people were so forward and zealous that the priests and Levites blushed to see themselves outdone by the commonality, to see them more ready to bring sacrifices than they were to offer them. This put them upon sanctifying themselves, that the work might not stand still for want of hands to carry it on" (2 Chronicles 30:15-17).

We get a blessed preview of the amazing grace of God from verses eighteen through twenty-two. The spirit of *repentance* was everywhere, but according to the law, "a multitude of the people [especially those from the Northern Kingdom who had not been present for the great revival in the first month] . . . had not cleansed themselves." The Passover was a feast for *the redeemed ones* in memory of their deliverance at the Red Sea, wholly by the mercy and grace of God. But humility and repentance were so profound that the unprepared ones felt constrained to "eat the passover otherwise than it was written" (verse 18).

Thank God for a man like Hezekiah, who could see "beyond the veil," as it were! He knew that God looked upon the people's hearts. So "Hezekiah prayed for them, saying, The good Lord pardon every one that *prepareth his heart to seek God,* the Lord God of his fathers, though he be not cleansed according to the purification of the sanctuary" (verse 19).

"And the Lord hearkened to Hezekiah, and healed the people" (verse 20).

The Passover was a seven-day feast of unleavened bread. *The people* kept it with gladness; even the priests and the Levites "prayed through" and "praised the Lord day by day, singing with loud instruments unto the Lord" (verse 21). And their kind, understanding king did not goad those priests and Levites for being "ashamed" in the beginning. Instead, he "spake comfortably" to them when he saw and heard them teaching the hungry people "the good knowledge of the Lord" (verse 22).

When the seven days were up, "the revival was still going well"—so well that "the whole assembly" decided to "run it another week" (verses 23, 24)! Apparently they were still rejoicing in the Lord when the fourteen-day feast was over (verse 25). There had not been such joy in Jerusalem since the time of Solomon's better days. *The ministry* was now in a spiritual condition to bless the people, and *the people's confidence* was restored so that they would listen to them—and all of their prayers were heard in heaven!

Fruits of the Revival

"Now when all this was finished, all Israel that were present went out to the cities of Judah, and brake the images in pieces, and cut down the groves, and threw down the high places and the altars out of all Judah and Benjamin, in Ephraim also and Manesseh, until they had utterly destroyed them all. Then all the children of Israel returned, every man to his possession, into their own cities" (2 Chronicles 31:1).

This revival goes on record as a success because the people went out and erased the evidences of their former sinful lives. Then Hezekiah could restore the priestly offices and functions more fully, since the ministry was now qualified to serve.

The financial system was next on the agenda for reinstitution. Hezekiah led the way as a good example (verse 3). Next he commanded that the Levites be given their portion according to the law, and the response was immediate and generous (verses 4 and 5). And it was not just those at Jerusalem, who might feel that the king could "keep an eye" on them. Those from the outlying cities of Judah, and those who had come down from Israel, brought their tithes in such abundance that "fixed expenditures" were provided for, with a "surplus," which was laid in "heaps" until after the "Feast of Ingathering" in the seventh month (verses 6 and 7).

Hezekiah questioned the priests and the Levites about the distribution of the "heaps." Truthfully they were not a "surplus," for their use was designated by the law. We will remember that the tribe of Levi had no land inheritance as did all the other tribes. The Lord Himself was their portion, and His plan for their sustenance was the tithes from all the tribes. The people had often failed through the years, and the Levites and the priests (who were of the tribe of Levi, of course) had suffered, having no land of their own from which to till out a living. This had been the case just prior to the great "revival"—which may have accounted for their slackness (perhaps *discouragement*), and their need for a spiritual lift. Now it would be different.

Azariah, the chief priest, and Hezekiah worked together to restore the financial system—both the tithes and the freewill offerings (2 Chronicles 31:10, 13, 14). A careful reading of verses ten through nineteen convinces us that no one who was eligible for support was overlooked. It was no small task, which accounts for the numerous appointments. And it is altogether fitting that verses twenty and twenty-one should have a place in the account:

"And thus did Hezekiah throughout all Judah, and wrought that which was good and right and truth before the Lord his God.

"And in every work that he began in the service of the house of God, and in the law, and in the commandments, to seek his God, he did it with all his heart, and prospered."

"Foreign Relations" Demand Attention

The king had other matters also claiming his attention. Probably early in his reign he was confronted with the Assyrian problem which his father had created for him. He may have felt that the people of God should not be tributary to any heathen nation. Since he had set out to serve God, he may have felt that he would trust Him to deliver Judah from this abominable subordination. So "he rebelled against the king of Assyria [Shal-maneser], and served him not" (2 Kings 18:7).

His "rebellion" probably meant that he stopped paying the tribute, and in no way showed any allegiance to the Assyrian king. Nothing is said about Shal-maneser's reaction. Problems with Israel probably overshadowed Hezekiah's independence. Also, Shal-maneser was not king very long. He beseiged Samaria three years, but apparently Sargon took his place before the actual captivity and exile of Israel. So the problems of transition took some time. It was in 721 B.C.—about five years after Hezekiah's accession—that Israel finally succumbed, and the captives were moved to Nineveh and other points.

During this time, Hezekiah "smote the Philistines" (2 Kings 18:8). Secular history links this with a complicated involvement of the Philistines with Assyria. Judah was only indirectly involved, but they helped deliver some of the cities which were oppressed.

By 713 B.C. (Hezekiah's fourteenth year), Sennacherib was king of Assyria, and he moved encampments into Judah (2 Kings 18:13-16; 2 Chronicles 32:1-8). The two accounts seem to be contradictory concerning Hezekiah's dealing with the seige. Historians hold that neither account is complete, yet both are true.

The author of 2 Kings portrays Hezekiah as submitting to Sennacherib without the least resistance. The author of 2 Chronicles does not even mention any such attitude. Rightly divided, we can clearly see that Hezekiah suffered a period of discouragement during which he tried to "buy peace," hoping to avoid the same type of takeover that had happened to Israel no more than eight years earlier. It is also clear that Hezekiah finally resisted Sennacherib. Perhaps we can trust *Josephus* to "synchronize" the two records:

"... Sennacherib made an expedition against him [Hezekiah] with a great army, and took all the cities of the tribes of Judah and Benjamin by force; and when he was ready to bring his army against Jerusalem, Hezekiah sent ambassadors to him beforehand, and promised to submit, and pay what tribute he should appoint. Hereupon Sennacherib, when he heard of what offers the ambassadors made, resolved not to proceed in the war, but to accept the proposals that were made him; and if he might receive three hundred talents of silver, and thirty talents of gold, he promised that he would depart in a friendly manner; and he gave security upon oath to the ambassadors that he would then do them no harm, but go away as he came. So Hezekiah submitted, and emptied his treasures, and sent the money, as supposing he should be freed from his enemy, and from any further distress about his kingdom. Accordingly the Assyrian king took it, and *yet had no regard to what he had promised;* but while he himself went to the war against the Egyptians and Ethiopians, he left his general Rabshakeh, and two other of his principal commanders, with great forces, to destroy Jerusalem. The names of the two other commanders were Tartan and Rabsaris."

There may or may not have been a time-lapse between Sennacherib's first and second expeditions against Judah. He was engaged in campaigns in other areas, so he sent an embassy made up of Tartan, Rabsaris, and Rab-shakeh, along with a great host, against Jerusalem—having saved the capital city till the last (2 Kings 28:17). Eliakim, Shebna, and Joah went out to hear what the embassy had to say.

Rab-shakeh boasted of the power and might of "the great king, the king of Assyria" (2 Kings 18:19), and at the same time belittling Hezekiah, the Egyptians (to whom Hezekiah had appealed for help, according to Isaiah 30:2-7), and even the Lord (18:22).

Eliakim made a plea for them to speak their negotiations in the Syrian language, since this was not a matter for the ears of the public (18:26), who could understand all that was being said in the Jews' language. But Rab-shakeh arrogantly violated the rules of ambassadorial conduct and declared that they had been sent to speak to the people. He then repeated his boastful barrage of accusations (verses 28-35).

Hezekiah had instructed his representatives to give the embassy no answer, so Eliakim, Shebna, and Joah rent their clothes and relayed the message to the king. Evidently the substance and threatening tenor came as a surprise to Hezekiah, who had put confidence in Sennacherib's earlier agreement, so he too "rent his clothes, and covered himself with sackcloth, and went into the house of the Lord" (2 Kings 19:1). Also, he sent Eliakim and Shebna to Isaiah the prophet, asking that he pray for Judah in this "day of trouble, and of rebuke, and blasphemy" (19:3, 4). Isaiah bade them return to their king with this word from God:

"Thus saith the Lord, Be not afraid of the words which thou hast heard, with which the servants of the king of Assyria have blasphemed me.

"Behold, I will send a blast upon him, and he shall hear a rumour, and shall return to his own land; and I will cause him to fall by the sword in his own land" (2 Kings 19:6, 7).

Rab-shakeh returned to Sennacherib when he failed to get a response from Hezekiah; but Sennacherib had been challenged by the king of Ethiopia, so he sent messengers again with a letter to Hezekiah (2 Kings 19:11-13). When Hezekiah had read the letter, he took it into the temple, "spread it before the Lord," and prayed that through it all the Lord would be glorified before all the kingdoms of the earth (19:15-19).

In another place, God and Isaiah were convening, and the Lord told Isaiah to send Hezekiah a second message: "That which thou hast prayed to me against Sennacherib king of Assyria I have heard." Then he proceeded with a copious answer concerning Sennacherib. (Read 2 Kings 19:21-28.) It is not supposed that His words were actually sent to the Assyrian monarch; but he would "sense" them when he "experienced" them! Hezekiah was further encouraged about the future, and about the Lord's defense of Jerusalem (19:29-34).

God had spoken; and "that night" *He performed!* " . . . The angel of the Lord went out, and smote in the camp of the Assyrians an hundred fourscore and five thousand [185,000]: and when they [the survivors] arose early in the morning, behold, they were all dead corpses" (2 Kings 19:35).

Among the dead were "all the mighty men of valour, and the leaders and captains" (2 Chronicles 32:21). All manner of conjectures have been set forth as to how this mighty army was slain. How foolish to trifle with "scientific" and "natural" suppositions when God has plainly given the answer—*the angel of the Lord went out and smote them!* Why should men desire to steal the glory?

With God's hook in his nose, and His bridle in his lips (2 Kings 19:28), "the great king, the king of Assyria" (2 Kings 18:28) "returned with shame of face to his own land" (2 Chronicles 32:21).

Returning to Nineveh, he went into the house of *his god;* and while he was worshipping, two of his own sons slew him with the sword (2 Kings 19:36, 37).

Hezekiah's Illness

"In those days was Hezekiah sick unto death" (2 Kings 20:1; 2 Chronicles 32:24).

The chronology fixes the date as 713 B.C. because of the fact that that was his fourteenth year as king (2 Kings 18:13), and his life was prolonged fifteen years, totaling twenty-nine (2 Kings 18:2). Since the account of the sickness is related entirely separate from other events of the period, there is little point in trying to explain it as having taken place before or after the first or second expedition of Sennacherib. However, if it had been at the time of the first, it might explain his failure to resist the Assyrian demands (2 Kings 18:13-16); and his miraculous recovery could account for his improved outlook as recorded in 2 Chronicles 32:2-8.

Whatever the sickness was, it was one that normally took the life. It is mentioned as a "boil" (2 Kings 20:7), but since boils result from different causes, we still do not know the root nature of the illness; and it doesn't matter, in the context of the incident, for "with God all things are possible."

The Lord's message through Isaiah was short and to the point—"Set thine house in order; for thou shalt die and not live." Any "unfinished business" spiritual or secular, would require immediate settlement. But Hezekiah was a man of prayer, so he prayed and "wept sore" (2 Kings 20:1-3).

His prayer was short, but many things must have sped through his mind. *Long life* was a special promise under the law; but he was only thirty-nine years old. *A good life* had become a rarity among the kings, but he had walked before God in truth and with a perfect heart. He probably as yet *had no son to succeed him.* (*Josephus* says he did not; and his son Manesseh, who did succeed him, was only twelve years old, being born after Hezekiah's recovery.)

But now we meet with something rather unexpected: "But Hezekiah rendered not again according to the benefit done unto him; for his heart was lifted up: therefore there was wrath upon him, and upon Judah and Jerusalem. Notwithstanding Hezekiah humbled himself for the pride of his heart . . . " (2 Chronicles 32:25, 26).

Somewhere in Hezekiah's short prayer and tears, God found an humbling of heart. Isaiah was not yet out of the court before the Lord gave him a new message for the king: "I have heard thy prayer, I have seen thy tears: behold, I will heal thee . . . and I will add unto thy days fifteen years . . . " (2 Kings 20:5, 6).

On the third day he would be able to go to the temple. And besides all this, there would be a deliverance out of the hand of Assyria. Isaiah then gave directions for the use of the fig poultice and gave the king his choice of a sign, which only God could effect. And He did effect it—by bringing the shadow on the sundial backward ten degrees (2 Kings 20:7-11).

An Unwise Confidence

The last half of Hezekiah's reign was comparatively uneventful. God blessed him with great wealth for himself and the kingdom (2 Chronicles 32:27-30). Only one event is recorded after his recovery. Some have tried to make this event an evidence of his pride *before* his illness, but 2 Kings 20:12 shows that it took place *after* he "had been sick."

Berodach-baladan, the son of the king of Babylon, sent Hezekiah "letters and a present"—*apparently* an expression of well-wishing, but *probably* in the hope of an alliance against Assyria, who was troubling both Babylon and Judah.

Hezekiah was pleased at their friendly gesture, and evidently saw in it the opening of diplomatic communications.

At any rate, he demonstrated such confidence that he "took them on a tour" of the royal premises, as though they were long-time, trustworthy friends. Whether or not they had an ulterior motive at the time, God knew the long-run consequences, so He sent Isaiah to show Hezekiah what he had done (2 Kings 29:13-19; 2 Chronicles 32:31).

The time would come when Babylon would overthrow Assyria and become a world power. Then they would come against Judah, as Assyria had done; and conditions would be such that God would allow Babylon to do to Judah exactly what Assyria had done to Israel!

Hezekiah's sons also (or at least his descendants) would be eunuchs in the palace of the king of Babylon. (See 2 kings 24:11-16 and Daniel 1:1-7, for examples of the fulfillment.)

Of course, Hezekiah was sorry, but it was too late. All he could say was, "Good is the word of the Lord..." (2 Kings 20:19). In His foreknowledge, God knew what would be. Hezekiah was glad that it would not be immediate.

The good king died in about 697 B.C. and was honored by being buried "in the chiefest of the sepulchres of the sons of David: and all Judah and the inhabitants of Jerusalem did him honour at his death" (2 Chronicles 32:33).

FOR OUR ADMONITION AND LEARNING

It is a sad commentary—and one not readily confessed—that "the people," or laity, are often more willing to obey the Scriptures than are the ministers. It was true in Hezekiah's time (2 Chronicles 29:34; 30:15). Many of *the people* were not "clean," because their kings had led them astray, and *the priests* had not been an example in purity. "The people" were ready for "revival," but the priests were unqualified. In our own dispensation, it is seldom "the people" who *introduce* heresies and false doctrines. They are "sheep," and they *follow* all too readily; but the so-called "shepherds" are to blame!

The "success" of a revival can be judged only after it closes (2 Chronicles 31:1). Are its *fruits* immediate only? What about after a month? six months? a year? ten years?

Satan's workings are so subtil that even the best of people are often taken in his snare, not realizing it until God makes them face themselves. Who would have thought of finding an exalted, prideful heart in a man like Hezekiah (2 Chronicles 32:25, 26)? But *God* saw it! The devil glories in making men "proud of their humility"!!!

—Lesson Twenty-two—

MANASSEH: FOURTEENTH KING OF JUDAH

Required Scripture Readings: 2 Kings 21:1-18; 2 Chronicles 33:1-20; Jeremiah 15:1-6 (judgment suffered after Manesseh's time).

Pronunciation Helps: Manasseh—ma-NASS-eh; Hephzibah—HEFF-zi-bah.

RELEVANT FACTS
Chief characters: Manesseh.
Time span: 55 years, beginning about 698 B.C.
Seat of government: Jerusalem.
Contemporary personalities: The prophet Isaiah. Also other prophets had spoken in advance of Manasseh's time, such as Micah and Hosea.
Lineage and family: Son of Hezekiah: Mother: Hephzibah. Wife: Meshullemeth (2 Kings 21:19). Son: Amon, only one named.
Accession to the throne: At age 12, about 698 B.C.
Death: Natural causes.

THE HISTORICAL SITUATION
The Assyrians had been quieted for the moment when the Lord heard Hezekiah's prayer and intervened for Judah. Something of a friendly association had developed (sincere or not) with the king of Babylon. Judah had enjoyed almost three decades of restored favor with God, along with much material prosperity.

But now Hezekiah was dead. He must have known the leanings of his son Manasseh toward evil. If so, there may have been those last hours when he shared Solomon's feelings:

"Yea, I hated all my labour which I had taken under the sun: because I should leave it unto the man that shall be after me.

"And who knoweth whether he shall be a wise man or a fool? yet shall he have rule over all my labour wherein I have laboured, and wherein I have shewed myself wise under the sun. This is also vanity " (Ecclesiastes 2:18, 19).

On the other hand, he may have been able to commit it all into the Higher Hand, knowing that he had done what he could in his own day and time. But a reign of a different kind lay ahead for Judah, as we shall see.

MANASSEH THE KING

Solomon had said, "Woe to thee, O land, when thy king is a child . . . " (Ecclesiastes 10:16).

And Isaiah had prophesied some forty years before Manasseh's time: "And I will give children to be their princes, and babes shall rule over them . . . the child shall behave himself proudly against the ancient, and the base against the honourable" (Isaiah 3:4, 5).

When the righteous are in power, such as Hezekiah, there invariably remains a Satanic element which does not cease to plot (underground perhaps) for a day when the truth and righteousness can once more be trampled under foot. It was so when Isaiah penned the following, in the very beginning of Manesseh's reign:

"And judgment is turned away backward, and justice standeth afar off: for *truth is fallen in the street,* and equity cannot enter.

"Yea, truth faileth; and *he that departeth from evil maketh himself a prey:* and the Lord saw it, and it displeased him that there was no judgment" (Isaiah 59:14, 15).

Manasseh seemed bent on undoing every good work his godly father had done (2 Kings 21:2-9). One historian reasons: "The group in power around the new king were for doing away with the religious reforms Hezekiah had made. Manasseh was too young to hinder them [at first] . . . He became a fanatical idolater, bringing a whole host of heathen practices into his realm."

He was, in his works, "a chip off the old block" of his grandfather Ahaz; perhaps worse, for apparently he set up the heathen altars and images *in the house of the Lord* (2 Kings 21:4, 7). He would have done better to have "shut the doors," as Ahaz had done.

Added also was the use of enchantments and witchcraft, seeking familiar spirits and wizards (2 Kings 21:6; 2 Chronicles 33:6). His wickedness was like an echo from that of

Jeroboam, "who made Israel to sin." Now it is written of Manasseh, "So Manasseh made Judah and the inhabitants of Jerusalem to err, and to do worse that the heathen, whom the Lord had destroyed before the children of Israel" (2 Chronicles 33:9).

God Sends the Prophets

"And the Lord spake to Manasseh, and to the people: but they would not hearken" (2 Chronicles 33:10).

He spoke *through* His prophets; but first He spoke *to* His prophets (2 Kings 21:10-15). *The Thompson Chain-Reference* chronology places only Isaiah within the years of Manasseh's rule (about 698 to 643 B.C.). Chapters fifty-seven through sixty-six carry the date 698 B.C.—Manasseh's first year. The chronologies of other historians vary.

This we know: The Bible declares that "the Lord spake by his servants the prophets" (2 Kings 21:10). So more than one prophet spoke concerning Manasseh's abominations and wickedness (21:11). He declared that He would bring such judgmental evil upon Jerusalem and Judah that it would be shocking to all the ears that would hear of it—not only upon the judged people, but upon the surrounding nations who would hear it. God's punishment would be commensurate with the evil that called it forth!

Judah was the chosen tribe, but God is no respecter of persons. If *Judah* stooped to the level of outcast *Israel,* He would measure *Jerusalem* with the same line with which He had measured *Samaria,* and with the same plummet with which He had measured the house of Ahab. If Jerusalem continued in the direction Manasseh was taking it, He would turn it upside down, scrape it empty, wipe it, and put it away (2 Kings 21:13)!

God would then forsake what would be left of His inheritance and deliver them over to their enemies—who apparently were already crouching to spring upon the prey (21:14, 15).

We have read that "they would not hearken to the prophets." Now we read: "Moreover Manasseh shed innocent blood very much, till he had filled Jerusalem from one end to another ... " (2 Kings 21:16).

Josephus says, " ... By setting out from a contempt of God, he barbarously slew all the righteous men that were among the Hebrews; nor would he spare the prophets, for he every day slew some of them, till Jerusalem was overflown with blood. So God was angry at these proceedings, and sent prophets to the king, and to the multitude, by whom He threatened the very same calamities to them which their brethren the Israelites, upon the like affronts offered to God, were now under. But these men would not believe their words, by which belief they might have reaped the advantage of escaping all these miseries; yet did they in earnest learn that what the prophets told them was true."

Another historian adds, "He [Manasseh] persecuted the pious people who were faithful to Jehovah, the true God. Jewish tradition says *he sawed the prophet Isaiah asunder."* We know, of course, that some of the men and women of faith, at some time in history, were subjected to this type of persecution, for the author of the *Epistle to the Hebrews* records it as follows:

"... Others were tortured, not accepting deliverance; that they might obtain a better resurrection:

"And others had trial of cruel mockings and scourgings, yea, moreover of bonds and imprisonment:

"They were stoned, they were *sawn asunder,* were tempted, were slain with the sword ... " (Hebrews 11:35-37).

Historian Dean Stanley puts it thus: "A reign of terror commenced against all who ventured to resist the reaction. Day by day a fresh batch of the prophetic order were ordered for execution. It seemed as if a devouring lion were let loose against them. From end to end of Jerusalem were to be seen traces of their blood. The nobles who took their part were thrown headlong from the rocky cliffs of Jerusalem."

Since Manasseh would not heed the voice of God through the prophets, He stirred up Assyria again, perhaps some eighteen to twenty years into his fifty-five-year reign. It is uncertain what is meant by the Assyrians having taken Manasseh "among the thorns." Some think he ensnared himself while trying to hide in his gardens, some thorny bushes preventing his escape until his captors were upon him. Others think the term is figurative; that he found himself in "a thorny situation"—"perplexed in his counsels and embarrassed in his affairs," says *Matthew Henry.*

Whatever the meaning, it somehow contributed to his being taken, bound with fetters, and carried to Babylon. (NOTE: Assyria and Babylon were vying for the status of "the world power." There seems to have been times when Babylon was tributary to Assyria; which may account for the Assyrians taking Judah's king to Babylon.)

Repentance in Affliction

"And when he was in affliction, he besought the Lord his God, and humbled himself greatly before the God of his fathers,

"And prayed unto him: and he was entreated of him, and heard his supplication, and brought him again to Jerusalem into his kingdom. Then Manasseh knew that the Lord he was God" (2 Chronicles 33:12, 13.)

The Bible record is exceedingly brief here. If we think only shallowly, it may seem that Manasseh "got by" with a lot of the very worst wickedness, and "got off" with very little chastisement. Again we are reminded that *men* do not see all that *God* sees; but God is just, right, and sovereign.

The truth is that God had not delivered him over to Assyria to *destroy* him, but *to bring him to the knowledge of the truth*—that the Lord is God. God was always mindful of His covenant with the house of David. Also, He probably remembered Hezekiah, the godly father of this impious son. He would bear a while longer with Judah! *Josephus* says:

"But then it was that Manasseh perceived what a miserable condition he was in, and esteeming himself the cause of all, he besought God to render his enemy humane and merciful to him. Accordingly, God heard his prayer, and granted him what he prayed for. So Manasseh was released by the king of Babylon, and escaped the danger he was in."

In Manasseh's prayer, God saw *true repentance* and *humility*. He was a pitiful wretch, reaping what he had sowed; but he had "come to himself" and acknowledged what he was in the sight of God. He begged for his life—yea, probably for his poor soul! And, coming to God in this attitude, He would in no wise cast him out! He not only forgave that wretched sinner, but also restored him to the throne of Judah. God had touched the hearts of the Assyrian authorities also; which reminds us of Solomon's words in Proverbs 21:1—"The king's heart is in the hand of the Lord, as the rivers of water: he turneth it whithersoever he will."

Housecleaning Time!

Manasseh returned to the throne a new man; not arrogantly, as though God had been obligated to him, but truly humble and determined to be the king he had so utterly failed to be before. He began at once to strengthen Jerusalem for what he must now have known would happen by and by—other enemy assaults!

But more important, he thoroughly purged the city and nation of the idolatrous system he had re-established during his early reign. Now, instead of being branded with the scourge of having made Judah to sin, he "commanded Judah to serve the Lord God of Israel" (2 Chronicles 33:16).

Following are excerpts from *Josephus'* re-characterization of the humbled king:

" . . . When he was come to Jerusalem, he endeavored, if it were possible, to cast out of his memory those former sins against God, of which he now repented, and to apply himself to a very religious life. He sanctified the temple, and purged the city, and for the remainder of his days he was intent on nothing but to return his thanks to God for his deliverance, and to preserve him propitious to Him all his life long. He also instructed the multitude to do the same, as having very nearly experienced what a calamity he was fallen into by a contrary conduct . . . . And indeed, when he had changed his former course, so he led his life for the time to come, that from the time of his return to piety towards God he was deemed a happy man, and a pattern for imitation . . . . "

FOR OUR ADMONITION AND LEARNING

God is true to His own Law: "Thou shalt not have in thy bag divers weights, a great and a small. Thou shalt not have in thine house divers measures, a great and a small. But thou shalt have a perfect and just weight, a perfect and just measure shalt thou have . . . " (Deuteronomy 25:13-15). He used the same line and plummet on Israel and Judah when the circumstances were the same. The Church will do well to remember this with respect to her type and shadow!

The old hymn says of Calvary, *"Mercy there was great, and grace was free; pardon there was multiplied to me."* The same God that was in Christ on the Cross was with Manasseh in Babylon. He needed mercy, grace, and multiplied pardon just as we did when we fled to Him who bore our sins. Sometimes we fail to understand the power of true confession and repentance in the mind and hand of a loving God. We must never begrudge the vilest sinner of God's forgiveness. Rather, we must remember the awful pit from which we ourselves were digged!

AMON: FIFTEENTH KING OF JUDAH

Required Scripture Readings: 2 Kings 21:19-26; 2 Chronicles 33:21-25.

Pronunciation Helps: Amon—AY-mon; Meshullemeth—me-SHULL-e-meth.

RELEVANT FACTS
Chief character: Amon.
Time span: 2 years, beginning about 643 B.C.
Seat of government: Jerusalem.
Contemporary personalities: The prophets Habakkuk and Zephaniah.
Lineage and family: Son of Manasseh. Mother: Meshullemeth, daughter of Haruz of Jotbah. Wife: Jedidah, daughter of Adaiah of Boscath. Son: Josiah, only one named.
Accession to the throne: At age 22, about 643 B.C.
Death: Slain by his servants (2 Kings 21:23-26).

THE HISTORICAL SITUATION
We do not know how many years Manasseh had left to restore the true worship of God after his repentance, but they were probably half of his long reign; perhaps more. Since Amon was only twenty-two years old when he came to the throne, he knew only by hearsay of his father's earlier sinful life.

The nation was turned over to him in good spiritual condition. Also, there had been no foreign intrusions for several years.

AMON THE KING

Amon's story is soon told. "... He did that which was evil in the sight of the Lord, as his father Manasseh did" (2 Kings 21:20). Since it is uncertain where Jotbah was, it would not be right to suggest that his mother Meshullemeth's influence may have caused his evil inclination. She may have been an Arabian from near Ezion-geber, at the northern end of the Gulf of Aqaba (Deuteronomy 10:7); but some would place Jotbah in Galilee, which was now Assyrian territory.

Amon restored idolatry, bringing back the images which Manasseh had made (2 Chronicles 33:22), and which, though they had been *removed,* had not been *destroyed.* As a result, Amon had a "head start," so he "trespassed more and more" (2 Chronicles 33:23). Whatever his two years gave him time to do, that he did.

But "his servants conspired against him" and cut his reign short, killing him in his own house. We are not told if the conspiracy developed because the servants were unhappy with his wickedness, or because of an ambition to put one of their own men in his place. We are told that "the people of the land" slew the conspirators (2 Chronicles 33:25). This may have been done to forestall the enthronement of an equally wicked king. At any rate, they selected a good one, though very young.

FOR OUR ADMONITION AND LEARNING

Sometimes it is considered "fanatic" to make a literal "housecleaning" after one is saved. But why not remove every vestige of the old life? In fact, the work of faith in the heart should constrain us to do so. Paul is emphatic in saying, "Therefore if any man be in Christ, he is a new creature [creation]: *old* things are passed away; behold, all things are become *new*" (2 Corinthians 5:17). If we are "a new creation" in heart, why should we want outward reminders of the life of which we are now ashamed (Romans 6:21)?

Be sure of this: Satan wanted nothing better than those *undestroyed images* with which to infiltrate the mind and heart of the next man on the throne!

—Lesson Twenty-three—

JOSIAH: SIXTEENTH KING OF JUDAH

Required Scripture Readings: 2 Kings 22:1 through 23:30; 2 Chronicles 34:1 through 35:27; Jeremiah, chapters 2 through 6 and 25:3-11; Zephaniah, chapters 1 through 3.

Pronunciation Helps: Josiah—jo-SI-ah; Jedidah—je-DI-dah; Adaiah—a-DAY-ah; Azaliah—Az-a-LI-ah; Meshullam—me-SHULL-am; Hilkiah—hill-KI-ah; Shaphan—SHAY-fan; Huldah—HULL-dah; Pharaoh-nechoh—FAY-ra-oh-NEE-co.

RELEVANT FACTS
Chief characters: Josiah; Hilkiah the high priest; Huldah the prophetess.
Time span: 31 years, beginning about 641 B.C.
Seat of government: Jerusalem.
Contemporary personalities: The prophets Jeremiah, Zephaniah, Habakkuk, and Huldah.
Lineage and family: Son of Amon. Mother: Jedidah, daughter of Adaiah of Boscath. Wives: Hamutal, daughter of Jeremiah of Libnah (2 Kings 24:31); and Zebudah, daughter of Pedaiah of Rumah (2 Kings 23:36). Sons: Johanan, the firstborn; Jehoiakim (Eliakim), second; Zedekiah (2 Kings 24:17), third; and Jehoahaz (Shallum—1 Chronicles 3:15), fourth.
Accession to the throne: At age 8, about 641 B.C.
Death: Slain by Pharaoh-nechoh, king of Egypt, or his archers.

THE HISTORICAL SITUATION
The situation here seems merely a repetition of the "ups and downs" of the Judean kingdom. *But not so.* At least, not in the eyes of God. True, Manasseh had put forth a sincere effort to undo his earlier fouling-up of the kingdom, only to have his son, Amon, foul it up again.

But the sovereign God, in His mind-boggling foreknowledge, had not been starting and stopping, then beginning all over again, each time a king was enthroned, or died, or was succeeded. Long before this He had declared, "I AM"! Israel's history—Judah's history—it was all one total panoramic view to Him. The time was at hand that certain things would be done which had been in the making since Judah's beginning—yea, before!

A good king—an upright man—comes on the scene facing a nation very much torn between two opinions; a nation that seemed always to be *changing its gods!* (See Jeremiah 2:11-13, written during Josiah's reign.) What would this man do? He would do what God had sent him to do, for here was *a king of prophecy.* More than three hundred years before this time, when Jeroboam, *Israel's* first king, "made Israel to sin," an unnamed "man of God" had prophesied that a child would be born of the house of David (Judah), "Josiah by name," who would destroy Jeroboam's idolatrous altar (1 Kings 13:1-34; see also Lesson Six on Jeroboam for review).

Would this prophetic king be able to save Judah, being "God's man" as he was? NO! IT WAS TOO LATE! (See 2 Kings 22:11-20.)

JOSIAH THE KING

"And he did that which was right in the sight of the Lord, and walked in all the way of David his father, and turned not aside to the right hand or to the left" (2 Kings 22:2).

One author (identified as "the son of Sirach") has written: "The remembrance of Josias [Josiah] is like the composition of the perfume that is made by the art of the apothecary: it is sweet as honey in all mouths, and as music at a banquet of wine. He behaved himself uprightly in the conversion of the people, and took away the abominations of iniquity. He directed his heart unto the Lord, and in the time of the ungodly he established the worship of God."

At so early an age, one wonders that nothing is said of him leaning on counsellors. There is only silence about the first eight years of his reign, but "the people of the land" had made him king (2 Chronicles 33:25), so they probably respected him highly, and behaved themselves toward him accordingly.

At age sixteen "he began to seek after the God of David his father" (2 Chronicles 34:3). *Josephus* says, "And when he was twelve years old, he gave demonstrations of his religious and righteous behavior; for he brought the people to a sober way of living, and exhorted them to leave off the opinion they had of their idols, because they were not gods, but to worship their own God. And by reflecting on the actions of his progenitors, he prudently corrected what they did wrong, like a very elderly man, and like one abundantly able to understand what was fit to be done . . . . "

The Purging of the Land

At age twenty "he began to purge Judah and Jerusalem" (2 Chronicles 34:3). The most careful expositors agree that this purging was the most *thorough* and *complete* of any that had ever been made. It extended to the extremities of the land, even into what had been the Northern Kingdom, where God had allowed a remnant to remain (2 Chronicles 34:6).

It appears that his sincere zeal in this nation-wide endeavor was so great that he accompanied those who were to do the works of demolition. The altars of Baalim were broken down "in his presence" (2 Chronicles 34:4), and when the work was complete, it is said that "he returned to Jerusalem."

The Repairing of the Temple

It may have taken as many as six years to do this purging work, for "in the eighteenth year of his reign [when he was 26 years old], when he had purged the land, and the house" (2 Chronicles 34:8), he gave special attention to repairing the temple. Evidently it ("the house") had already been cleansed of Amon's pollutions, but, like any neglected or misused structure, it needed the attention of "carpenters, and builders, and masons" (2 Kings 22:6), as well as "artificers," or skillful craftsmen (2 Chronicles 34:11).

This project involved the providing of finance also (2 Chronicles 34:9, 10). The honesty and faithfulness of the workmen are noteworthy; "there was no reckoning with them of the money . . . because they dealt faithfully" (2 Kings 22:7; 2 Chronicles 34:12). Considering the testimony of the prophets—that Judah was definitely in a declining spiritual state—this honesty and dependability must have sprung from the workmen's love and respect for their king.

The Book of the Law Is Found

During the temple-repairing process, Hilkiah, the high priest, found "a book of the law of the Lord given by Moses"

(2 Chronicles 34:14, 15). It is clear that the book had been lost during the intermittent "backsliding" of the kings, and apparently even of the priests—as before Hezekiah's time. Considering that "the book of the law" was available only in handwritten copies, and few in number, this discovery was really an occasion for rejoicing. But when Shaphan, the scribe, took it to the king and began to read from it, Josiah "rent his clothes" (2 Chronicles 34:19). One expositor has this to say:

"Josiah recognized that Judah had done, and was still doing, exactly those things against which the threatenings of the Law were directed—had forsaken Jehovah, and gone after other gods, and made themselves high places, and set up images, and done after the customs of the nations whom the Lord had cast out before them. He could not therefore doubt but that the wrath of the Lord 'was kindled'; but would it blaze forth at once?"

Josiah commanded the high priest and others, "Go ye, inquire of the Lord for me, and for the people, and for all Judah, concerning the words of this book that is found..." (2 Kings 22:13).

This meant that they should inquire of a prophet; so they went to a prophetess named Huldah who dwelt nearby, explaining to her the king's concern and request (2 Chronicles 34:22). Her reply was an emphatic "Thus saith the Lord." It was in two parts: *First,* concerning "this place" and "the inhabitants thereof." God would bring evil upon them for their sins; and this time His wrath would not be quenched (2 Kings 22:16, 17). *Second,* personally to king Josiah, God would spare him the heartbreak of seeing His unrelenting pronouncement come to pass; He would let him die in peace before His wrath would be outpoured (2 Kings 22:18-20).

The People Hear the Law

Matthew Henry comments: "Josiah had received a message from God that there was no preventing the ruin of Jerusalem, but that he should deliver his own soul; yet he did not therefore sit down in despair, and resolve to do nothing for his country because he could not do all he would. No, he would do his duty, and then leave the event to God...."

Just what could he do with fourteen remaining years of kingship in a nation whose doom already had been pronounced?

Seemingly, he moved on the biblical premise: "Whatsoever thy hand findeth to do, do it with thy might; for there is no work, nor device, nor knowledge, nor wisdom, in the grave, whither thou goest" (Ecclesiastes 9:10).

The *nation* could not be spared, but perhaps there were *individuals* who would receive encouragement. The finding of the book of the law had resulted in this inquiry, so Josiah decided that everyone should hear it for himself. Calling for a gathering, "he read in their ears all the words of the book of the covenant" (2 Chronicles 34:30). Then he made a covenant to keep that law, and "caused all that were present in Jerusalem and Benjamin" to promise to do likewise (2 Chronicles 34:32, 33). Whether or not they were sincere, they had been given one more opportunity to choose the right way. Josiah at least derived this satisfaction: ". . . All his days they departed not from following the Lord, the God of their fathers" (2 Chronicles 34:33).

He continued his reformations, little by little discovering and destroying all traces of idolatry and sodomy (2 Kings 23:4-14). In the process, *as the Lord would have it,* he came to the altar at Bethel, where Jeroboam had made Israel to sin by setting up the golden calves—as has already been mentioned in the beginning of this lesson. Not one word of "the man of God" to Jeroboam had fallen to the ground; and though Jeroboam had been dead almost three centuries, and Israel at large was in the land of her captivity, yet God's confirmed Word is on record, that we in these last days might fear the Lord.

The Keeping of the Passover

Much had been done in this eighteenth year of Josiah's reign, but he would do one more thing. They would keep the Passover feast (2 Kings 23:21-23; 2 Chronicles 35:1-19). In making preparations, the ark of the covenant was put in its place in the temple, probably having been impiously removed during the reign of an ungodly king.

2 Chronicles, chapter thirty-five, would teach us that Josiah spared nothing to make this feast wholly acceptable unto God, according to God's detailed instructions in the book of the law.

"And there was no passover like to that kept in Israel from the days of Samuel the prophet; neither did all the kings of

Israel keep such a passover as Josiah kept, and the priests, and the Levites, and all Judah and Israel that were present, and the inhabitants of Jerusalem" (2 Chronicles 35:18).

Gathered Unto His Fathers

Josiah is not to be criticized for the move which resulted in his death, for in all probability it was of the Lord.

The great Assyrian Empire was about to fall to the Babylonians. Pharaoh-nechoh, king of Egypt, was en route with his army to assist the Assyrians in their fight. Judah lay between, and Josiah "went out against him" (2 Chronicles 35:20). Pharaoh-nechoh sent out ambassadors to assure Josiah that there was no quarrel against Judah; that they only wanted to pass through and go on to the Euphrates.

For some reason not explained, Josiah would not hearken, so the battle was engaged in the valley of Megiddo. "And the archers shot at king Josiah [even though he was disguised]" (2 Chronicles 35:23). He was sorely wounded, and his servants took him in a chariot to Jerusalem, where he died.

We have already seen that the prophet Jeremiah was a contemporary of Josiah. Jeremiah lamented this loss, and wrote down his lamentations, which apparently have been lost. (NOTE: The biblical book, *"The Lamentations of Jeremiah,"* seems to have been written at the time of Judah's captivity and exile, more than twenty years later. However, it could be possible that the lament referred to above is included—here and there—"in the lamentations.")

The next twenty-three years would have held nothing for the good king Josiah. So God had graciously gathered him to his fathers—in peace.

JEHOAHAZ: SEVENTEENTH KING OF JUDAH
(Also Called Shallum)

Required Scripture Readings: 2 Kings 23:31-34; 2 Chronicles 36:1-3; Jeremiah 22:10-12.

Pronunciation Helps: Jehoahaz—je-HO-a-HAZ; Riblah—RIB-lah.

RELEVANT FACTS
Chief character: Jehoahaz.
Time span: 3 months, in about 610 B.C.
Seat of government: Jerusalem.
Contemporary personalities: The prophets Jeremiah and Daniel.
Lineage and family: Son of Josiah. Mother: Hamutal, daughter of Jeremiah of Libnah.
Accession to the throne: At age 23, in about 610 B.C.
Death: Not altogether known; dethroned before his death. See Jeremiah 22:11, 12, where he is called Shallum, and where it seems to indicate that he died in captivity.

THE HISTORICAL SITUATION
Pharaoh-nechoh probably proceeded to Assyria, whence he had started when Josiah had briefly detained him. It is reasonable that he would return over the same route—perhaps after about three months.

So little is said about this brief period that we can only say that Jehoahaz inherited a well-ordered kingdom; but just beneath the surface, the end was virtually in sight. If Josiah's reformation acts were not finished according to his plans, they would never be!

JEHOAHAZ THE KING
According to the genealogy in 1 Chronicles 3:15, Jehoahaz (Shallum—Jeremiah 22:10) was Josiah's youngest son. It is written that "the people of the land" anointed him and made him king (2 Kings 23:30). We are told nothing about Johanan, the oldest, who would have been the heir, so he may have been dead. At any rate, Jehoahaz's two other brothers would eventually serve as king.

Jehoahaz "did that which was evil in the sight of the Lord" (2 Kings 23:32). *Josephus* characterizes him as "an impious man, and impure in his course of life." Ezekiel 19:3, 4 is said to refer to him (Shallum), and to portray him as a persecutor.

But he had little time to do either good or evil. Pharaoh-nechoh (possibly returning to Egypt) may have seen his opportunity to make Judah tributary. *Josephus,* and others, say that the king of Egypt "sent envoys to Jerusalem, and summoned Jehoahaz to his presence at Riblah, in the territory of Hamath [some 180 miles north of Jerusalem]. Jehoahaz obeyed the summons; and Nechoh, having taken possession of his person, 'put him in bands' [2 Kings 23:33], and carried him off to Egypt, where he died [2 Kings 23:34]."

The Bible says that "the king of Egypt put him down at Jerusalem, and condemned the land" (2 Chronicles 36:3). In other words, he was deposed as king, and the land was put under tribute. The king of Egypt made Jehoahaz's brother Eliakim king over Judah, changing his name to Jehoiakim (2 Chronicles 36:4).

FOR OUR ADMONITION AND LEARNING

God is not in a hurry. All eternity is His. He is "longsuffering to us-ward, not willing that any should perish, but that all should come to repentance" (2 Peter 3:9). Even though, in His foreknowledge, He knows what the end will be, it is as though He is reluctant to let His judgments fall on those who deserve them.

But men often seem to "force His hand," daring Him in their unbelief. *Israel,* in a sense, cut herself off some one hundred thirty-five years ahead of *Judah.* Now Judah was playing "the treacherous sister" (Jeremiah 3:6-11)! God was waiting in Josiah's time. Judah could not be spared, but the God of love halted at the threshold.

Yes—God seems slow. But when the "due time" arrives, *He acts quickly!!!*

—Lesson Twenty-four—

JEHOIAKIM: EIGHTEENTH KING OF JUDAH
(Also called Eliakim)

Required Scripture Readings: 2 Kings 23:34-37; 24:1-6; 2 Chronicles 36:4-8; Jeremiah 22:13-23; 25:1-11; 26:1-24; chapters 35 and 36; 46:2-12 (battle between Egypt and Babylon).

Pronunciation Helps: Jehoiakim—je-HOY-a-kim or Eliakim— e-LI-a-kim; Zebudah—ze-BOO-dah; Pedaiah—pe-DAY-ah; Chaldees—KAL-dees.

RELEVANT FACTS
Chief character: Jehoiakim.
Time span: 11 years, beginning about 610 B.C.
Seat of government: Jerusalem.
Contemporary personalities: The prophets Jeremiah and Daniel.
Lineage and family: Second son of Josiah. Mother: Zebudah, daughter of Pedaiah of Rumah. Wife: Nehushta (2 Kings 24:8). Sons: Jehoiachin and Zedekiah (not the Zedekiah who succeeded him)—(1 Chronicles 3:16).
Accession to the throne: At age 25, in about 610 B.C. Made king by Pharaoh-nechoh, king of Egypt.
Death: Manner uncertain (2 Kings 24:6). 2 Chronicles 36:6 indicates that he was carried away to Babylon, but historians say that the king of Babylon did not carry out this intention. Jeremiah 22:18, 19 and 36:27-32 seem to indicate that he died in Jerusalem.

THE HISTORICAL SITUATION
Under the circumstances of being a vassal state to Egypt, it would seem that Jehoiakim would rather not have been king; but in the light of Jeremiah's characterization of his lifestyle (Jeremiah 22:13-17), he must have enjoyed the luxurious honor.

It was a time of "world turmoil." Assyria had lost its power to Babylon and Egypt; and during this reign Egypt would succumb to Babylon. It was *then* even as *now* (twenty-six centuries hence): Each world power despised the people of God, but all wanted their land and possessions. No power on earth could have withstood them, much less overcome them, *if they had only been true to their God.* Theirs was the only true and living God, yet they would rather serve idols and "other gods." This they did much of the time; and they were doing so in Jehoiakim's time.

JEHOIAKIM THE KING

The Bible Briefs
Except for the prophet Jeremiah's numerous chapters pertaining to Jehoiakim, and Judah's spiritual state during his reign, the biblical historians who wrote 2 Kings and 2 Chronicles were very brief.

"And he did that which was evil in the sight of the Lord, according to all that his fathers had done" (2 Kings 23:37).

Pharaoh-nechoh, king of Egypt, made him king instead of his brother Jehoahaz. He readily paid the tribute to Egypt, taxing the land to raise it (2 Kings 23:35).

In the fourth year of his reign, Egypt lost out to Babylon, and "Nebuchadnezzar king of Babylon came up, and Jehoiakim became his servant three years: then he turned and rebelled against him" (2 Kings 24:1).

It was nothing new for God to make foreign powers His instrument of chastisement and judgment against His erring people; and it is only reasonable that He used Nebuchadnezzar to authorize the "bands" from other vaassal nations to go against rebellious Jehoiakim and Judah. In that sense—the truest sense—"the Lord sent against him bands" of Chaldees, Syrians, Moabites, and Ammonites, to *destroy* Judah "according to the word of the Lord, which he spake by his servants the prophets" (24:2).

Emphasis is added by something of a repetitive statement— "Surely *at the commandment of the Lord* came this upon Judah, to remove them out of his sight, for the sins of Manasseh, according to all that he did" (verse 3). It was not the long-deceased Manasseh's personal sins that God was remembering, but the type of sin that he had introduced, and which was still being practiced. One *W. G. Sumner* has observed:

"The sins of Manasseh had become a designation for a certain class of offences, and a particular form of public and social depravity, which was introduced by Manasseh, but of which generation after generation continued to be guilty."

This "certain class" of sins has been noted as: (1) idolatry accompanied by licentious rites [which were not "new"], (2) child-murder, or sacrifice to Moloch [the offering of children as human sacrifices], (3) sodomy [which was not new in Manasseh's time], and (4) the use of enchantments and the practice of the magical arts [which Manasseh had no monopoly on!].

Probably the "hallmark" of the sins of Manasseh was the "wholesale" slaughter of the prophets, priests, and other godly people—"the innocent blood that he shed; for he *filled* Jerusalem with innocent blood; *which the Lord would not pardon*" (2 Kings 24:4).

That this was going on during Jehoiakim's reign is clearly seen from Jeremiah 26:20-24, where the story is told of the prophet Urijah's death at the king's own hand. And Jeremiah himself narrowly escaped.

The Bible record of Jehoiakim's death is abbreviated—he "slept with his fathers" (2 Kings 24:6). 2 Chronicles 36:6 states that Nebuchadnezzar "bound him in fetters, *to carry* him to Babylon," but history says this was not carried through. Jeremiah's prophecies undoubtedly came to pass, indicating that he died infamously in Jerusalem (Jeremiah 22:18, 19), and that he died with "none to sit upon the throne of David" (36:30). His son Jehoiachin was made king but was not allowed to remain, as we shall see.

Other Historians Comment

Following are excerpts from *Zondervan's Pictorial Bible Dictionary:* "Jehoiakim was an oppressive and thoroughly godless king.... The prophet [Jeremiah] wrote at the direction of the Lord the dooms of Judah and other nations (Jeremiah 36:1-32). When the princes heard these words, they let Jeremiah and his clerk Baruch hide themselves, then when the king heard the words of the book [of Jeremiah], he cut out the leaves which displeased him and burned them, with the result that the book of Jeremiah was rewritten and enlarged. Jehoiakim died in disgrace, 'buried with the burial of an ass' (Jeremiah 22:19)."

Josephus comments: "He was of a wicked disposition, and ready to do mischief; nor was he either religious towards God, or good-natured towards man . . . When Nebuchadnezzar had already reigned four years, which was the eighth of Jehoiakim's government over the Hebrews, the king of Babylon made an expedition with mighty forces against the Jews, and required tribute of Jehoiakim, and threatened upon his refusal to make war against him. He was affrighted at his threatening, and bought his peace with money."

Concerning his death, *Josephus* says: "When he [Nebuchadnezzar] was come into the city [Jerusalem] . . . he slew such as were in the flower of their age, and such as were of the greatest dignity, together with their king Jehoiakim, whom he commanded to be thrown before the walls, without any burial; and made his son Jehoiachin king . . . . "

FOR OUR ADMONITION AND LEARNING

In this late-Twentieth Century, we see nations rising and falling, and others clinging to false hopes as negotiators "speak lies at one table" (Daniel 11:27). *Commentator W. Clarkson* writes the following, inspired by conditions in the time of Jehoiakim:

"A strong and self-respecting people falling into servitude, bowing its head to an utterly relentless power which has no other force than that of the sword and the war-chariot—that is a melancholy spectacle indeed. It may profitably suggest to us the question—*What is the real cause of a nation's fall?* And it will be found, on inquiry, that while this may be due to overweening ambition, it is much more likely to be ascribed to indulgence, to demoralization, to the weakness which must attend moral and spiritual deterioration. Simplicity and purity of life, sustained by Christian principle—this is the one security against decline, subjection, and ruin."

JEHOIACHIN: NINETEENTH KING OF JUDAH
(Also called Jeconiah)

Required Scripture Readings: 2 Kings 24:6-16; 2 Chronicles 36:8-10; 2 Kings 25:27-30; Jeremiah 22:24-30.

Pronunciation Helps: Jehoiachin—je-HOY-a-kin; Evil-merodach—EE-vil-MER-o-dak; Nehushta—ne-HUSH-ta.

RELEVANT FACTS
Chief character: Jehoiachin.
Time span: 3 months and 10 days, in about 599 B.C.
Seat of government: Jerusalem.
Contemporary personalities: The prophets Jeremiah and Daniel.
Lineage and family: Son of Jehoiakim (Eliakim). Mother: Nehushta, daughter of Elnathan of Jerusalem.
Accession to the throne: At age 18 (2 Kings 24:8), in about 599 B.C. (NOTE: 2 Chronicles 36:9 gives his age as 8 years old, but historians and chronologists hold to age 18.)
Death: Not known. He was carried away to Babylon (2 Kings 24:15; see also 2 Kings 25:27-30).

THE HISTORICAL SITUATION
Nebuchadnezzar had already deported some from Jerusalem, including Jehoiakim. Heavy tribute was being paid to Babylon. "And the king of Egypt came not again any more out of his land: for the king of Babylon had taken from the river of Egypt unto the river Euphrates all that pertained to the king of Egypt" (2 Kings 24:7). Judah was an absolute tributary to Babylon, even though the captivity and exile was still eleven years away.

JEHOIACHIN THE KING
After his father was killed, Jehoiachin was made king by Nebuchadnezzar, says *Josephus,* who also explains the siege of Jerusalem (2 Kings 24:11) as follows:

"But a terror seized on the king of Babylon, who had given the kingdom to Jehoiachin, and that immediately; he was afraid that he should bear him a grudge, because of his killing his father, and thereupon should make the country

208

revolt from him; wherefore he sent an army, and besieged Jehoiachin in Jerusalem; but because he was of a gentle and just disposition, he did not desire to see the city endangered on his account, but he took his mother and kindred, and delivered them to the commanders sent by the king of Babylon, and accepted of their oaths, that neither they should suffer any harm, nor the city; which agreement they did not observe for a single year, for the king of Babylon did not keep it, but gave orders to his generals to take all that were in the city captives, both the youth and the handicraftsmen, and bring them bound to him . . . and when they were brought to him, he kept them in custody, and appointed Jehoiachin's uncle, Zedekiah, to be king . . . ."

Although Jehoiachin "did evil in the sight of the Lord" (2 Kings 24:9), *Josephus'* characterization as "of a gentle and just disposition" probably indicates that he simply allowed the set pattern of idolatry and superstition to continue, making no effort at reformation during his short reign.

Jeremiah's prophecy was emphatic about the rejection of Jehoiachin (Coniah, or Jeconiah—Jeremiah 22:24-30). This may have been less for personal reasons than because of the "closing in" of God's ultimate judgment on Judah. At any rate, Jehoiachin was shown favor in Babylon after thirty-seven years of captivity (2 Kings 25:27-30 and Jeremiah 52:31-34).

It seems certain that it was God who brought this favor about. Evil-merodach had succeeded his father, Nebuchadnezzar, as king of Babylon. In his first year as king, he "did lift up the head of Jehoichin king of Judah out of prison." (See Genesis 40:13, 40, where the same phraseology is used.)

It seems that there were other captive vassal kings in Evil-merodach's court, and that he treated them well. *The Pulpit Commentary* suggests: "An honourable position and probably a seat of honour was assigned to each; but the highest position among them was now conferred on Jehoiachin . . . Evil-merodach supplied suitable garments to the released monarch instead of his 'prison garments,' and Jehoiachin arrayed himself in the comely apparel before taking his seat among his equals."

Jehoiachin enjoyed the privilege of eating at the king's table the rest of his life. The "continual allowance given him by the king" daily could have had reference to his food (Jeremiah 52:34), and possibly also a financial allotment.

The thirty-seventh year of his captivity, according to our chronology, would have been about 552 B.C., and he would have been about fifty-five years old. We do not know how much longer he lived, but according to Jeremiah's prophecy, he died in Babylon.

FOR OUR ADMONITION AND LEARNING

In life's darkest hours, God breaks through with rays of *hope*. The despairing saints are thereby reassured that God knows and cares. The sinner is thereby given another opportunity to repent, being reminded that "while we were yet sinners, Christ died for us" (Romans 5:8).

Jehoiachin's long imprisonment was known to all the Jews then living in Babylon. The favor shown him might well have come through to their minds as a witness that the prophesied *seventy years* would come to an end at last. While most of those who had come to Babylon would then be dead, their posterity would be privileged to restore the homeland—if they would.

ZEDEKIAH: TWENTIETH KING OF JUDAH
(Also called Mattaniah)

Required Scripture Readings: 2 Kings 24:17-20; 25:1-7; 2 Chronicles 36:10-21; Jeremiah 21:1-10; 25:5-14; 27:2-22; Ezekiel 12:1-16; 17:12-21.

Pronunciation Helps: Zedekiah—ZED-e-KI-ah, or Mattaniah— MAT-a-NI-ah; Hamutal—ha-MOO-tal.

RELEVANT FACTS

Chief character: Zedekiah.
Time span: 11 years, beginning about 598 B.C.
Seat of government: Jerusalem.
Contemporary personalities: The prophets Jeremiah, Ezekiel, and Daniel.
Lineage and family: Third son of Josiah and Hamutal, and brother of Jehoiakim. Sons: See 2 Kings 25:7.

Accession to the throne: At age 21, about 599 B.C.

Death: Not known. He was deported to Babylon, according to *Josephus,* along with many of his subjects. Ezekiel 12:8-13 indicates that he was carried to Babylon blind, and died there.

THE HISTORICAL SITUATION

Jehoiachin's short reign had brought no changes worthy of note. The first deportation of captives took place at the time Jehoiachin himself was taken to Babylon.

The Bible record in Kings and Chronicles is abbreviated, but there are several chapters in Jeremiah and Ezekiel pertaining directly to Zedekiah and Judah's situation at the time. The truly interested student will want to pursue the study in those areas of the Scriptures.

It will become apparent that the prophecies are not always in consecutive order. Some references may not use the king's name, but much study and research has been done by historians and expositors. In most instances, their conclusions seem sound.

In the writings of Jeremiah it can be seen that Zedekiah was unstable and vacillating in the face of conflicting influences by true and false prophets. This makes him seem unqualified as a ruler. Perhaps so. However, little could be expected of one who "did that which was evil in the sight of the Lord, according to all that Jehoiakim had done" (2 Kings 24:19).

ZEDEKIAH THE KING

The Bible characterization of Zedekiah's first nine years as king is severely condensed into two significant statements: (1) "... And humbled not himself before Jeremiah the prophet speaking from the mouth of the Lord" (2 Chronicles 36:12), and (2) "For through the anger of the Lord it came to pass in Jerusalem and Judah, until he [God] had cast them out of his presence, that Zedekiah rebelled against the king of Babylon" (2 Kings 24:20).

Another passage brings the above statements together, but intensifies the suspense: "and he also rebelled against king Nebuchadnezzar, who had made him swear by God: but he stiffened his neck, and hardened his heart from turning unto the Lord God of Israel" (2 Chronicles 36:13).

The Prophets Speak

The brunt of the captivity would have been greatly alleviated had Zedekiah hearkened to and heeded God's instructions through the prophets Jeremiah and Ezekiel. The burden of their message was that Zedekiah should submit to *the king of Babylon,* for God had made *him* His servant (Jeremiah 27:6-13).

To a very great extent, the people of Judah could have lived as Babylonian captives right in their own land instead of being removed to Babylon; but they would have had to live in submission and obedience to Nebuchadnezzar and his successors. However, through Zedekiah's stubborn rebellion, the second and final deportation was made in 587 B.C., about five hundred eight years after Saul had become king.

Zedekiah covenanted with Nebuchadnezzar ("swear by God") to be subject and pay tribute, but by believing false prophecies he rebelled, or broke the covenant. (Compare 2 Chronicles 36:13 with Ezekiel 17:12-21.)

In response to Zedekiah's rebellion, Nebuchadnezzar and his troops besieged Jerusalem until *famine* and *pestilence* resulted. This was in the ninth year of Zedekiah's reign (2 Kings 25:1-7). A comparison of 2 Kings 25:1-7, Jeremiah 39:1-7, and Ezekiel 12:3-13 gives clarity to the events at the time of and following the siege.

(NOTE: The following passages from Jeremiah are enlightening in connection with this era: Jeremiah 21:1 through 22:9; 24:1 through 25:11; 27:1 through 28:17; and chapters 34, 37, 38 and 39.)

Summarizing—

Zedekiah's wavering position was provoking to Nebuchadnezzar. This moved him to *overthrow* Judah and carry all but the poorest of the people into exile. The prophets' warnings were ignored—even despised (2 Chronicles 36:15, 16). Therefore Jerusalem was devastated, even to the burning of the house of God and the king's palace, and the breaking down of th walls of the city (36:17-19).

Only "the poor of the land" were left "to be vinedressers and husbandmen" (2 Kings 25:12).

FOR OUR ADMONITION AND LEARNING
In conclusion of the course, it may be worthy of note—after observing the total corruption of the *withdrawing* Northern Kingdom contrasted with the comparative righteousness of the "remnant" Southern Kingdom—that *Judah was God's beloved,* called out from the larger chosen Israel.

In New Testament theology, *Judah* might be thought of as *a type of the Church* as "an holy nation," called out from among "all nations" to whom Christ was sent as the Redeemer.

"He came unto his own, and his own received him not.

"But as many as received him, to them gave he power to become the sons of God, even to them that believe on his name" (John 1:11, 12). Amen.

THE KINGS AND KINGDOMS OF ISRAEL AND JUDAH

Test Questions

1. There were _____ kings in all; _____ before the division; _____ of Israel; and _____ of Judah.
   (53 43 4 23 19 5 20 25)

2. This course covers a period of about _____ years, according to the *Thompson Chain-Reference* chronology.
   (805 508 1,095 587)

3. The first king of the United Kingdom was _____;
   the first of the Northern Kingdom was _____;
   the first of the Southern Kingdom was _____.
   (Samuel Saul David Jeroboam Rehoboam Solomon Hezekiah Ahab)

4. The last king of the United Kingdom was _____;
   the last of the Northern Kingdom was _____;
   the last of the Southern Kingdom was _____.
   (David Jeremiah Solomon Zedekiah Zachariah Hoshea Jehu Jehoiachin)

5. Write "True" or "False" before each statement:
   (   ) Most of the kings were good men.
   (   ) The United Kingdom began about 1095 B.C.
   (   ) The Divided Kingdom dated from about 975 B.C.

6. A. The kingdom was first demanded by _____.
   (Samuel Jeroboam the people God Rehoboam)
   B. The idea of having a king was _____ to God at the time.
   (pleasing displeasing of no importance)

7. Write the correct name in each blank:
   a. _____ hid himself "among the stuff."
   b. _____ was anointed king while he was a shepherd boy.
   c. _____ was noted for his great wisdom.
   d. _____ was the king who "should not have been."

8. Write "True" or "False" before each statement:
   (   ) Saul was of the tribe of Benjamin.
   (   ) David was of the tribe of Dan.
   (   ) Solomon was the son of David and Michal.

9. Match by writing in the numbers from the second column before the names in the first column:
   (   ) a. Jehu   1. Made the golden calves.
   (   ) b. Jeroboam I   2. Listened to the younger men.
   (   ) c. Hoshea   3. Coveted a man's vineyard.
   (   ) d. Rehoboam   4. Said, "Throw her down!"
   (   ) e. Ahab   5. Went into captivity in 721 B.C.

10. Fill the blanks below from the list of places:
    (Jerusalem Jericho Shiloh Hebron Shechem Gilgal Samaria Ramah Gibeah Bethel)
    a. Saul's seat of government _____.
    b. David's first seat of government _____.
    c. Solomon's seat of government _____.
    d. Jeroboam I's first seat of government _____.
    e. Ahab's seat of government _____.

11. A. Nadab, son of Jeroboam I, was assassinated by _____.
       (Baasha Elah Zimri Omri)
    B. Elah, fourth king of Israel, was slain by _____.
       (Ahaziah Ahab Zimri Jehoram)
    C. _____, eighth king of Israel, died from an injury received in a fall through a lattice.
       (Omri Jehu Ahaziah Jehoahaz)
    D. _____, fifth king of Israel, committed suicide.
       (Jehoram Zimri Elah Shallum)

12. Write "True" or "False" before each statement:
    (   ) Jehu's wife was Jezebel.
    (   ) There was a 3 1/2-year drouth during the reign of Ahab.
    (   ) Jehoash, twelfth king of Israel, visited the prophet Elisha during the prophet's illness.
    (   ) Jeroboam II was Israel's longest-reigning king.

13. Match by writing in the numbers from the second column before the names in the first column:
   (   ) a. Manasseh
   (   ) b. Asa
   (   ) c. Rehoboam
   (   ) d. Hezekiah
   (   ) e. Abijam
   (   ) f. Jehoshaphat

   1. Said, "I will chastize you with scorpions."
   2. Reproved Jeroboam I from the top of a mount.
   3. King of Judah 55 years.
   4. Judah's first righteous king
   5. Life extended fifteen years.
   6. Had affinity with the house of Ahab.

14. A. Judah's only "queen" was _____.
       (Jezebel   Athaliah   Maachah)
    B. _____ was hidden six years in the temple.
       (Joram   Joash   Jotham   Uzziah)
    C. _____ instituted a successful financial plan for the repairing of the temple.
       (Joash   Asa   Amaziah   Jehoram)
    D. _____ turned to the idols of Seir (Edom) after God had given him a great victory.
       (Ahaziah   Azariah   Amaziah   Ahaz)
    E. _____ was stricken with leprosy when he tried to intrude into the office of the priesthood.
       (Hezekiah   Jehoshaphat   Uzziah   Ahaziah)

15. Put an X before each statement that applies:
    Events in Manasseh's reign over Judah include:
    (   ) Used enchantments and witchcraft.
    (   ) Filled Jerusalem with innocent blood.
    (   ) Repented and humbled himself greatly.
    (   ) Was carried to Babylon, then released.

16. Write "True" or "False" before each statement:
    (   ) Ahaz shut the doors of the temple.
    (   ) Hezekiah reopened the doors.
    (   ) Jotham was a wicked man.
    (   ) Hezekiah observed the Passover in the seventh month instead of the first.

17. A. The priests and the Levites had their offerings restored to them during the reign of _____.
    (Jehoshaphat   Jotham   Josiah   Hezekiah)
    B. _____ spread a letter from the king of Assyria before the Lord.
    (Jotham   Asa   Uzziah   Amon   Hezekiah)
    C. The reign of _____ was prophesied more than 300 years ahead of time.
    (Josiah   Jotham   Manasseh   Ahaz)

18. Circle the right answers:
    A. During whose reign was the book of the law found?
    (Amon   Josiah   Jehoahaz   Jehoiakim)
    B. During whose reign did the angel smite 185,000 Assyrians?
    (Jehoiachin   Joash   Menahem   Hezekiah)
    C. Which king was diseased in his feet?
    (Jehu   Ahab   Asa   Amon)
    D. Who held the greatest Passover feast since the days of Samuel?
    (Josiah   Jotham   Zedekiah   Uzziah)

19. Write "True" or "False" before each statement:
    (   ) Jehoiakim was made king by Pharaoh-nechoh, king of Egypt.
    (   ) Zimri reigned only seven days.
    (   ) Zachariah was the last king of Judah.
    (   ) Jehoiachin was honored by the king of Babylon after thirty-seven years of captivity.

20. Match by writing in the numbers from the second column before the names in the first column:
    (   ) a. Nebuchadnezzar   1. King of Assyria in Hezekiah's time.
    (   ) b. Tiglath-pileser   2. King of Egypt in Jehoiakim's time.
    (   ) c. Sennacherib   3. King of Babylon in Zedekiah's time.
    (   ) d. Pharaoh-nechoh   4. King of Assyria in Ahaz' time.

NAME _____

ADDRESS _____